Harry Wat

ERIC BALL
THE MAN AND HIS MUSIC

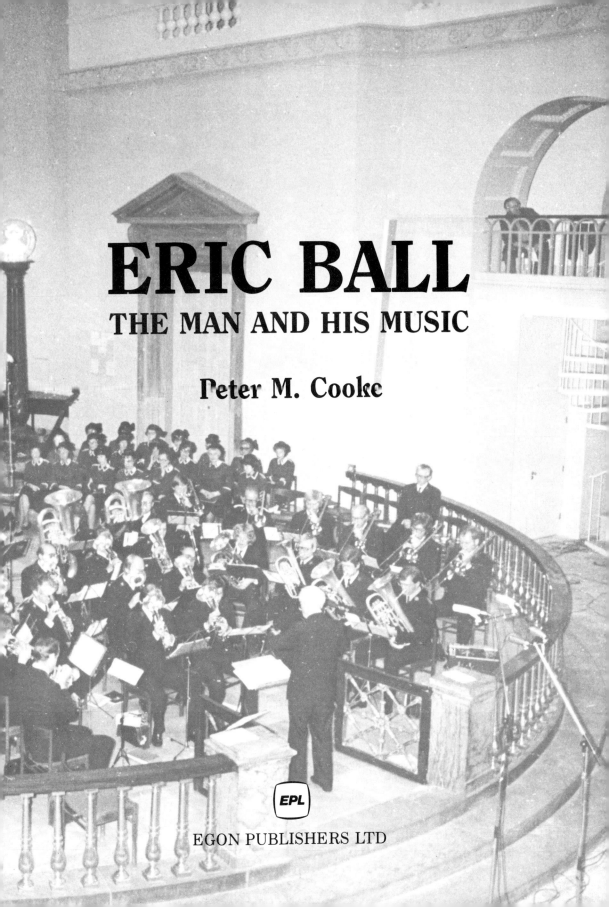

ERIC BALL
THE MAN AND HIS MUSIC

Peter M. Cooke

EPL

EGON PUBLISHERS LTD

Title page photograph:
Eric Ball conducts Copenhagen
Temple Band in the cathedral,
1979.

Published in 1991 by
Egon Publishers Ltd
Royston Road, Baldock, Hertfordshire SG7 6NW
England

Copyright © 1991 The General of The Salvation Army

ISBN 0 905858 56 5

Designed by Campion Design, Baldock, Hertfordshire

Printed by Streetsprinters
Royston Road, Baldock, Hertfordshire SG7 6NW
England

Contents

There is music which searches the unfathomed depths
Of the innermost soul of man –
Stirs joy indescribable, unmeasured woe –
All the lure of the unattained we know.
Time is lost in eternity –
Death and life one entity –
All the aeons of struggle and pain –
All life's barren and transient gain –
The divine, indestructible spirit of man, stirs again
As the chords rise and fall.

'Eric – an appreciation' – E. May Pyke

Foreword

Eric Ball was the kind of deeply considerate man who found friends without seeking them, and it was not necessary to know that he was an exceptionally gifted person to realise that here was someone wholly admirable. He never sought to impress, yet did so, simply and naturally, quite apart from his musicianship.

In him, grace was the first quality we noticed. I remember discussing with him originality in music, and he somewhat gloomily remarked, 'My music's derivative,' so I reminded him that the very greatest composers were 'derivative'. Bach studied all his precursors and often copied out their works; he was the sum, the climax of two centuries of music. Beethoven derived from his musical fathers – Bach, Handel, Haydn, Mozart, and we can see this in his mightiest works. After finishing his last quartets, perhaps the greatest music in existence, he said he hadn't studied enough, though he did add with a modesty that Eric would have appreciated, 'Thank God there's less lack of imagination than before!' The real artist uses what he finds – he doesn't try to start from nowhere. Eric's work had its own stamp, the result of his ability to make fresh use of what he knew. At length we concluded that originality escapes those who attempt to fabricate it. His originality lay in being innocently himself.

His sensitivity made him into a vegetarian, something else that drew us together. He saw clearly that unless we stop visiting suffering and death on our speechless, defenceless fellow creatures, we can never hope to stop doing it to each other. It is the first step we must take on the road to being a civilised, pacific species.

I remember Eric as mentor (in my youth), brilliant musician, humane man – an unforgettable combination of qualities. All who knew him have in them part of him, the part that shone from his personality, that at once taught us about the meaning of music and about living. He would have warmed to Carl Nielsen's simple but profound words, 'Music is the sound of life'.

This book will be welcomed by all who knew and loved Eric Ball – and they are many.

Robert Simpson

Acknowledgments

Obviously, no book writes itself, and it is impossible to write a book of this nature without a great deal of help from a great many people.

My first thanks must be to The Salvation Army's archivists in London, Melbourne, New York and Toronto for their help in supplying material hitherto unpublished as well as that which has appeared in print. Lieut-Colonel and Mrs Norman Bearcroft and the staff of the bands department at the UK Territorial Headquarters were unfailingly helpful and encouraging.

To members of the Ball, the Bryan and the Millest families, who lent family photographs (and particularly to Joan Moreau in the USA); to Lloyd Bates, Connie Clark, Noel Frost and Bob Getz; to friends of Eric and Olive from Southall Citadel days; to Geoffrey Brand (of R. Smith & Co) and Peter Wilson of *British Bandsman* who gave permission to reproduce copyright material; and to those whose personal stories hopefully enliven these pages giving flesh to what would otherwise have been a skeleton, my deep gratitude.

Peter M. Cooke

Introduction

(Thoughts suggested by the test piece 'English country scenes')

The buzz of conversation which hums around the interior of the Royal Albert Hall subsides as Band No 999 comes on to the platform. You idly think that the members look elegant, rather than smart, in their grey jackets with their dark-gold facings. You lean back in your chair, and, having listened to the piece 998 times already, wonder what new thing can possibly be said by Band No 999.

As you listen, the scenes already made familiar by the previous renderings rise before you. You relax and are half asleep, when, all of a sudden, a solo horn-player splits a note. You half expect a sharp intake of breath around the hall, but it doesn't come. Perhaps the rest of the audience is half asleep as well. The music pursues its course. Now they romp home in a rollicking *finale* as you once heard a BBC commentator say of a similar piece years ago.

The audience breaks into applause and you join in. It was a good interpretation on the whole. Pity about that split horn note though. Hopefully the adjudicators were half asleep, too. . . .

* * * * *

The scene changes. You are at the village fête. You spurn the fortune-teller's tent and the rummage stall; you ignore the guess-the-weight-of-the-cake contest and the coconut shy. Like every honest Englishman you hate fêtes. You make for the band stand.

Here players elderly and young are flung together in a piece whose attack and release leave much to be desired. Farmer Wellborn's horn and Postman Hornet's cornet are out of tune every June; why should this year be any change?

The range of music is limited and small; the parish hall in which they rehearse is worse than anything you've seen. But the village square rings with crotchets and quavers. No one wavers. They're all in at the attack. Crotchets and quavers can't answer back!

* * * * *

Sunday mornings and we twist the kaleidoscope to show a street scene in an industrial town. The sound of music is heard, plaintively at first, and then more melodiously, as the late-comers tune their instruments to the sound. It is a local Salvation Army band holding one of its open-air meetings.

The children stop their play; the dogs begin to bark; the music stops, as a member of the group exhorts his unseen listeners behind their curtains to hear the good news of the Gospel of Jesus Christ. An anxious woman comes to the gate and asks the band to go away - her husband is dying.

Immediately the captain goes in with the woman to offer comfort to her, and spiritual sustenance for the husband who is about to walk 'the last long mile of all'. At the gate the bandsmen quietly pray for the group inside the house. The captain promises to come back later in the day to discuss plans for the funeral.

* * * * *

'And once again the scene is changed . . .'. You are at the sea-side. Citizen of an island race, the call of the running tide is ever clear and ever beckoning. But again you spurn the deckchairs and the beach-cricket; the candy-floss and the rock-sellers; cockles, welks and winkles have no charm for you, as you make your way once more to the bandstand.

You notice, idly you tell yourself, with no prejudice and with no mote (or even grain of sand) in your eye, that there is a girl cornet-player. Third cornet of course. What is more, she has long, auburn tresses. Equally idly, you hope that she doesn't get them tangled in her valves in the trickier passages. . . .

The band strikes up. At first it is the usual 'Overture to *Zampa*' and the trombone solo, 'The acrobat'. You yawn, and are about to continue your walk, when you hear something a little more adventurous. Was that 'Journey into freedom' you recognised? You stay a little longer. Next comes '*Quid pro quo*' – that double-trio for cornets and trombones – and you see your girl cornet-player is in it, and she's not bad, not bad.

A sudden, manacing roll of thunder not caused by the percussionist, and a sudden splash of rain on your cheek, and the storm is upon you. The girl cornet-player's auburn tresses flow out behind her like those of a carved mermaid on a carved prow of a carved sailing ship. You wonder whether the band might play next that same composer's, 'Through storm to safety', but don't stay to find out. It has been another typical British summer's day. . . .

* * * * *

One last snapshot of English life comes before us. It is Remembrance Day and the British Legion Band is leading the service at the local war memorial. 'O God, our help . . .' is played and Psalm 90 is read. 'The last post' rends the air and heads are bowed for two minutes' silence. You hope like anything that the bandsmen notice in time that a mischievous little boy is pulling all the bandsmen's tuning slides out a fraction of an inch. Fortunately they do, though fortunately for the little boy they don't realise that it is *he* who has perpetrated the mischief. . . .

* * * * *

And behind all this, smiling benignly, almost proprietorily, is a little, slight, white-haired figure, with his hands in his pockets, his lips now jutting slightly. We do not need to ask who he is. And this is the story of his life, his music, and his influence.

ONE

Eric the Boy

The year 1901, with the death of Queen Victoria, marked the end of an epoch. The age which bore her name had been a long period of ever-increasing prosperity for Britain; of gradual, uninterrupted, not always peaceful transition from the old to the new society, and of peace and security for the country in her most important foreign relationships. The South African war and the Boxer uprising in the Far East had embroiled Britain in foreign adventures, but these were now over. At the Queen's death the monarchy enjoyed a position of respectability it had not done for almost 200 years.

The second decade of the new century would involve the world in the greatest catastrophe in its history: the First World War. In a single generation came the motor car, the wireless, the conquest of the air and new forms of exploration of the world beneath the sea. Speed and mechanism destroyed the older habits of life and thought, and gave birth to the urbanisation of the landscape. Throughout the world, nations and races were linked up too suddenly for their own peace, and national ambitions found ready to hand new weapons of conquest and of self-aggrandisement.

On Britain's domestic front, Prime Minister Balfour's Education Act of 1902 added another layer to the edifice of national education begun in 1870, though he was to incur the wrath of nonconformists who considered it wrong that they should have to contribute to Church of England schools. Thus began the decline in the Unionist Party's fortunes which was to lead to its rout in 1905 and the beginning of the last Liberal Government in the country's history.

So far as The Salvation Army was concerned, the years of its greatest expansion were over, but the seemingly inexhaustible William Booth was still finding fresh fields to conquer. In January 1901 (when he was close on 72 years of age), officers were appointed to Alaska. In 1902 and 1903 the work commenced in various parts of Central and South America.

On Wednesday 28 October 1903 Emma Booth-Tucker, daughter of William Booth, and joint leader, with her husband, of Salvation Army work in the United States, was killed as a result of a railway accident. The train carrying her from Kansas City to Chicago left the rails and crashed into a huge water tank. She died as a rescue train was on its way to the spot.

On Saturday 31 October 1903 Eric Walter John Ball was born at Kingswood, near Bristol, England.

* * *

The Lord thy God in the midst of thee is mighty. Yes, bless his Name. When Mr Booth told me I was to go to Kingswood, and what a bad place it was, my heart sank within me. But when I was in the train I gave myself afresh to God willing to go anywhere with Jesus . . . Our startling bills were put about the town, causing a great deal of excitement, people wondering who we were. When we commenced on the Sunday morning there were hundreds waiting for us. I got up to give out the hymn, but my heart sank within me, and I could not move my lips; but at last the victory was gained, the power of God came down mightily, and while I was talking numbers were weeping. In the evening we had a mighty time, people weeping all over the place.

After we had done talking we went into the prayer-meeting and then I spoke to a young man, and asked him to give his heart to God. He fell on his knees, weeping bitterly, and crying out at the top of his voice for mercy. The blood was applied, and he got up and told us he was saved, and the next night spoke in the open air. Praise God.

One dear woman told me the burden of her sins was more than she could bear. I asked her to let Jesus take it off. She fell on her knees and cried, 'Oh, Lord take this burden away. I will do anything to get rid of it. Oh, Lord do take it, do save me, I am so unhappy, I cannot live like this, do help me. I believe, I will believe, I do believe.' Glory. She got up, with the tears running down her face, and said, 'The burden is gone, I am so happy.'. . .

Another young man came to our meetings. He was deeply convinced. He cried for mercy. He soon got saved through believing. He said he used to be a runner, but now he has given me his running clothes. He says he was once running down to hell, but now he is running up to Heaven. Oh, may God keep him faithful.

I went up to another great man and said when are you going to start for Heaven? He said, 'To-night'. Hallelujah! He started in good earnest, and if you were to hear him it would do your heart good.

Eric's three paternal uncles, left to right, Amos, George (who gave him his first music lessons) and William, with Eric's father, Jack. In the foreground, are his grandparents, Ester and Daniel Ball.

Money and tracts thankfully received by yours in the battle field,

EMILY J. HALL

Ten Mile Hill, Kingswood.

This report, which appeared in *The Salvationist* dated 1 July 1879, reads oddly these days, but it is included to show the ground from which Eric Ball sprang, and its influence upon his music. It was preceded by a much more precise report in the previous issue, dated 1 June 1879:

> **Kingswood** – The opening was blessed. Chapel full; hundreds could not get in. Many convicted and some saved. Already they are pulling down the side wall in order to get more room for the people. Sister Hall is in good spirits, and she says 'Kingswood is getting converted.' Hallelujah!

This is the first mention of Kingswood, Corps No 98. Less than a year had passed since The Salvation Army, known first as The Christian Mission, had come into being. Even Bristol Citadel Corps, known as 'Bristol I' at first, did not open for another year. A corps with only two digits in its number is historic indeed. Not too many have survived. Yet Bristol Kingswood salvationists march on 112 years later. Eric Ball, one of its most famous sons, was to return in 1979 to lead part of its centenary celebrations.

Was 'Ten Mile Hill' a misprint for 'Two Mile Hill'? For in the local newspaper which circulated on the very day on which Eric Walter John Ball was born the following advertisement appears:

SALE OF FREEHOLD PROPERTY AT
TWO MILE HILL, KINGSWOOD, BRISTOL
GEO. NICHOLS, HOWES, YOUNG,
ALDER & CO

Have received instructions to SELL by AUCTION, at the
BLACK HORSE INN, KINGSWOOD HILL on WEDNESDAY
Next, November 4th, at 7 o'clock in the Evening, the under-
mentioned
FREEHOLD PROPERTY,
Viz:
Lot 1 – The commodious HALL, with SCHOOLROOM adjoin-
ing, known as the

SALVATION ARMY BARRACKS,

Situate at TWO MILE HILL, on the Corner of the Main Road
and REFORMATORY ROAD, to both of which it has important
frontages.

The Hall itself is a commodious building, and is erected in a
substantial manner, and together with the schoolroom adjoining forms an excellent premises for manufacturing purposes.

Lot 2 – A Large YARD, together with the SHEDS erected the
constituate at REFORMATORY ROAD, and adjoining the rear
of the last Lot.

The Mines and Minerals are reserved.

For further particulars apply to the Auctioneers, 43 Broad
Street, Bristol, or to

Messrs. ATCHLEY
Solicitors,
Clare Street Bristol.

Happily, it appears that The Salvation Army purchased the
freehold, for almost 100 years later salvationists still worship
at Two Mile Hill.

That same newspaper records that '. . . At a special meeting on Wednesday evening the Kingswood Urban District
Council discussed the advisability of applying for a pro-
visional order for Electric lighting, the application of a
private company for a similar order having been notified . . .
Seven voted against the making of the application and six for.
Mr A.F. Moon then gave notice to rescind a resolution passed
at a previous meeting in favour of the application.'

Well done, Mr Moon!

Local historians tell us that pin-making was a major industry
in Kingswood in the 18th and 19th centuries, 'a multitude of
the poor population' earning subsistence wages in small
workshops or in their homes. Hat making and boot and shoe
manufacturing were among other local industries. Some of

the workers in these would have been among the converts who 'cried for mercy' in early-day meetings at the Salvation Army barracks!

And among them were Daniel Ball, and his wife, Ester.

Daniel Ball kept a smallholding of about three or four acres (now a housing estate), on which he grew vegetables. These he supplied to his son Jack's shop.

We do not know whether he thought he was 'too bad a sinner' or that the burden of his sin was 'more than he could bear' (to use the picturesque language of those *Salvationist* reports). What we do know, however, is that when he became converted he donned, in the equally picturesque manner of converts of those days, a jersey embroidered with 'Salvation Army' on the front and 'Under New Management' on the back!

Daniel Ball remained an active salvationist until his seventies, later becoming a member of the Kingswood Evangelical Mission. This mission had, like the salvationists, a band, whose bandmaster, Albert Smith, liaised regularly with the salvationists to ensure that both groups did not hold open-air meetings in adjacent streets at the same time. Eric himself later visited the Mission to preach, to teach its band and lead band weekends. When Albert Smith died, in February 1954, Eric conducted his memorial service, at which Olive, Eric's wife, sang a solo, and Eric conducted the band in arrangements of two Handel choruses.

Daniel's wife, Ester, was also an active salvationist for many years, with her husband pioneering Army work in the Thornbury and Bristol areas. She was a friendly woman who knew and was known by most folk in Kingswood and Thornbury. On Sundays she would, like many others, wear a black straw hat, having a crimson band around it with 'Salvation Army' emblazoned on it in yellow.

Her photograph recalls Francis Evans's lines in *A Book of Salvationist Verse* 1963:

> But her eyes were pools of sweetness,
> And her face sang of God's peace.

But she was a forthright woman, who would tell a preacher 'to preach Jesus and not pad your sermon with too much nonsense!'

Of the 16 children born to Daniel and Ester Ball, Jack was the eldest. In 1902 he met and married Lily Bryan. She was three years his senior, having been born on 12 August 1876 into a baptist family in Aston, near Birmingham. She was a Salvation Army captain, who had held appointments at the old Drury Lane Slum Post and in Brighton and Bristol before becoming second-in-command of the Kingswood Corps. Eric used to say that it was love at first sight – 'My father saw and heard my mother preaching in an open-air meeting, and decided "that's the one for me!" '

Lily Bryan, along with some of her sisters, joined The Salvation Army at an early age. She had a great influence on Eric, as had her sister, Emily. In old age Emily wrote down her memoirs (such heaven-sent material for a family-tree researcher or social historian!) and extracts from her 'Story of a Life' are here presented:

I cannot remember anything of my infancy, but from facts that have been kept, I have learned that I was born at 'Enfield Highway', Middlesex, at the back of the Gun-makers' Arms. My first recollections are of a small house (near a railway) where I lived with my father and mother, two sisters and two brothers . . . We must have been quite poor for I can remember my mother taking in . . . washing . . . My next recollections are of our living in an off-licence, the property of my father's brother [this must have been in Aston] . . . My mother had the care of the shop, beer and tobacco, and my father had charge of the coal yard connected to it and a big coal round . . .

It was here my father got into bad company and ways, and child as I was, I can well remember my mother's grief and patient endurance. My father always went on Saturday evening to collect the accounts from his coal rounds, which I was then able to book in on his return, ready to pay over to my uncle on Monday morning; but one fateful Saturday (soon after my youngest sister was born) he failed to return or bring in any money, and my poor mother had to face my uncle's wrath and hear his dreadful threats about my father. For weeks we carried on and did our best, but as there was no one to see to the horses or serve the people on the rounds, my uncle soon got rid of them . . .

A letter arrived from my father, saying that he had tramped to London, got converted at Charrington's hall at Mile End, and that, as soon as he could get work, he would send for us all . . . My father had a dreadful time, but eventually got a job in London and then started to screw and save to send for us . . . The goods had gone off, when on the Saturday, my sister, who had been at work, came home ill; the doctor diagnosed it as small-pox which was then raging . . . My mother and her young baby were kept back for quarantine and on the Monday morning a brother of my mother's came and took us to London. We met my father at Paddington station and we were all taken to an empty house at Wapping . . .

After a few weeks it was decided that I had better go to work and a job was found for me learning 'book-folding' at two shillings and six pence [12-and-a-half pence] a week for 12 months. I liked my work and patiently waited for the time when I should be on 'piece' work and be able to earn a little money to help my mother, who was having a dreadful struggle . . .

I had been five weeks out of my apprenticeship . . . when very suddenly one Saturday evening, while my father was out at a prayer-meeting, Mother was taken ill and died before we could get any aid. I used my bit of money for our mourning and my father had to borrow the money for the funeral, which again kept us poor for some time . . .

In a month or two, Father decided we had better move nearer to his work [which by this time was back at Enfield] so again we moved . . . It all ended in Father's marrying again and then life was anything but happy for my young brothers and sisters and one by one they left home and we were scattered to various parts. I too left home and took a job as a general servant, and though I remained two years, the job was hard and often unpleasant.

During this time I had become acquainted with The Salvation Army and decided to become a soldier . . . I took another job as housemaid for a year, and then became a candidate for Salvation Army officership. I was accepted, and by the time I was 20 I was a captain in charge of a slum post.

I spent a happy year doing my best for God and the people, then I met and married my husband, with whom I spent 41 years of comradeship, being all the time a happy salvationist, and both of us working as local officers until a short time before my husband's death . . .

One gasps in astonishment that so much could have happened to one girl in one lifetime; at the abject poverty of the family. If she had had all these situations before she was 20 (I have omitted part of her narrative describing the period Emily was looking after the children between her father's two marriages) whatever age was she when she was apprenticed as a 'book-folder'? Eric's mother shared the same background which inevitably contributed to the strength of character which many, including Eric, testified in later years, belonged to Lily Ball.

But what of Jack Ball, Eric's father? He has been variously described as 'a holy terror'; 'an adventurer, whose "adventures" were usually non-productive money-wise'; 'everybody's favourite uncle'. His photographs show him as being of upright carriage and smart, even elegant appearance, with a small moustache, now short and clipped, then longer and waxed at the ends.

'He could never stay in one place for long; how my poor mother coped with the continual moving around I'll never know', Eric said in later years. The family moved from Kingswood to Godalming (in Surrey), and from Surrey to Buckinghamshire; from Buckinghamshire to Middlesex; from Middlesex to Kent; from Kent to Clapham in south

Eric's mother, Lily Ball.

Eric's father, Jack Ball.

Eric's father, Jack Ball.

London; from Clapham back to Bristol – 'about 14 moves in all!' Eric's youngest brother, Don, remembers, ruefully. 'Then, finally, Mother put her foot down; "I'm *not* moving again!" '

For a time Jack Ball managed a chain of small grocer's shops in the Hanwell and Southall areas owned by one Howard Roberts. Eric used to weigh out the sugar, slapping the blue bags down on the counter to 'settle' the contents, deftly folding the necks of the bags and turning the corners in firmly to secure the package. One can imagine him cutting the cheese with the wire cutters such shops used to have, or packing butter, shaping it first with wide, flat, wooden knives into convenient 'pats'. No pre-packed groceries in those days! ('And it was very much a case of "open at all hours!"' says Don.) It is easy, too, to think of Eric delivering orders on a rickety old bicycle, themes from Beethoven sonatas or Bach fugues running through his mind in time to the turn of the wheels.

But Jack Ball was nobody's fool. Eric used to tell a gleeful story of a man who would come into the shop and, while Jack's back was turned, help himself to small items. One day he saw the man slip an egg into his pocket. When it came to adding up the bill, Jack exclaimed, 'and a farthing for the egg you've taken!' – slapping the pocket in which the egg lodged. Eric does not tell us whether the customer ever returned to the shop, or whether he put in the bill for having his jacket cleaned!

Don Ball remembers, too, a time when they kept a shop in Harmondsworth. It was 'a real village superstore, with a horse pulling the breadcart', to use his own words. 'The same horse pulled the village fire engine, and from which-ever bell rang, the horse knew which vehicle he would need to pull and went to the right one.' He remembers the time when they kept a chicken farm, and one of the chickens was having difficulty in swallowing something. 'My father did no more than shove the chicken between his knees, cut open its stomach, then its gizzard, removed the offending object and sewed the bird up again. The bird then fluttered off to join the others, quite happy – much more so than it had been a few minutes previously!'

For a time Jack and Lily Ball kept a cafe in Coldharbour Lane, Slough, and Don remembers his father putting sticks of rhubarb through the mangle preparatory to making wine. He also remembers his father hiding the bottles under the stairs, and the corks blowing out when the wine fermented. He remembers the resulting mess on the floor: 'Mother wasn't very pleased!'

During this period Eric lodged with his Uncle Tom (Thomas Bunn, the corps treasurer at Southall Citadel) and Auntie Emily (the corps's first home league – women's group – secretary). This 'Auntie Emily' is she whose memoir is reproduced on a previous page. Uncle Tom had become a salvationist at Kennington Lane in 1891, much to the sur-prise of his relatives, who were business people of some standing in the district. He served as an officer until the pas-sing of his father, and, before transferring to Southall Citadel, served for a time at Lambeth Slum Post.

In December 1898 a crop of posters had appeared in and

The Salvation Army

WEDDING

OF

CAPTAIN BRYAN
and ENVOY BUNN

Conducted by

Adjutant and Mrs. BROWN

(South London's Chancellor),

at the

MILLWALL BARRACKS

MALABAR STREET, on

Tuesday, December 27th.

Marriage Feast, 4.30 p.m. - Admission, 6d.

Wedding Ceremony, 6.30 p.m. „ 3d.

TICKETS MAY BE OBTAINED FROM ANY LONDON SLUM OFFICER.

J. HAY, D.O., London Slums.

Above left: Eric's uncle and aunt, Thomas and Emily Bunn.

Above right: Poster advertising the wedding of Eric's aunt and uncle, Emily Bryan and Thomas Bunn.

around the Millwall Barracks in Malabar Street, announcing that Adjutant and Mrs Brown would conduct the wedding of Captain Bryan and Envoy Bunn there on Tuesday, 27 December. Admission to the Marriage Feast, at 4.30 pm, was 6d; that to the Wedding Ceremony, at 6.30, was 3d. (They feasted before the ceremony on that occasion!) The *War Cry* reporter described the event:

They have had a wedding at Millwall – Captain Bryan to Envoy Bunn. There was a real slum 'banquet', and 300 people crushed themselves into the barracks to hear the bride and groom say what they thought of salvation.

Auntie Emily was afterwards to serve as young people's sergeant-major (Sunday-school superintendent) at Southall I, and, for a time, as corps cadet guardian (youth group leader) there, a post which Eric was himself to occupy for a time.

Eric obviously held his uncle and aunt in affection; when Thomas Bunn died, in October 1939, Eric conducted the funeral.

Eric's own father died in the summer of 1936. An announcement in *The Bandsman and Songster* for 5 September of that year mentions that, 'Whilst staying at Bristol, Mr Ball, the father of Adjutant Eric Ball, was taken seriously ill. He regained consciousness, and a recovery was expected, but we regret to announce he had a relapse and was promoted to Glory [The Salvation Army's term for the death of a salvationist] on Wednesday 19 August.' Lily Ball had a long period of widowhood ahead, for it was not until 6 October 1968 that she died. During part of her widowhood she kept a cafe in Southall, and took in paying guests. Her husband had died without being able to make financial provision for her, and the hard life she had endured in earlier days returned.

Some criticism has been made of Eric during this period. Never one to interest himself in the financial aspects of life, he apparently neglected his mother financially at a time when she needed his support. Not that *she* herself would have criticised him; she is remembered by corps officers at Hayes, at which corps she was latterly a soldier, as being a tough, independent old lady, a strong personality, totally blind, but well in control. She was able to cook for herself until the end of her life, and would knit, with white yarn, on very large needles. On the day before her death she was out doing her shopping; Eric's old friend John Hunt conducted the funeral.

Mrs Ball was at various times and at various corps, owing to their constant changes of address, young people's sergeant-major and home league treasurer. She is recorded as being a talented musician and public speaker. Some of her song-poems appeared in *The War Cry* in the 1890s.

Lily Ball felt keenly the pain of her son's resignation from officership, but had no criticism of the Army. She treasured a large photograph of him conducting massed bands in the Crystal Palace, as she did her silver star badge (she must have been one of the first to be admitted to the Order of the Silver Star, by which The Salvation Army honours mothers who give a child to officership). It must have given her great grief when she had to stop wearing it following Eric's resignation, though she would have born this with the same fortitude as her other misfortunes.

There is a picture of Eric, taken when he was a child of three. He was bewitchingly pretty, with curly, golden hair down to his shoulders (as was not uncommon for boys in those days). In the picture he is wearing a thigh-length knitted garment, a kind of tunic, and he holds a sort of wand in his hand. He looks as though he is about to dive into a dewdrop, swing on a cobweb, or attend on the Fairy Queen. Then we look at the eyes – already with that faraway expression we will see so often in later years – and we imagine he is

Left: Eric Walter John Ball, aged 3.

Above: Harold Ball, aged 2.

dreaming of a symphony for the elfin orchestra to play. We look at the lips, already thrust forward slightly, as they are in so many of his later photographs, and we feel that it is, perhaps, the horn-calls that are going through his mind!

The three sons who formed the Ball family all pursued different professions. Eric, the eldest (born in 1903) was, as we know, a musician. Harold (1908–1976) was a civil servant, in the Admiralty during the war, and later in the then Ministry of Education; he took early retirement and served the Bible Reading Fellowship for a number of years. Don (born in 1919) was a consulting railway engineer who, following a long period with British Railways, went 'private', fulfilling a number of contracts in the Middle and Far East.

Harold's son, John, admits that 'My father and my Uncle Eric did not always agree on matters religious, my father's views being decidedly those of a high churchman, and Uncle Eric's being, to say the least, somewhat unorthodox . . . They would have long discussions on the few occasions they met – few because of Uncle Eric's professional and other engagements – and sometimes their conversations became somewhat heated. But they always parted good friends. My father always wanted to enter the full-time ministry, but was never able to do so.'

In a letter to friends in later years, Eric said,

> . . . my formative years were variable, for my parents were often moving from here to there, so day-school work was sketchy. 'Composition' (essays) was my best subject I think, and I am always thankful for tonic sol-fa, which was the only school music I experienced . . . then there was the Army, and for a year or two the junior band at Ealing. Living in the country when I was about 12, there was no Army, but a methodist church and some piano lessons and a little mathematics with harmony and counterpoint with the local anglican organist, a retired teacher. No school – that was the end of my schooldays!
>
> Then, at 14, an office-boy's job, and organ lessons at the church; then on to Dartford and Holy Trinity Church, playing for the hymns on 11 November 1918 [Armistice Day]! [Interestingly, he mentions, in another letter, taking part in a holiday procession with Ealing Junior Band on the day, in 1914, that war was declared.] Then to a small town nearby [Erith], linking up with the Army again (against my wish!) and so, by . . . recommendation, to Judd Street [The Salvation Army's trading department in Britain], and ultimately the Music Editorial Department.
>
> My musical education was very sketchy: some piano lessons here and there, of variable standard, and also the organ, which delighted me. While at Judd Street, I also did a little private

Edith and Harold Ball, Eric's
sister-in-law and brother.

Eric's ARCM certificate.

THE ROYAL COLLEGE OF MUSIC,

PRINCE CONSORT ROAD,

SOUTH KENSINGTON,

LONDON, S.W. 7.

December, 1924.

A.R.C.M. EXAMINATION, 1924-25.

———

Mr. *Eric W. J. Ball*

I beg to inform you that you have obtained the requisite number of marks to entitle you to a Certificate of Proficiency in

Theory of Music

Results of Optional Harmony and Counterpoint Papers cannot be communicated until some days after the Examination is ended.

CLAUDE AVELING,
Registrar.

Maximum Marks	Pass Marks	Marks obtained
300	225	240

Grammar of Music ....

Figured Bass ....

Addition of Melody to Unfigured Bass ....

Southall I Band on the occasion of its visit to Guernsey, CI, 1921. Eric can be seen, with E flat bass, on the far right of the picture.

teaching of piano, in order to help pay for theory lessons from a correspondence college in Nottingham. So I have not to my credit a full technical education at college or university level, but was to some extent self-taught. I sat for the ARCM diploma in about 1924 or 25 – in theory of music, and scraped through (I must search for my certificate!) . . .

Such a search would have revealed his diploma to have been awarded in 1924.

Eric's first job was as a junior clerk at the Staines Linoleum Company. Many years later an elderly gentleman, a former employee at the same firm, remembered '. . . a boy named Ball, quite musical, and showing such flair that the chief cashier allowed him to extend his lunch-hours in order to run along to the Parish Church to practise the organ'. Little did this chief cashier realise what a prodigy he had in his office! But the Army and brass band worlds have reason to thank him for the degree of perceptivity he *did* evidence, and the kindness he showed!

There were musical influences on both sides of the family. His paternal Uncle George taught him to improvise at the piano. (This uncle unfortunately became what is euphemistically termed a 'gentleman of the road', who tramped the lanes of England, sometimes presenting himself at his brother's shop, and doing odd jobs to earn a little money. Years later, when Eric was conducting a brass band concert in Manchester, Uncle George, then working as a public-house pianist, met up with his nephew, who acknowledged his gratitude.) His maternal Uncle Walter took him while still a child to an organ recital in a local church. Eric was carried away by the music he heard, and resolved that one day he would make music like that.

The first reference we have to his 'making music like that' is during a visit Southall Citadel Band made to Guernsey. Eric was the piano/organ soloist and accompanist. Frank Clayton, a bandsman at Southall in those days, remembers a local reporter writing that 'the accompanist, Salvationist Ball, is an excellent musician who memorises his selections on the pianoforte'. In actual fact the reporter was mistaking 'memorisation' for improvisation. At this time Eric would take a song and create a descriptive piece with it. One of the band's favourites was a sort of fantasia, 'Stilling the storm'. Taking the song 'A little ship . . .' he would go through it, verse by verse, through the storm, and the calming of the sea. Throughout, the phrase 'a little ship was on the sea' could be heard above the storm, and during the calm. This piece was sometimes rendered on the organ.

This time spent at Southall was the first settled period of Eric Ball's life (and even that was interrupted by a short period 'south of the river' when he instructed Upper Norwood Band), and thus deserves a chapter of its own.

TWO

Eric and Olive

Southall Citadel Corps commenced with an 'invasion' of salvationist 'troops' from Hounslow, and the first meeting-place was a loft above some stables, which was fitted out with a platform, seats, some windows, and gas lighting.

The actual opening was on 24 September 1885, and the Grecian Corps Band joined the first open-air meeting. They marched to the High Street, and stopped between the George and Dragon and the White Hart public houses, to form a ring right across the road. It was not long before a few converts were won, and the ranks increased in number. Open-air meetings were subsequently held in other parts of the town.

Among these early stalwarts were Edward ('Ted') and Rosetta Hill. If Ted did not actually commence the band he was one of its earliest members. Mrs Hill was herself a member of the Hounslow Corps before transferring to Southall and they were Nos 1 and 2 on the corps roll there for many years.

Ted was a born musician who in his youth worked at the gas works in winter and in the brick fields in the summer. His daughter Rosalind, afterwards to become Mrs Phil Catelinet, still speaks with affectionate pride of how her father wrote music on the bricks he helped to make. Years after his death, when his house was being redecorated, layers of wallpaper were stripped away, to reveal a stave drawn on the walls, which he had used to teach the first bandsmen their notation. Afterwards he took a correspondence course with Richard Slater (known affectionately to salvationists as 'father of Salvation Army music'), and won prizes with his compositions. The band selection, 'Echoes from Calvary', was one of his 'winners'.

In 1912 Southall Citadel Band had the privilege of marching behind the cortège in the funeral procession of William

Booth, and on the photograph of the occasion, Band Inspector Ted Hill's tall figure can be seen in front of his band. Many years later Olive Ball was watching a video-transcription of the film made of this event. Suddenly she recognised her father, Albert Dorsett, marching with the band. She was scarcely able to contain herself in her excitement, and almost unable to believe what she was seeing. Her host ran the section of the video through again, and she was quite enraptured by the sight of her father marching with the band behind the Founder's cortège!

Ted Hill was the Band Inspector (a lay-salvationist working full time in the interests of bands and bandsmen in Britain) for a number of years; his appointment took him away from home on divisional tours, checking band inventories and leading practices. 'He would be away from home for three weeks and back for one before being off again,' Rosalind remembers. His death from cancer in 1925 at the relatively early age of 56 was a great sorrow. His wife was to survive him for about 28 years. They are both buried together at Havelock Cemetery, Southall.

Phil and Rosalind Catelinet were themselves lifelong friends of Eric and Olive Ball, Olive's sister, Elsie, being a bridesmaid at their wedding. They served as officers for some years, being trained in the famous Awakeners Session of cadets of 1934/35 ('Come on, you half-asleep Awakeners!' Phil remembers their training commissioner, Samuel Hurren, telling them.) Phil has nearly 200 band pieces to his credit, the Bible Picture 'Saint Peter' being 'all the rage' in the thirties. His *air varié*, 'A Sunbeam', is still heard from time to time. The 1986 edition of *The Song Book of The Salvation Army* ensured new life for the song 'With my heart so bright in the Heavenly light' (No 402) for which Phil provided the lilting music with its male-voice counter-melody, originally written for his fellow-cadets to sing on the march.

Phil was later to pursue a career as a professional musician, notably as a tuba player with the Philharmonia and London Symphony Orchestras. Vaughan Williams wrote his tuba concerto for him and dedicated it to him. Later Phil was Professor of Brass at the Carnegie-Melon University, Pittsburgh (USA). During part of this period he and Rosalind were bandmaster and songster leader respectively - Rosalind having already earned her spurs as singing company leader at Southall Citadel.

Rosalind remembers, somewhat amusingly, though seriously at the same time, that her 'engagement ring' was their grand piano. At that time there was only enough money for a ring *or* the down-payment for the piano, and, of course, the piano won. (Phil went on to become a noted pianist.) She was glad it did, for a ring would have given them no protection from the falling ceiling in war time, as did the piano. The instrument was the only item of furniture they took with them to America in 1956.

Phil and Rosalind Catelinet returned to England in 1977, and still attend meetings at Ramsgate Corps as often as health allows.

While they were there Southall Citadel was 'a nest of singing birds' with all sorts and conditions of musical and other personalities, and remained so for many years. Most of them influenced Eric strongly. When Songster Leader Peppiatt died in 1955, for instance, Eric wrote in *The British Bandsman* of how the songster leader had once taken him aside, and gently and firmly dealt with him on the unfair weapon of sarcasm. Eric never forgot his advice, wondering what his future might have been had he done so.

Among the song writers connected with Southall were Brigadier Joseph Buck, himself a great friend of Eric, and writer of the words of one of the latter's most popular songs, 'Love stands the test'. Set first for male voices, it was later re-arranged for mixed voices, and later still found its way into the present Salvation Army song book.

Ivy Mawby was another song-writer at Southall Citadel. Her parents, the Memmotts, were officers in the now defunct Salvation Army Assurance Society, and were also local officers at Southall Citadel. Thus she was brought up in the corps, but entered training as an officer from Southall Broadway, returning to the Citadel for her marriage, in 1929, to Captain Arthur Mawby. Sadly she was widowed in 1943, but then went on to to hold influential appointments on her own, in the editorial department at International Headquarters, and from 1955 until her retirement in 1963 as National Home League Secretary.

Early in her officership Ivy Mawby developed her interest in words. She began writing songs for which her name will live – 'Grant us thy peace' and 'Jesus answers prayer' being among her most popular. They all reflect the deep spiritual values she cherished and sought to develop. Like Joseph Buck, her parents are buried in Havelock Cemetery.

Close by is the grave of Albert and Susan Dorsett, parents of Olive, later to become Eric's wife. Of Albert and Susan Dorsett the stone says 'they grew old gracefully' – as accurate a description of them, it is said, as anyone is likely to find. With them lies their younger daughter, Elsie, who, according to the inscription on the stone, 'entered the Summerland' on 15 September 1942. She was 34.

Albert Dorsett, who was born at Long Crendon in Buckinghamshire, and commenced his career as a musician there, was a stalwart of Southall Citadel, a member for 68 years, and a horn player in the band. He retained his love for band music all his life. He was No 1 on the corps roll for a long time, and would often, in later years, wear his tunic indoors in case, as he would say, the 'Heavenly summons' might catch him unawares. He was promoted to Glory on 10 October 1955, and his wish to be buried in uniform was fulfilled.

The story is told that Albert vowed to the Lord that he would preach the gospel in the streets of Southall and Hanwell, in uniform and alone if necessary, and he often did so. Norman Bearcroft, the well-known Salvation Army composer, said, as a five-year-old, 'I'll stand with him!' – and he did, complete with a little Army flag on a stick!

Jill Bearcroft, Norman's wife, grew up in Southall Citadel (Norman's parents were the corps officers there for a period), and she speaks equally warmly of him. 'He would testify in the meetings, and sing little solos in a funny, cracked old voice. On one occasion he stood up and sang the chorus "Running over . . . my cup's full and running over" and we teenagers in the songsters nudged each other, saying, "Off he goes again!" or words to that effect. But then he said, as he testified, "But the cup's got to be *full* to be of any use. Who wants a cup that's only *half full?*" It shot an arrow into my heart, and I knew that this was my call to officership.'

It was while Erik and Maria Leidzén were staying with the Balls that Albert Dorsett received the 'Heavenly summons'. Olive, who had nursed her father devotedly, had left the house this particular morning to do a little shopping. When she returned she noticed that the house was even quieter than usual, but cheerfully asked Maria if there had been any visitors. 'Not in the accepted sense of the word,' Maria told her, quietly, and then broke the news that 'there has in fact been a Heavenly Visitor'.

Susan Dorsett served for 56 years in Southall Citadel (or Southall I as it was known in earlier days). Like her husband, she was a local officer (a lay-salvationist who holds office in corps on a part-time basis), fulfilling several functions at various times, and, as the *War Cry* tribute said at the time of her promotion to Glory on 10 July 1957, 'performing her duties with devotion. Her influence on her neighbours was particularly marked and her work in the home league will long be remembered.' In her younger days she was a pretty-featured woman, and had a lovely voice. She was a songster for a number of years.

Ivy Mawby — wedding-day picture.

Southall I Singing Company in 1927. Olive, the leader, is seated in the middle; Rosalind Catelinet stands behind her, just to the left.

Olive Dorsett was born on 29 March 1902 and was converted at Southall Citadel on 22 October 1914. Early photographs show her to be a winning little girl and young woman, with a beguiling smile. She became singing company leader in 1921, and retained that appointment until entering training for Salvation Army officership. She had a good company of young singers and they all loved her.

It is probably impossible to put a date on the beginning of 'an understanding' between Eric and Olive. They were both so busy about their various tasks in the corps (in those days it was very much a case of 'every night at the Army'), and Eric was immersed in studies and composition as well. There is in existence a letter he wrote to her:

My dear,
  When you read this, you will have already heard that which I have been intending to ask you for weeks past; and I shall have your answer.
  Whatever that is, this letter will do no harm, so that I will give it to you in any case; because I wish to give you a thorough idea of my intentions and feelings in the matter I have brooked to you this evening.

Eric and Olive's wedding photograph.

I can promise you nothing materially. You perfectly understand me, don't you? I can promise you no expensive presents, outings (which, by the way, don't seem to trouble you much); and I can promise you no definite end to our friendship – at least at present. What I can promise you is, long, leisure hours in which you may be forced to make your own amusement, during which time my studies will hold me from you; and also I can promise you a lasting, staunch friendship, and unfailing respect, and I will stand by you in everything as long as you may wish it.

So that, you see, I have nothing material to offer you, but I have that – if you will take it – that will last through the ages, and will not leave anything for regret.

Will you make your final decision on this letter?

Eric

Hardly the most romantic of proposals! But at least Olive was under no illusions as to Eric's love for her, and for problems the future might bring. Both were to be fulfilled. Their love and loyalty to each other never wavered throughout the years, and although there must have been many hours of loneliness, there were times of intense joy in his achievements and pride in the way he was fêted through the years.

Olive retained her clear singing voice for many years, and would from time to time feature the song, 'Clear skies', as a solo, with its lilting chorus:

> Clear are the skies above me,
> Pure are the joys within,
> Boundless the grace that keeps me
> Free from the power of sin;
> Walking each hour with Jesus,
> Held by his mighty hand,
> Pardoned, the past behind me,
> Before, the Gloryland.

Many years later, Eric was to compose a theme-and-variations cornet solo on this chorus and dedicate it to Olive. It would be nice to think of it as her testimony through life, and nothing would seem to contradict that possibility.

'Happy the bride the sun shines on!' – or so runs the old adage. Whether or not the actual sun shone on that April day when Eric and Olive were joined in holy matrimony by Eric's head of department, Frederick Hawkes, it can safely be said that the Sun of Righteousness did so, and continued to do so in the long years ahead. Though their skies were not always cloudless, they walked each hour with their Saviour, and were content.

At some time during the celebrations (during which his cousin, Joan Moreau, remembers 'his [Eric's] radiant, shining face'), Fred Hawkes said the following:

An event of this kind provides a suitable opportunity for the expression of some words of appreciation and gratitude for past efforts in the shape of what has already been accomplished as well as to express our kindest wishes and best hopes for the future.

Life – at whatever period we view it – consists of past, present, and future. The past can never be altered or lived again, the present largely depends upon the past, the future is what we shall make of it.

Speaking for Bandmaster Eric Ball I can say with the greatest confidence – *he has done well*. I can emphasise that statement and say he has done *very* well! . . .

He has worked hard and made good with the result that providing he so plans it his future is, I believe, secure.

He has worked hard at his studies and consequently has laid in a good foundation of musical knowledge which will stand him in good stead in the days to come.

As a sign of assiduous devotion to study it is well known that a short time ago he passed with distinction the very exacting examination connected with the Royal College of Music and is now entitled to add to his name the letters *ARCM*.

He has not merely crammed his head with musical knowledge but has also given evidence that he is able to create and compose music and has already laid the foundations of what I believe will in the future become a considerable output of both instrumental and vocal compositions.

His services in this connection are already widely known and much appreciated, and if his abilities remain consecrated to God's service a future of great usefulness lies before him.

A rare photograph of Southall I Band with Eric as its bandmaster.

May I say to Mrs Ball that we extend to her the hand of welcome. It will be her duty and privilege to assist her husband in every possible way and if she does this she will also share in the success that will attend her husband's efforts.

Prophetic words indeed! Then it was off to the brief honeymoon at Bridge Cottages, Shoeburyness, and finally to their first married home, with Albert and Susan Dorsett, though not before a visit to the studio of the local photographer for a suitable pictorial record to be made. In this connection a curious little story is told. The members of Southall Citadel Band formed a guard of honour for their bandmaster and his bride, and the inevitable confetti was thrown. Unfortunately Eric swallowed a piece which lodged in his throat, and he was unable to speak properly for three days. It will be remembered by many who knew him that his throat was always somewhat sensitive.

Eric's first appointment at Salvationist Publishing and Supplies Ltd was in the Music and Instruments Department. Buying and selling sheet music and brass instruments might not have been his idea of the height of bliss or achievement, but he was, at least, working in a musical environment, and 'you never know what lies just around the corner'. Here he would have met the redoubtable Charles Coller, an officer who became a salvationist at Regent Hall in 1885. Charles Coller was a member of the Household Troops Band on its first campaign in 1887, and later played trombone in the International Staff Band. He was the contributor of more than 200 songs to *The Musical Salvationist*, and 10 of these had musical settings by Eric Ball.

Indeed, Eric's first contribution to that publication was a setting of Coller's words – a song called 'Joyful hallelujah's'. Eric himself despised the music in later years, as so many poets and composers reject their early work, saying that it was a bad tune. Not that Coller's words on this occasion were all that marvellous! A later joint effort, 'Christ my companion', published in 1924, was more successful, and went on to become an Army 'classic' of its day. Its chorus could well sum up Eric's testimony, both at this time, and throughout his life:

> Lord, thou shalt my Companion be,
> My loving, mighty Friend;
> Grant I may walk and talk with thee,
> Till trav'lling days for me shall end.

Another lifelong friendship started from this period, and this was with Freda Webb, later to become Mrs Freda Lambert. Freda remembers Eric from corps cadet (youth group) days, which takes us back to his teenage period. She played the violin, and even at the approach of 90 has a musical voice and good sense of pitch. She played in the National Orchestra, of which Eric was later appointed conductor, but long before this she and Eric were travelling around London and the surrounding area with Archie Burgess, an officer at SP&S Ltd, who played the concertina.

Eric with (left) Connie Clark and (right) Freda Lambert.

From time to time down the years salvationists, usually officers, have formed 'parties', usually made up of up-and-coming musicians, to give programmes, conduct weekend meetings etc, and such was the case with Archie Burgess. Freda remembers special afternoon programmes given by this particular trio in the Hyde Park Hotel for Salvation Army subscribers, when they accompanied the munching of cucumber sandwiches with selections from *Iolanthe* among other 'suitable' items. The word 'suitable' is placed in quotation marks because it is almost unbelievable today that at that time Salvation Army musicians would play such music, even when making up a trio of violin, piano and concertina at the Hyde Park Hotel. They would certainly have been considered unsuitable fare for programmes given in a Salvation Army hall, where the choice of items to be played was very limited.

Indeed, Freda Lambert remembers being taken to task not too many years after this for playing something considered unsuitable in a Salvation Army programme and being asked to submit for permission all the music in her repertoire. Months went by, and she was having to ignore numerous invitations to play on programmes, until finally she wrote to the 'powers that be' – only to receive all her music back, with the stern decree that '. . . the regulation still applies in this particular case'. History does not tell us whether Freda ever played anything more adventurous than Handel's *Largo* on a Salvation Army platform – as a solo at any rate.

But she remembers an end-of-term concert at Trinity College, where she was a student, at which Eric accompanied her, and then their having to hurry away to play at the Salvation Army hall at Shoreditch. They had to change hurriedly from evening dress to Salvation Army uniforms – almost *en route* so as not to be late for their appointment. She recalls, too, a hilarious occasion when she, Archie Burgess and Eric were travelling to an appointment on an open-top bus (such luxuries as motor cars were almost unheard of for salvationists at that time) when Archie carried her violin, and Eric her music. They got up from their seats quickly, fearing to go past their stop, being in an unfamiliar district, when Eric picked up her music case *upside down*, so that all manner of 'the things we girls carried in our music bags in those days' fell out, along with her music.

Eric was 'a brilliant sight reader' at the piano, to use Freda's own phrase, and could chat away to his audience while he was improvising or playing an item from sight – chat which had nothing to do with the music: 'what he had had for his tea that day, or the price of fish,' Freda says. He would improvise in this fashion on well-known Salvation Army choruses, to the delight of his audiences. She also remembers him as 'a wonderful speaker – too deep for me though!'

Eric's pianoforte improvisions were legendary, and stories about them are legion. A favourite device of his was to ask members of the congregation to name a favourite chorus. Three such choruses would be chosen and woven into a pianoforte (or, occasionally, organ) solo. Writing many years later than the period under review, one correspondent mentions putting forward for this purpose his mother's favourite chorus, 'The cross is not greater than his grace', and speaks of being 'transfixed' by the result.

Typical of his kindness is a story told by salvationist-musician Bram Thornett, and his decision to play Haydn's 'The heavens are telling' as a concertina solo during a week-end's meetings led by the SP&S Band – an ambitious choice for anyone and on any occasion. Eric was to accompany him at the piano, which they found to be in poor condition, and half a tone flat. Eric did no more than take the music to his 'billet' during the lunch interval and transposed the music to C sharp major to accord with the concertina which was, of course, of fixed pitch.

Among the numerous headquarters bands and singing brigades which proliferated in the earlier decades of this century was the Salvation Singers. This group operated from the old Trade Headquarters in Kentish Town, and then, from 1911, when the Judd Street premises opened as SP&S Ltd, from that building. The group was 'legalised' by a Minute issued by the Chief of the Staff in 1904, the leader being Alfred Braine. Henry Hall, later to become the well-known dance-band leader, and at that time employed in The Salvation Army's Music Editorial Department, was featured with the brigade as a concertina soloist. Eric became pianist to the Salvation Singers in 1924. Olive was a member too, and can clearly be seen, with her customary smile, on one of the official photographs, as can Eric himself, and his friend for so many years, Sam Hooper.

Eric was still a junior employee at Judd Street when Sam arrived to join the tailoring department. Still young, he yet

came with some experience of the world, for he had served in France in the First World War, having joined up well before reaching the official minimum military age. He had seen destruction and death, and had witnessed the devastation of men's ideals and conduct, but his grounding in the Christian faith – in his family circle, and in the old corps at Exeter – had brought him through.

Now he had come to London, joined the corps and the band at Wood Green, and also the Salvation Singers, as a welcome reinforcement to the bass section.

During the return journey from a visit to the Channel Islands with the Singers a group formed in a sheltered corner of the ship to pass away the time singing songs from their repertoire. Sam, half in fun, was conducting. Not long afterwards, finding that Southall I Corps needed a songster leader, Eric mentioned Sam as being suitable to fill the gap, and he was appointed. A very efficient brigade was the outcome. In those days choral training in the Army was poor. Even well-known brigades had a 'brass band style'. Sam Hooper, already a choralist by instinct and by training, now took further private lessons with well-known tutors, and became interested in a new style of singing which was at that time becoming popular.

The Salvation Singers, 1926. Eric is in the middle of the third row from the back, with Olive on his right, and Sam Hooper on her right.

Southall I Songster Brigade in 1933. Olive is second from the left, front row; Eric stands immediately behind Songster Leader Sam Hooper.

The resulting 'sound' of his brigade made impact, and it was this 'sound' that he took with him to several other corps down the years, including Leigh-on-Sea, Clapton Congress Hall, Regent Hall, and Hanwell.

His fine bass voice and warm emotional approach to solo work were particularly impressive. Eric himself remembered with secret glee his and Sam's adventures in humorous ditties and spirituals, and Sam's duets with Doris Coles – whose was an equally compelling voice and personality. These latter could literally 'swamp' a congregation with sound and emotion. But Eric remembered most of all Sam's singing in a morning holiness meeting, 'O touch me again Lord' or 'Ah, then I knew' (Eric's own setting of Fanny Jolliffe's words).

Sam's speaking voice, too, was rich and expressive in monologues such as the anonymous 'Ballad of Calvary'. He handled a G trombone as to the manner born, was a founder-member of the Salvationist Publishing and Supplies Band, playing G trombone during the whole of its existence. He was excellent company; liked and could tell a good story and had an infectious laugh. He could hold an opinion firmly, even stubbornly, and found it difficult to suffer fools gladly. Afterwards, Eric himself was to say that 'Sam has been a good and loyal friend, especially when one was away from Army circles; and he loves his Lord.' What finer tribute could anyone pay to a friend than that?

Later in life Sam Hooper was to carve himself another niche in the Army's hall of fame by his work with the music camps (afterwards known as summer schools of music) for girls, held mainly at Sunbury Court, Middlesex. His skills at table tennis also made him a popular figure among students. As 'Uncle Sam' Hooper he made a lasting impression on innumerable young lives.

When he felt that, due to age, he must 'call it a day' so far as that activity was concerned, his successors were Muriel Packham (later to become Muriel Yendell), and, in time, Don Osgood.

Don, his brother Bert, and their father, Bert Osgood senior, were all redoubtable 'Southall-ites', all great characters in their own right, all supremely loyal to their corps and to The Salvation Army, all having lives interlinked with that of Eric Ball. Bert senior was a lasting influence on Eric, and Eric's life had the same effect on Bert's two sons.

By now Eric was serving his second term as bandmaster at Southall I. He himself later admitted that he was too young for the first term. Between whiles he instructed Upper Norwood Band, at its bandmaster's request. In some ways he had the best of both worlds in this: the privilege without the responsibility of leadership.

It was not long, however, before he was back at Southall. It is quite possible that he merely went over to Upper Norwood to conduct band practices, and probably stayed overnight, travelling in to the office the next morning. This was in the days before the type of commuting which is the order of so many of today's City men. Few people had motor cars at that time, and Eric never did have one.

During this period Eric formed a small orchestra at Southall, consisting of two or three violins, two mandolines, two clarinets, a couple of trumpets, and Olive on cello. The music used consisted mainly of hymn tunes, simple marches and so on, arranged by Eric himself. It was always a joke, then and in later years, a joke shared by Olive herself, that Olive could only use a bow, and could not 'finger-stop' a string, so that the range of keys and musical styles was some-what limited: every chord which contained a note for the 'cello had to use a note which could be played on an open string. This imposed quite a discipline on Eric as an arranger!

But Eric was not alone in this. When his own beloved Elgar, as a teenager, was writing his 'Wand of youth' music for a group of friends, mainly children, to play, he found that for one movement the double-bass player had to play another instrument, so that he had to use a stand-in for that one movement. This player could also only play on open strings (and only three strings at that). Later commentators who examined the original scoring (which was changed later for publication) testify to there being no limitation on the shifting-harmonic style of that particular movement, and nothing to distinguish it from others in the composition.

The Southall Orchestra gave at least three programmes 'away from home': one at Yiewsley, which also featured Eric as organ soloist, and two at Chalk Farm. The reporter said that on the second occasion the playing had 'considerably improved' since the previous visit! Chalk Farm Corps went on to form its own orchestra, and there were others formed at other corps during this time, notably at Nunhead. Gradually they all disappeared, even that at Nunhead, though this survived until the fifties, some of its members forming the nucleus of The National Orchestra, of which Eric was appointed conductor in 1935.

No survey of Southall I Corps, or of the life of Eric Ball, would be complete without mention of his cousin, May Pyke, née Sandford, since she was such a powerful influence on him, as were most of his mother's family, and co-writer with him of so many well-known Salvation Army songs.

Emily May Sandford, to give her her full maiden name, was a daughter of Clara Bryan, sister to Eric's mother. She was born in Hayes on 28 May 1893, and was thus 10 years Eric's senior. He was said to be 'a little bit in awe of her' – she was a deeply spiritual woman, much loved by all who knew her.

She became an officer, and held command of three corps in Norfolk, Swaffham being one of them. She would invariably come home to find items of food on her doorstep – a live lobster, fish, vegetables etc, without which she would not have survived as the corps were very poor, and officers' salaries were not guaranteed in those days.

All this led to a breakdown in health which brought her to an appointment at National Headquarters, in the then Naval and Military Department. Here she became a member of a brigade which sang spirituals almost exclusively and which was the first to sing at meetings led by General Bramwell Booth in the Westminster Central Hall. But a further period of ill health led to her resigning her officership after about five years. A six-week coma left her with impaired hearing and grey hair.

She was a talented woman: interested in poetry and drama, she wrote a number of poems, sacred and secular, and a number of plays in later years. She was corps cadet guardian at Southall I.

Eric's cousin, May Sandford as a cadet, and later, as she will be better remembered, as Corps Cadet Guardian May Pyke.

In 1919 she married Edward Charles Pyke, a semi-invalid following the First World War, and extremely neurotic. The marriage was not successful and the couple separated. May's daughter emigrated to America in 1946, and her mother followed her later that year. She found it difficult to settle as a salvationist in America, so later became a methodist, serving as an unofficial pastor, preaching, taking radio services, conducting outlying district services – everything except weddings. May Pyke died on 24 August 1949.

Of her song-writing, May Pyke once wrote, 'I have to write what I *feel*. I cannot string together certain phrases in order simply to make rhyme, or to set mere *words* to music. I am sure this makes the songs more useful, yet, at times, it means that they are rather too introspective for publication.' This is the woman who wrote the words of such 'Eric Ball classics' as 'Begin the day with God', 'Service and sacrifice', and 'True life' – the latter with its deeply challenging last verse:

> Life is a solemn duty
> To God and our fellow-man,
> Something to be accomplished
> As nobly as we can.
> Life is a charge committed
> To each as a sacred trust,
> And all an account shall render
> To the God who is always just.

The song calls forth from its composer music of deep feeling – a melody strongly chromatic, and striking harmonies to match.

Her daughter testifies to the benefit of 'a wonderful Sunday-school teacher at Southall – my great-auntie, Emily Bunn [that same Emily Bunn to whom Eric owed such a lot], the young people's activities at Southall and the influence of all the salvationists with whom Mother associated at IHQ . . . I've tried (and continually strive) to live up to the principles Mother taught me and which I learned from exposure to some wonderful people, especially during my childhood.'

These are just some of the people who were such a influence on Eric in his formative years, and to whom he had such cause to be grateful.

THREE

Eric the officer

Only a few months after joining the staff of Salvationist Publishing and Supplies Ltd, Eric moved 'upstairs' from the music counter to the Music Editorial Department, where he was to remain for close on 28 fruitful years. By this time he had already written 'for my own delectation', to use his own words, 'sonatas, overtures, and even a symphony or two'.

Eric had already had dreams of becoming a cathedral organist, and perhaps, too, a concert pianist, having already given organ and piano recitals. He afterwards recalled hiring a village hall, and having the thrill of seeing the local country gentry turning up in their traps and motor cars to hear him. But the most vivid memory of the occasion was the fact that, after paying all expenses, there was 10 shillings profit for himself!

He had also been fortunate in having met in his youth a number of outstanding musicians from whom he received much help, one in particular a Belgian military officer whom he had met in the First World War – a man with an excellent musical education, who showed great interest in him and who introduced him to aspects of music he had hardly dreamed existed. Tuition of this order and the assistance he received from his correspondence course all proved helpful to his studious mind.

But most of what he was able to do by now, so far as musical composition was concerned, was the outcome of close personal study and the rigid rule of self-criticism, besides hearing the finest music of all kinds.

Eric himself referred to this period in his life as 'his university', even though on one later occasion he added the wry comment that 'I sometimes think that we were under the twin jurisdiction of General William Booth and Ebenezer Prout! We never heard any Debussy there – or even any Delius!' It is easy to understand why; only during his time were the boundaries of Salvation Army music being pushed gradually outwards.

His earliest duties were mundane enough: typing and filing correspondence, hardly likely to fulfil his dreams of being a professional musician. But he also had the opportunity to study the scores of leading Salvation Army composers from Britain and abroad, for as well as having access to those of, say, Richard Slater and Arthur Goldsmith, he would also have to hand the music of, for instance, Klaus Østby of Norway, with its overtones of Greig, and Jules Vanderkam, of Belgium, whose selection, 'My fortress', was a classic of its period.

Another of his duties as a junior member of the department was to go along to R. Smith & Co, the publisher of brass band music, then at 210 The Strand, to obtain a copy of each new championship test piece immediately on publication. Eric was expected to sit at the piano and play the score from sight. This was good experience, and something he was ever afterwards grateful for. He always composed 'in score' on the page, knowing instinctively that the tone quality of each instrument he used was what he had in mind.

It was in September 1881 that William Booth had realised that some kind of 'department' would need to be set up to control the phenomenal 'octopus' that had come to birth following the appearance of the first Salvation Army band in the market place at Salisbury in 1878. Thus, Fred Fry, private secretary to Commandant Herbert Booth (who is considered by many to have been the most creative of all the Founder's children, and certainly the most musical) who was at that time in charge of the men's side of the officers' training home at Clapton, was appointed to produce music to meet the growing needs of corps brass bands. This responsibility was in addition to his existing duties.

There is no space here to permit a complete account of the department: its story has been fully told in *Play the music, play!* (Brindley Boon). The early struggles to produce printed music and the saga of the personalities are the material of a book of its own. By the time of Eric's arrival there a veritable industry was flourishing, and the amount of material being produced was extraordinary. This is still the case.

Eric joined a team consisting of Fred Hawkes, Albert Jakeway and Phil Catelinet, all working full-time in the office, and George Marshall, working part-time, mainly on proofreading, direct from home.

Richard Slater and Arthur Goldsmith had preceded Fred Hawkes as heads of the department; the results achieved by these men in terms of musical output, their influence upon

Fred Hawkes, Head of The Salvation Army's International Music Editorial Department at the time Eric came to work there. He conducted Eric and Olive's wedding at Southall in 1926.

'Heads bent over their work ...'
Left to right: Arthur Bristow,
one-time Assistant Head of the
International Music Editorial
Department, Fred Hawkes, Head,
Eric, and typist Chris Chalker.

Salvation Army music, and, in turn, upon the music of the brass band movement as a whole, is immeasurable. Present-day 'giants' such as Ray Steadman-Allen testify to the work of Arthur Goldsmith, for instance, whose name is almost forgotten among rank-and-file musicians today because his musical style has gone out of fashion.

Fred Hawkes himself was Head of the department from 1913 to 1936, and has been described by Brindley Boon as 'a progressive architect' under whose direction 'there was a consistent pressing forward to supply the ever-growing need of Army bandsmen, not only in the matter of output but also in the type of music demanded by advancing enthusiasts'.

The *Festival Series Band Journal* was inaugurated by him in 1923, his own selection, 'Gems from the "Messiah" ', being the first number in that series. He had already introduced the *Second Series Band Journal* two years previously. This was later renamed the *Triumph Series*. It would be interesting to know how many readers of this book, and how many brass players, 'cut their teeth' on compositions in this series! Solos with pianoforte accompaniment were now being published, mainly transcriptions of previously published material with band accompaniment. The theme-and-variation solo and the *air varié*-type of composition were introduced in his time – as was the tone poem.

Albert Jakeway, who had come to the department follow-ing a period of work in Czechoslovakia, continued there until his retirement in 1958; he was Head from 1952 until that year. When he joined it the *Band Tune Book* (1930 edition) was being prepared; his first task was to copy the tune 'For I'm going!' He is probably the most prolific of Salvation Army composers in terms of published items.

George Marshall's name is a legend in itself; how this giant of a man, who lay crushed in body under a fall of rock in a mine under the sea, lived to contribute so much to Salvation Army music is an inspiration to forthcoming generations. Sadly, his music is little performed these days.

The remaining member of the team, Phil Catelinet, remembers those days so well: the hard work they were engaged in; the fun they had ('sometimes, when the boss was out, we'd play golf in the office, using his umbrella as a club, a ball of string as a golf-ball, and a waste-paper basket as the hole'). 'And there were Eric's famous colds as well!' he recalls with a wry smile.

It is important to realise that, though so many people 'recall' Eric and his colleagues 'at work on their wonderful compositions', it wasn't like that at all. In any branch of pub-lishing editors and their assistants have little time to spend on their own work, 'wonderful' or not – they are far too busy preparing other contributors' items for publication. Most creative work takes place during an editor's leisure hours. Though the days of the midnight oil are gone literally, figura-tively they remain, and more is accomplished in those times than most of the world is aware of. But Eric wasn't physically strong, and he tended to catch very bad colds, sharing them, in his magnanimity, with any and everyone he came into contact with. Thus, at the slightest sneeze, he would be packed off home, and there he would remain for at least a fortnight.

'And then he would walk into the office with the score of a brand-new composition, looking the picture of innocence in the meantime, while we'd all look at each other, across the tops of the proof-pages we were reading, and wonder how long it was going to take him to go through the pages which were waiting for him,' Phil continues. 'It could have led to resentment, but it never actually did so.'

Ray Steadman-Allen makes the same kind of observation. 'There were the times when he had been commissioned to write a sessional song for cadets, and the training college "powers that be" would be calling for the song ready for rehearsals to commence, and not a note had been committed to paper,' he says. 'And then Eric would go down with one of

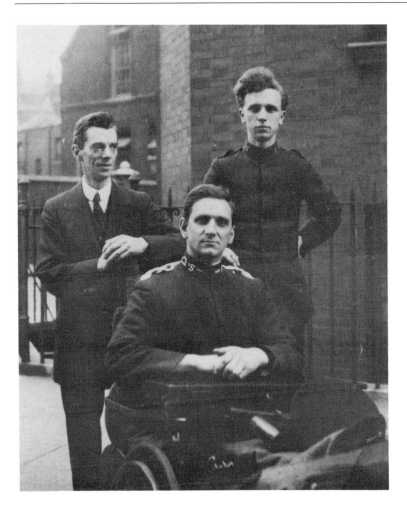

Eric, right, with George Marshall. The man on the left has not been identified.

his colds, and return with not only the music of the sessional song in his briefcase, but other things besides!'

In an interview published in *The Bandsman and Songster* in 1930, Eric said that he was not subject to inspiration at all times, saying that 'no musician is, and even when inspirational ideas come it still remains for them to be given form and arrangement. This is where good workmanship and the development of the artistic sense are essential. I always try to make music that is worth playing, worth listening to – something more than mere surface noise; music that makes a definite appeal to the best and highest in the human soul.'

A glance at the list of his publications, even up until then, reveals how he was being true to his ideal. Such band items as 'Adoration', 'A soul's awakening', 'The old wells'; and songs such as 'True life', 'As the palm tree', 'Christ my companion', 'Welcome, happy morning', 'Service and sacrifice' show skilful handling of melodies in the band pieces, and sensitive setting of words in the songs. All these, indicative of further quality to come, are almost unsurpassed in their own right.

In 'Adoration', for instance, he produces a selection which, while, in his own words, is 'one of praise and thanksgiving' is 'hardly of the "free and easy" type so often associated with these subjects, but an attempt . . . to musically suggest reverent worship and adoration.' Of the music of this 'early period', however, the *air varié* 'The old wells' is the greatest favourite, and is still often played in programmes.

Analyses of these selections may be found at Appendices E and F.

Noel Frost, a friend of Eric for close on 60 years, tells an interesting story concerning the band selection, 'A soul's awakening'.

This item, not played nowadays, and possibly worth reviving, illustrates musically the sentiments of the well-known Army song which begins 'O, the bitter pain and sorrow'. Its introduction and first verse depict the experience of one who, while declaring his self-reliance, yet feels his hopeless state. After the first verse the awakening of his conscience is described, but he temporarily quietens his soul by admitting 'Some of self and some of thee'. Verse 3 shows him almost wholly accepting Christ, 'Less of self and more of thee'. A rather elaborate section follows, depicting the resolute decision to face the whole matter out, his soul again becoming a battleground for the forces of good and evil, until, almost exhausted by his conflicting emotions, the band breaks into the last glad verse:

> Higher than the highest heavens,
> Deeper than the deepest sea;
> Lord, thy love at last has conquered –
> Grant me now my spirit's longing:
> None of self and *all of thee*.

We shake our heads and gasp in incredulity at the realisation that Eric was not yet *twenty-three* when this item was written. It is a typical example of Eric Ball's music being ahead of its time, and of its probing upwards and outwards in an effort to illustrate emotions hitherto unexplored musically.

Nottingham Memorial Halls Band, of which Noel Frost was then a member, was marching back to the hall, following its regular Sunday afternoon open-air meeting. Bandmaster Vickers was wondering what piece his band would play in the 'free-and-easy' meeting to follow, when a noisy, verbose,

Founder
William Booth

International Headquarters,
London E.C.4.
MONDAY,
23rd May, 1927.

My dear Comrade,

I felt the Demonstration on Saturday
night to be a real success, and your contribution
to it was certainly worthy of commendation. I
congratulate you on the setting you gave to those
striking words written by my daughter, the Colonel.

I trust that God will use you more and
more. In the words of the Founder "Soul-saving music
is the music for me", and I hope we may look to you
for even more of it.

God bless you!

Yours sincerely,

W. Bramwell Booth.

Band Instructor Eric Ball.

aw

24th May 1927.

My dear General,

I thank you most sincerely for your
letter of commendation regarding my effort towards
last Saturday night's Demonstration at the Albert
Hall, which has greatly encouraged me.

You may be assured that my continued
efforts will be directed for the Glory of God and
the Salvation of the People, and that I shall take
full advantage of all the opportunities for service
offered me by The Army.

Yours sincerely,

Eric Ball.

GENERAL BRAMWELL BOOTH.

drunken woman of notoriously questionable morals, staggered out of a public house and followed the band to the hall and into the meeting. The bandmaster announced to his men that they would play 'A soul's awakening'. The piece was duly played.

Ada Goode was noisy during the meeting, but quietened down during the playing of the band. As the music reached its climax in the lines 'Higher than the highest heavens, deeper than the deepest sea', she staggered to the mercy seat and knelt there. After a few minutes she stood to her feet, a new person. She never touched drink again; she sent her common-law 'husband' packing; she became a salvationist, commenced wearing uniform and remained a true, loyal, hard-working soldier of Nottingham Memorial Halls Corps until her promotion to Glory, some 50 years later. Such is the power of music, when 'the Spirit breathes upon the notes'!

So far as Eric's songs are concerned, it was not always good words to which he added his gilded touch. Those of 'Plunge in the fountain' may have been considered a liability, with

Above left: Letter of thanks from General Bramwell Booth to Eric.

Above right: Copy of Eric's reply. Always 'the encourager' it is good to see him gaining encouragement from his leader.

their exploration of the imagery of the blood shed on Calvary, and were possibly distasteful to the composer:

> Come all to the fountain Christ opened for sin,
> Break through every hindrance and plunge boldly in.

Yet by his forthright, shapely melody, and interesting part writing, he manages to produce a song which was a classic in its time.

'Classics in their time' is a description which might apply to a number of his songs from this period. 'Service and sacrifice' was a great favourite in holiness meetings a couple of generations ago, the plaintive melody of the first half of each verse echoing the sentiments of the words, before the whole choir sings of 'the voice eternal' which speaks to every 'eager, impetuous heart', the message of 'the voice eternal' forming the chorus:

> He who would follow the Son of Man
> Must take up his daily cross;
> Must walk a lonely way, and steep,
> Must for Christ suffer loss.
> Even to Calvary the way may lead,
> 'Twill call for sacrifice, for sacrifice indeed.

The song is one of those 'chicken-and-egg' conundrums; one wonders which came first, words or music. One suspects it might have been the music, for the words are not cast in any regular metric pattern. But they match perfectly, and the tiny cross-rhythm on 'Son of' in the chorus (a triplet of quavers against a dotted quaver and a semi-quaver) is extremely subtle. So much so that one wonders how often it has been observed in performance:

Another favourite choral work of Eric's which dates from this early period is 'Break forth into joy' which uses verses from Isaiah 52. An analysis of this music may be found at Appendix G.

Having regard to what was to follow, it is significant to find that for Eric Ball himself the idea of Salvation Army officership held no real attraction. In his candidate's papers, he says that '. . . I have been privileged to work for God and the Army in a musical capacity and am happy in the knowledge that my efforts *have* been of use to the Kingdom. My application for officership is now made as the outcome of the invitation by certain officers and in the hope that I may be increasingly useful to God by taking this step. Officership, as such, holds no appeal for me – only the hope that I may be used more by God as an officer. That constitutes my call.'

In August 1927 Eric and Olive Ball entered the Victors Session for training.

The International Training Garrison was situated at Clapton, though, to quote *The Salvation Army Year Book* for that year, '. . . the men have, during recent years, been accommodated at the Conference Hall at Mildmay Park, some half-hour's walk away . . . . The cadets, who this year number approximately 500, come from various social ranks and from an astonishingly large number of trades and professions.' The garrison was at that time presided over by the colourful Charles H. Jeffries, an outstanding convert from the early days of The Salvation Army, who had commanded his own batallion of the 'Skeleton Army' – bands of ruffians who set themselves up in opposition to salvationists. After his conversion he became an equally outstanding Salvation Army officer.

Jeffries was among the early officers sent to Australia, where his appointments included that of social services secretary. He also filled various posts in the British Territory at various times, including those of provincial commander and field secretary. He was the first territorial commander for Northern China, and first Principal of the International Training College (when training work moved from Clapton to Denmark Hill in 1929), and British Commissioner from 1931 to 1935. He had a tremendous influence wherever he went, and whatever Eric's misgivings as regard to officership might have been, he could not fail to have been impressed by his leader.

At the training garrison Eric and Olive would have had their own quarters, along with the other married cadets, but Eric would have joined the men for classes, and Olive the women. Occasionally they would have gone away together to lead weekend meetings, and at other times separately, Eric with the single men and Olive with the single women. Harry Warren, now a retired commissioner, living in Australia, remembers Eric playing E flat bass in the cadets band. Occasionally, the bandmaster, William Sansom, and deputy bandmaster, Frederick Harvey, would hand the baton to Eric and the bandsmen would enjoy his rehearsals. Harry Warren remembers him taking the band with great feeling through his own 'Adoration' selection.

Harry Warren was in those days called upon from time to time for vocal solos in the Clapton Congress Hall, and remembers Eric as 'a most sensitively helpful accompanist', on one occasion transposing at sight one of Eva Booth's songs, 'You and I', into a lower key to match the soloist's voice. On a Good Friday Harry was singing 'Come to this Man of Sorrows', when he 'dried' in the middle of a verse, and needed to substitute 'off the top of his head'. Eric cleverly covered for him at the piano.

In 1977, former members of the session met in reunion at Upper Norwood Corps, for a public meeting, moving for the next day, Sunday, to Sunbury Court, Middlesex. Eric and Olive were among those who attended. For the occasion he wrote a special song, full of nostalgia, but at the same time full of hope and reconsecration for the future. It appears to have vanished, but it fell gratefully on the ear on the occasion.

Training days for the Balls did not last for long. Like members of the staff of The Salvation Army Assurance Society, they were required to serve for only half a session in training, and a letter to Richard Wilson, the commissioner at SP&S Ltd, dated 20 December 1927, says, 'In accordance with word we have received from the Chief of the Staff, this comrade is to be made a captain and appointed to the SP&S Ltd. We have forwarded his marching orders to Commissioner Jeffries who in due course will hand them to him and Captain Ball is to report himself to you on Monday, January 2nd.'

Reunion of officers and cadets of the Victors Session at Sunbury Court, 1977. Eric and Olive are seated front row, far left.

Again, all these years later, it is interesting to read on his cadet's Final Certificate, under his 'Training Garrison Report', such remarks as 'Has fair education and ability – in first classes for all subjects and has done good work and shown some progress'. Under 'Leadership', we find 'Does good work on the field, self-possessed, has a definite message, voice not too strong'. And under 'Character' we read, 'Gives evidence of spirituality and character, has responded well to training, shown an excellent spirit and ability, developed along lines of real salvationism and is promising.'

So Eric and Olive commenced the next part of their lives together.

FOUR

Eric and Eva

Erik Leidzén, the noted salvationist-composer, once described the 1930s as a golden age of Army music-making and in many senses he was right.

It would appear from the Army's press that the thirties found 'something musical' for salvationists to do almost every week. There were programmes by the ISB; there were programmes by other associated headquarters bands; there were the Assurance Songsters; there were 'days' at the Alexandra Palace; there were small parties of salvationist-musicians visiting corps up and down the land. *The Bandsman and Songster* (and its successor *The Musician* in its early days) published profiles of soloists who were available to visit any corps which cared to invite them.

Bob Hamlett, of Middlesbrough Citadel, remembers a 'Southall Citadel' weekend at his corps, held during the thirties. Horace and Evelyn Mead were the corps officers at Middlesbrough, and both were doughty 'Southallites', so it was not unnatural for them to invite Eric Ball, Phil Catelinet and Sam Hooper to lead a weekend's meetings for them. And with such 'troopers' as these to lead it, how could it be anything but 'fantastic' as Bob remembers, more than 50 years later!

The thirties were certainly the golden age so far as Eric Ball's Army service was concerned.

A somewhat terse footnote in *The Bandsman and Songster*, 27 October 1928, following an item entitled, 'At close quarters with the *Second Series Journal*', had stated that 'A combination known as the "SP&S" Band, attached to Judd Street Headquarters, has now been formed, and, as opportunity arises, will visit different centres to demonstrate the possibilities of the *Second Series Band Journal*.' By 5 January 1929 the band had led weekend meetings at Sholing, Winton, and Derby II, and at the last-named corps, 'its personnel of seventeen players,

led by Captain Eric Ball, the Band, playing only the *Second Series Journal*, gave this well-known corps, in the words of Bandmaster Foster at the conclusion of the weekend's meetings, "a real treat" ' (*The Bandsman and Songster*). 'The Scout Leader' had been among marches played; the singing of Bandsman Hooper, the monologues of Bandsman Childs, also the pianoforte duets by Captain Ball and Bandsman Catelinet 'were well received' according to the same report.

By June of that year the band had conducted an 11-day tour of the Channel Islands, commencing at Southampton and including various corps on Jersey and Guernsey.

Arthur Bristow, a one-time member of the band, has his own memories of its activities: 'The band came into existence . . . as a result of 16 employees of SP&S Ltd being sent to Halesworth in Suffolk where the 1,000th Salvation Army band had recently been formed,' he wrote in *The Musician* many years later. 'The men travelled in the bright red furniture van using chairs from the various offices. It was not intended at that time that the band was to be permanent, and its first weekend away was to Winton, where the then Adjutant Frederick Coutts was the commanding officer.'

He goes on to say that 'A point of note is that this was the first band to be equipped with Model "C" overcoats, each one being tailored so that the hems of all the coats were the same distance from the ground.' In the early stages its uniform

The SP&S Band, with its only bandmaster, Eric Ball, taken in 1930. Sam Hooper can just be seen seated, far left.

SP & S Band on the march, 1929.

was a plain blue tunic with the well-known 'S' in blue embroidered on the collar, and the SP&S monogram on each epaulette. Later the band was equipped with red tunics with white facings.

By the time of the band's visit to the Channel Islands it was becoming a firmly established part of Army life, taking part in national musical events, and, from 1931, sharing with the International Staff Band the responsibility of preparing and presenting new band manuscripts to the International Music Board. Soon after the outbreak of the Second World War the band was discontinued, because the majority of its members were being called up for national service. It is maintained by some, 50 years later, that the band's discontinuance could have been caused by rivalry with the International Staff Band.

But the SP&S Band is held in affectionate memory by all who were concerned with it. Noel Frost, a member of Stapleford Band, recalls how, as a rebellious teenager, he heard it on campaign at nearby Nottingham Memorial Halls, at which corps he was then a soldier. He was wondering whether to sever his link with the Army. 'The SP&S Band transformed my life,' he declares, and he is a salvationist still.

The band travelled extensively during its term of activity, and its sole bandmaster was Eric Ball.

Many years later, in a feature 'My heart stood still', a correspondent, Wally Horwood, wrote in *The British Bandsman* of how 'as a very shy youth in 1939' he tiptoed to the bandroom door at Judd Street. 'The band were indulging in a pre-practice warm-up. Then an immediate silence as the conductor rapped his baton. Suddenly the band crashed into the splendid *fortissimo* of his own [Eric Ball's] lately published tone poem "The triumph of peace". I am sure my heart stood still as I was engulfed by that welter of glorious sound and to this day the memory returns whenever I hear a brass band in full stride.'

It is interesting to look at the programmes presented by the band. At Southampton Citadel, for instance, on Saturday 18 March 1939, Bramwell Coles's 'Under two flags' opens the programme; his 'descriptive selection', 'Pilgrimage', is included, as well as Eric Ball's 'Biblical tone poem', 'Exodus', Albert Jakeway's selection, 'Gems from Gounod', and Erik Leidzén's meditation, 'The cross'. There is a trombone solo, 'The priceless gift', a cornet duet, 'Deliverance', and a euphonium solo, 'Song of the brother'. There are three songs, 'Reign, Massa Jesus', 'Were you there?' and 'The gospel train', from Sam Hooper, a monologue, and, preceding the last band item, a song by the vocal party, 'By the way of the cross'.

Thus there is variety, and only four 'heavies' out of a total of eight items in which the whole band participates.

The Sunday afternoon programme opens with the bandmaster's own tone poem, 'The triumph of peace', and includes the cornet solo, 'Tucker', the *air varié*, 'A sunbeam' and the 'study', 'St Peter' (the last two of these by Eric's friend and office-colleague Phil Catelinet). Albert Jakeway's selection, 'Memories of the past', and, finally, Bramwell Coles's march, 'Sons of the Army', are played. There have also been another monologue, and a song, 'Ah, then I knew', from Sam Hooper. Again, not too heavy a programme, and one with considerable variety. By now the band's personnel has increased from 17 to about 25 players, to cope with the bigger numbers.

It has been said that composers of test pieces for the brass band championships would go to Eric and the SP&S Band with their music and ask him to 'run it through' with the band. For obvious reasons they were unable to go to, say, Brighouse and Rastrick, with the same request, since all test pieces were kept strictly 'under wraps' up until a certain date. But composers would want to know how their pieces

Cartoon of Eric, drawn by his friend, Cyril Kingston, for *The Bandsman & Songster*, 1929.

sounded, and in this way Eric met Arthur Bliss and others, contacts which would, unknown to him at the time, serve him well later.

At this time Eric was still very much involved in life at Southall Corps, being corps cadet guardian there at the beginning of the decade.

Rosalind Catelinet, who was one of his corps cadets, remembers him in that role. 'Well, yes, we thought he was pretty good!' she says. 'There were about 30 of us at one period. Eric had two sergeants [helpers] to assist him – Albert Dorsett with the boys, and Susan Dorsett with the girls. We had a wonderful time doing all the things corps cadets do.'

The thirties were the years when Eric Ball was proving himself indispensable in so many directions: as a composer, conductor, soloist or accompanist at piano or organ (and sometimes all of these), as a reporter of national events for the Army's press, as the author of stimulating articles, as a public speaker, and, towards the end of the decade, in 1937, as an international visitor at a Salvation Army music camp in the United States of America.

Frederick Coutts writes in *The Bandsman and Songster* (23 November 1935):

. . . The ever-welcome Songster Leader Hooper sang about

'The sergeant on the door of the dear old Army hall,
The sergeant on the door with a cheery word for all . . .'

We could do with a few more such sergeants who would relieve the stranger within our gates of a good deal of embarrass- ment. I hope the broad hint of the chorus was widely taken; and if memory lapsed for a moment in verse three, the lapse only served to show how skilfully Captain Ball at the piano could cover it up, and how courageously the songster leader could recover to go on to one of his robust and triumphant conclu- sions. (The songster leader felt his throat giving way after the singing of the first line, and stopped for a moment to recover himself. It was not a lapse of memory, as many others thought. – Ed)

This now leaves the quintet and the Salvationist Publishing and Supplies pieces – 'Recollections' and 'Exodus'. The piece for piano and strings charmed us all. It would not be fair to make special mention of any one of the five players – they were Mrs Joseph Hoy, Songster Peggy Brown, Captain Ball and Bandsmen J. Lewis and P. Burgess – and the choice extracts from Schubert were familiar enough to interest everyone, and yet were played in so delicate a fashion that the conscience of the strictest musical purist could not be offended.

Now what about the Band of Salvationist Publishing and Supplies? Its conductor is the last man to want fulsome praise. It would be offensive to him. Yet, when in response to the continuous

cheering the bandsmen rose to their feet at a word from Captain
Ball, I felt it was the audience who ought to have risen in salute
to one of the Army's greatest musicians. He should not have
stood to us . . . .

These were the years of 'Exodus', of 'Songs of the morning' and of 'The King of kings'; of the character-study songs
'The lifeboatman' and 'The door sergeant', written for Sam
to sing, of Scripture settings such as 'The whole armour of
God' and 'Psalm 150' (even though the latter was not published until 1940), and, most of all, of those splendid
sessional songs, such as 'Torchbearers', 'The awakeners',
'Liberators', 'Guardians of the covenant', 'Enthusiasts', and
(again in 1940), perhaps the greatest of them all, 'Hold fast!'
For the first three of these he worked with Albert Orsborn,
then Chief Side Officer for Men at the International Training
College; then, when Albert Orsborn went to New Zealand as
chief secretary, William Leed was his collaborator. He
worked with Kaare Westergaard on 'Hold fast', a song which
deserves special mention.

(Each session of cadets, whether in Britain or other parts of
the world, has its own name – a name which is regarded
proudly by the officers trained in that particular session.
Though some of their names fall rather quaintly on modern
ears, they were not regarded so by the cadets who formed
them. They resolved, in the words of their songs, to bring
'light to wanderers . . . out there!' or to 'awaken' people to
their need of God; to help liberate the masses from the
power of sin, or to 'hold fast' to their call to God's service.)

In 'Hold fast', Kaare Westergaard gives us a cosmic picture
of the forces of evil in conflict with the legions of light, a
picture which is illumined by Eric's unmistakable music.

What newly commissioned officer could dream of resigning after singing such a sessional song, an analysis of which
appears at Appendix H! Sadly, quite a few, for the vision
soon fades for some after all. Some would reach their first
appointment only to find that all their male members had
enlisted or been called up for military service (for it was war
time). They would feel there was nothing they could do but
join them. Others would grow discouraged at the conditions
they found at their appointment, especially during these days
of added hardship due to the war.

The song is a tiny masterpiece of almost mini-cantata pro-
portions. It will be remembered, too, that since the Hold
Fast Session was commissioned just after the outbreak of the
war, the words of the song would have special significance for
singers and hearers alike. It is somewhat ironic to note,
though, that the session was to have had a different name.

Somewhat late in the day General Eva Booth decided on a change of name to 'Hold Fast' – so that if she had herself 'held fast' to her original decision, the song would never have been written. As it was, words and music had both to be completed in a great hurry.

What a writer of 'good tunes' Eric was!

When scored as the first movement of his suite, 'Songs of the morning', his song, 'Welcome, happy morning', takes us almost into the enchanted world of the Mendelssohn 'Midsummer-night's dream' music:

Elgar himself would not have been been ashamed of the intensely lyrical music to May Pyke's words, 'Begin the day with God'; it is so similar in style to his own *Salut d'amour* that it could almost be considered as a kind of first-cousin to it:

There is music written in a superbly broad fashion for Eric's setting of John Oxenham's words which begin 'Peace in our time, O Lord . . .'. And even Sir William Walton might have been pleased to call his own this theme from 'Torchbearers' when called on to write a coronation march:

All these have that unmistakable stamp of a good tune. The average listener (and the university professor, for that matter) may not be able to sum up exactly what it is that makes 'a good tune', but average listener and university professor alike recognise one when they hear one! And they certainly hear one in any of these examples, and in any of a hundred-and-one of Eric Ball's melodies!

And what a 'chooser' of good tunes he was! – in his classic selection, 'The King of kings', for example, when he depicts the conquering power of Rome with crashing fanfare figures. How unerring is his choice of melody to depict the Nativity of Christ: Gounod's ingenuous little song, 'Bethlehem' ('*Dans cette étable*'). And how unerring his choice of soprano cornet to play it to us! Only the flugelhorn might have been more appropriate – but that is only opinion; most would agree with the composer's own choice. And how delicious is the rocking accompaniment for the other instruments! Perfection indeed:

But he follows that with a highly original choice for the ministry of Christ; possibly a tune little known even when he was choosing it, since it dates from 1889. But it was exactly right, since its words echo the prophecy of Isaiah of the Suffering Servant:

> To heal the broken heart he came,
> To free the captive from his chain;
> The blood he spilt when he was slain
> Brings guilty sinners home to God:

And after the cruel, surly cries of the crowd, in 'Crucify him, crucify him', have reached their climax in a chord which reputedly caused members of the first audience to hear it to run from the Regent Hall with their hands to their ears, crying 'What is happening to Army music?', how appropriate to have the solo cornet sounding utterly broken in heart and in spirit in the tune, 'Calvary', 'O come and look awhile on him'. No other tune would have conveyed quite so utterly the pathos of the scene:

Then, 'when the hurly-burly's done' of the previous movements and their interludes, and 'when the battle's lost and won' of the Saviour's life and man's redemption, what better tune than 'Diademata' – 'Crown him with many crowns'? Even that isn't enough: Eric Ball manages to weave into his final cadences phrases of the much-loved Easter song 'He arose, he arose . . .' to depict not only the resurrection but the ascension of Christ. The Saviour's train of triumph is now complete.

Not every salvationist-composer has had the privilege of having his work praised by no less a composer than Sir Edward Elgar, but it *did* happen to Eric Ball. The organist of Canterbury Cathedral, hearing the SP&S Band play his *air varié* 'The old wells', asked for a copy of the score, and took it to show Sir Edward, a personal friend of his. Both agreed that it was a splendid piece of brass band scoring, and Sir Edward wrote to Eric, saying that it was 'free and sane and open-airish – all three good objectives'.

Not only was Eric Ball conductor of the SP&S Band throughout the 1930s, but in 1935 he was appointed conductor of the National Orchestra. This was in succession to Harold Zealley, who had been given another appointment in the United States.

The first appearance of this group under his direction was at the National Songster Festival, at Clapton, on 25 January 1936. Mrs Joseph Hoy was leader of the violins, of whom there were five others. There were also two violas, a cellist, a double-bass player, and a pianist, who was the then well-known Joyce Kyle. On that occasion the group played the overture to Handel's 'Messiah'. 'The absence of woodwind and brass made the contrapuntal work . . . very difficult to appreciate,' says the writer of the official report. What he would have made of modern performances on original instruments one is left to wonder. 'The Party was much more successful in "A Keltic [*sic*] lament" and in the *andante* movement from Mendelssohn's Violin Concerto. Mrs Joseph Hoy was the solo violin. Her tone was really beautiful, and in her double-stopping she displayed technical efficiency of a high order.'

Few persons at the Royal Albert Hall on Monday week worked as hard as did Captain Eric Ball. He was present at both the dedication and commissioning of the cadets, and in addition to contributing a succession of voluntaries on the grand organ, accompanied the congregational singing, and provided picturesque interludes during the pageant, *The Captivity and Liberation of Mansoul*, a striking adaptation from John Bunyan's *The Holy War*. For the actual commissioning ceremony the captain left the organ-loft, reluctantly, we dare avow, to conduct [the] Salvationist Publishing and Supplies Band, which supplied occasional martial music, and thus helped to maintain the fervour of this memorable event in the lives of some 400 young evangelists.

'The Song of the Liberators', specially composed for the session by Colonel Albert Orsborn and Captain Eric Ball, was sung by all the cadets under the leadership of Adjutant Will Harrison.

(*The Musician*, 23 May 1936)

This was at the commissioning of cadets in May. To be accompanist, conductor, and composer of the most import-ant song, all on the one occasion, 'can't be bad' as they say!

The SP&S Band gave a programme in the Central Hall, Barking, early in 1935. The Mayor was in the chair; members of the local branch of the British Legion, some 400 of them, with their standards, had marched to the hall, headed by Barking Band. The playing of the visiting band, the euphonium solo, 'Wondrous love', and the vocal items of the band, were an inspiration to the large crowd which attended. 'But Captain Eric Ball's salvation appeal will long be remem-bered,' the *Bandsman and Songster* correspondent reported.

Bandmaster Sidney Hill, of Wandsworth, reporting a year later in the same newspaper the national songster councils held in the Clapton Congress Hall, said of his talk, that 'to many he was revealed in a new light as, with quiet eloquence born of conviction, he placed before us "The value of the wider vision." Hitherto unexplored vistas were opened up before our eyes as he spoke of music, poetry, personal cul-ture, and their place in service and worship. And when he said, "I want to speak of the things of the Spirit," we experi-enced a thrill greater than any we have felt on hearing some of his wonderful compositions. As this young apostle of sanctified modernity talked of the deep things of life we of the passing generation felt that the future of the Army was safe in the hands of his kind.'

Later that year Eric was being pressed into service as a journalist, writing reports for the editor of *The Bandsman and Songster* (6 July issue) of a Youth Festival of Music and Song at the Alexandra Palace:

At 6 30 pm, on to the orchestra of the Great Central Hall are trooping young people's bands and singing companies which have just marched past the General. There is chatter, hubbub, *heat*! The audience, mainly adults, quickly fills the vast auditorium, and well before the advertised time we are waiting for the com-mencement of the Festival. The platform is a patchwork of dark reds and blues, relieved by the brighter red of the uniforms of the Swedish Staff Songsters. Programmes used as fans give a bizarre sense of mirage to the upper orchestra; and through it all peals the organ, at which sits Bandsman Kent, who is doubtless experiencing that unmoved, detached sense of power so well known to those who love the seclusion of the organ-loft; and in spite of the noise and chatter, he plays well, not noticeably per-turbed by the fact that very few in the audience seem to realise the standard of musicianship that is being exemplified.

7 pm – The General! A blare of brass, and the bands sustain a

long, joyous unison; the waving of hundreds of programmes, and right at the outset her personality is stamped upon the proceedings.

And now the Festival sets off with a kind of rhythm which rarely falters to the end, so that in spite of the heat our interest hardly flags, and even those constantly-moving programmes become an accepted part of this festival of restless, daring youth, for daring these young folk are, in the music they choose, in the way they tackle it, and in the gravity with which they self-consciously fill their places as the musicians of the day; and all the time there is hammered into our minds – 'The Future! The Future!! The Future!!!'

And, everywhere, his tone poem, 'Exodus', was being played and heard. In the official report of the Bandmasters' Councils Festival, 1936, the writer comments:

It is a good thing to withhold [an item] from publication if high standard of interpretation will make it easier to play when it is actually in the hands of the bands. The gain will be all the greater when, as in this case, the band rendering the music is conducted by the composer, who is thus able to give the correct interpretation. In spite of distracting echo effect this was the most inspired performance that I have heard. I am fortunate in having a pianoforte score before me. An analytical criticism bar by bar will convey little to my readers, but a reference to the 'programme' of the item may give some enlightenment. Excellent tonal effects are given in the 'In bondage' picture; ponderous and powerful tone without anything blatant indicating the spirit of 'Imperial Egypt' and the successive moods indicative of 'Israel's despair', the warning 'Death motif', and the seemingly Egyptian triumph demand more than ordinary imagination and interpretation from the players. True sympathy is established between conductor and men, and a glance reveals how quickly the latter respond. 'The night of the passover' theme, with its haunting melody, is delicate in its rendering, and when the music again rises in intensity the Band reveals inspired playing. The selection as a whole calls forth team work, and all players must lose their identity. One may, however, be permitted to especially refer to the soprano who, at one moment with brilliance of tone and execution and at another with lightness and grace, reveals himself as an outstanding player. He is an artist, and I thank him for his work. The 'Thanksgiving' theme, with its old Hebrew strain 'The God of Abraham praise', finds the band in no way tired, and though the character of the piece needs a 'programme' to rightly interpret all its meaning and to quicken the imagination, those who hear it know that its rendering is of the highest standard. In some of the movements the finest band playing of the evening was revealed.

Eric was apparently in great demand again at the 'Great Coronation Festival' (to celebrate the coronation of King

George VI and Queen Elizabeth – the present Queen Mother) the next year. He conducted the massed bands for the opening song and the closing chorus and led them through '. . . a very fine rendering of the "Coronation" march, and the really wonderful interpretation of the meditation "Rock of Ages" which, of course, had never been unitedly rehearsed. The trombones of each band playing unitedly were most effective, as also was the soulful cornet solo of Bandsman H. Dilley, stealing above the accompaniment of the band like a bird hovering above the gentle hum of city traffic.'

It is Arch Wiggins, editor of *The Bandsman and Songster*, who is waxing so lyrical in his report, and in the next paragraphs telling us that 'When Songster Marjorie Hughes sang her two pieces, "Lord of every perfect gift" and "The charm of the cross", in a voice of flute-like clarity that filled the huge building and entranced the great audience into perfect stillness, it was the adjutant who accompanied her with masterly touch on the piano.' He continues, 'When that unassuming young songster leader, Jack Haynes, of Twickenham, rippled his sticks with lightening dexterity across the hard wooden notes of his xylophone and brought forth music, real music, it was Adjutant Ball who, with equal facility, rippled the ivory keys of the piano in accompaniment.'

He goes on to tell us of Mrs Joseph Hoy playing again the slow movement of Mendelssohn's Violin Concerto, and how 'the adjutant again sat at the piano . . . of how Adjutant Eric Ball appeared in yet another role, that of composer-conductor, when he took his band through the intricacies of two of his latest works ['Exodus' and 'Songs of the morning'], and of how 'the other bands present seemed mediocre in comparison with that of SP&S, and they would be the first to admit it'.

Tom Giles, a former member of the International Staff Band, has vivid memories of this period:

> I was in a taxi going from Judd Street to the recording studios with Commissioner Jolliffe, Colonel Hawkes, and Eric, to record 'Consolation' to reveal my trial qualities, and also to record 'A happy day' and 'Jesus is strong to deliver'. 'Consolation' was recorded, but after two and a half hours spent in an endeavour to record the other numbers the work had to be abandoned. Eric felt the accompaniments to these solos were unpianistic. He phoned his friend Phil Catelinet and asked him to appear at the studios the next morning when the recordings were completed.
>
> It was while we were in that same taxi that Commissioner Jollife asked me to record 'Tucker', whereupon Eric immediately volunteered the services of the SP&S Band to accompany. Then

the feud started, because the International Staff Band claimed
first priority. However, Eric was granted permission, and it was
then that I found what a dynamo he was. Three nights for three
weeks we worked in rehearsal.

My other great experience with him was going with the then
British Commissioners, Charles Jeffries and Rich, to conduct
Bandsmen's and Songsters' Councils at Birmingham, Manchester,
and Glasgow. Always in the preceding Saturday evening festivals,
when there would be anything from 1,500 to 2,000 in the congregation, there would be a request for me to play a slow melody
solo, e.g. 'Lord with my all I part' or something similar. Eric
could make the massed bands sound like a mighty organ in their
accompaniments. I have seen him white with emotion during
the interpretation of such music as 'The King of kings'.

Another typical story of a similar, personal, nature which
belongs to this period, showing something of the influence
Eric Ball shed all around him, is told by Winifred Backhouse,
a retired Salvation Army officer, living at Hadleigh, in Essex:

As a teenager, just before the war, I worked at the head office
of The Salvation Army Assurance Society. At one of our weekly
meetings for prayers, Adjutant Eric Ball was the speaker. I have
never forgotten his words. He started off by saying, 'I have to
confess to you a sin – the sin of boredom. But then I ask myself,
"Why should I be bored? I have hands that I can use" ' (and he
stretched out his hands and looked at them, and we could see
him using those expressive hands, to conduct the band, or play
the organ). He went on to speak about having eyes to see, a mind
with which to think, and so on, ending, 'So why should I be
bored?'

He certainly captured our attention, so much so, that after all
these years I can still see him standing there before us. He
became a 'hero' for at least one teenager!

Another such teenager, working at Judd Street, was Vera
Marlow, now Vera Lawrence, who remembers that her duties
occasionally took her to the Music Editorial Department
where Eric, Albert Jakeway, and Frederick Hawkes could be
found, heads bent low over their work.

Eric would always stop whatever he was doing – never complaining – and either receive my messages or tell me where he
wished me to put them. He always acknowledged me as one of
the 'Judd Street juniors'.

One day – I remember it as though it were yesterday – General
Evangeline Booth arrived. She had written the words and music
of a song, based on Isaiah 35, 'Streams in the desert', and
wanted the SP&S Band to play it to her. In subsequent years I
realised that it was a tone poem, arranged by Eric, for full band,
based on her initial song. I can see it all now, though it was many
years ago: the General and her fellow-officers walking through

into the Assembly Hall. They came out later, with Eric Ball walking by her side. His face radiated happiness; the General was apparently delighted with what she had heard.

I suppose we young teenagers could be forgiven for stopping our work just to stand and stare. I can still see them in that procession. Such memories always come back to me when I see the names of Eric Ball and Eva Booth.

General for slightly less than five years, this remarkable, striking, flamboyant, gifted daughter of the Founder was named 'Eveline', but always thought of herself as being 'Evangeline', and was popularly known as 'Eva' by the rank and file of The Salvation Army. The cry of the cockney down-and-out – 'Lor' bless yer Miss Eva' – is perhaps the subject of an apocryphal story, but it sums up the feelings of hundreds, if not thousands, of people – sick, sad, lonely, dying, whom she encountered, loved, wept over, prayed for, in Britain, in Canada, and in America. She could quell a riot by wrapping a United States flag around herself, she could hold an audience of thousands spellbound by her oratory, she could write verses and music. It has been said that, each morning, as she arrived at International Headquarters, a trumpeter sounded a fanfare.

Eric himself wrote in *The Musician* of 25 December 1965 of his contacts with Evangeline Booth.

He had not met her before she became General, yet all his life he had felt a strange interest in this spectacular personage of whom he had heard so many fascinating stories. She had often been spoken of in his family circle, for his mother had, as a cadet in the training home in the 1890s, given some small personal service to 'Miss Eva', and the tale was often told, to the end of Mrs Ball's life. Then, like so many of his generation, he came under the spell of the presence and oratory of the Commander from the USA during some of her rare visits to Britain. Five hundred cadets at the International Training Garrison in 1927 would, if they had been asked, have followed her to the ends of the earth, hypnotised by her stories, her humour, her rolling phrases, her authority, her humanity.

Soon after she arrived in London to take up the office of General, she made it known that she wished to see Eric. It was not sufficient merely to call at her office. He was to meet her one morning at Wimbledon Station – a long way from his home. To this rendezvous the General's car brought her from her home in Esher, Surrey. At Wimbledon an officer alighted, his interview completed, and Eric entered the car to meet and talk with the General on the way to International Headquarters. When they arrived, he was courteously dis-

adjt Eric Ball. With deep appreciation of all you have meant to the music of the armies. Keep it up.
Evangeline Booth
1937

SONGS OF

THE EVANGEL

GENERAL EVANGELINE BOOTH

New and Enlarged Edition

COPYRIGHT

PUBLISHED BY
SALVATIONIST PUBLISHING & SUPPLIES, LTD.
JUDD STREET, KING'S CROSS
LONDON, W.C.1
MADE IN ENGLAND

Title-page of *Songs of the Evangel,* the book of songs on which Eric worked with Eva Booth, signed by her.

missed. Further meetings were even stranger, in that, for some reason never revealed to him, he had to keep them secret. He was to work with the General on the final edition of a collection of her songs, *Songs of the Evangel.* This was being thoroughly revised and a few new songs added.

He was never in at the birth of a new song. Bramwell Coles would see the General and bring back a sketch of the new work. He was a man who could keep his counsel, and he would not tell his staff how the General conveyed her musical ideas, whether by writing, by playing on organ or piano, or by singing. 'The General does not want you to see how she first writes a song. She says you would laugh at her!' he told them, mysteriously. The sketch of the new song would be handed to Eric to work on, and then placed with the rest of the material for the book. Then he awaited his call!

This would come in a strange way. One morning the phone would ring. It would be a call from International Headquarters: 'Go out of the building to a call box and phone Lieut-Commissioner Richard Griffith.' (Richard Griffith was the General's private secretary.) This Eric did. His instructions were: 'The General would like to see you at 2 pm. Tell no one at all'. This included his commissioner, it would seem! The General would graciously request the use of the sitting-room in the caretaker's flat at the top of the IHQ building. There, hidden away, they would sit together at the piano. Eric would play her songs, and they would discuss them, criticising, amending. She would accept criticism readily, but she knew what she wanted.

'You don't like that chord, do you Ball?' she would say.

'No, General, I don't.'

Smiling, her hand on his arm, she would say, 'But I *want* you to like it!'

A couple of hours would pass by, and then Eric would go home, earlier than if he had been at his own desk.

Meanwhile, at Judd Street, there would be trouble. Ball had gone off again, without a word. Next morning he would be summoned to a superior.

'Where were you yesterday afternoon?'

'Oh, just – out – on private business,' he would reply.

The superior would shake his head. 'You know, all this will go against you, and your promotion comes up in a year or two!'

It was following one of these clandestine interviews that the phrase 'tone poem' came into Salvation Army phraseology.

General Evangeline had written an extended version, for band, one of her *Songs of the Evangel* – 'Streams in the desert'. Eric had tactfully altered a chord progression here, a phrase there. Now it was almost – but not quite – ready for submission for publication. 'I feel it needs a – sort of – title,' he told her.

'But it has a title – "Streams in the desert",' the General replied.

'No – that isn't what I mean. A sort of descriptive title. You see, it isn't a march, or a selection or –'

'No. You're quite right. Then what is it?'

Eric looked out of the window, with those faraway eyes. 'I think the phrase "tone poem" describes it,' he said.

'Yes, "tone poem" – I think I like that.'

'But *they* won't like it,' he told her.

'Then they'll *have* to like it. You say "tone poem" – I like "tone poem" – "tone poem" it shall be!'

And 'tone poem' it was.

But what of her songs? Were these her own work? Eric was asked that many times. He spoke as he found. There was no doubt about her talent for music – but a person who is at once a public orator, administrator, Commander, and, at last, General, has not the time to perfect musical techniques. The *ideas* were certainly there, her very own; Eric and she interpreted them together into the language of music. He, or others who helped her, could not (so he said) have written 'I bring thee all', 'The star in the East', 'His love passeth understanding'. Without her these songs, and many others, would never have been heard, and the Army would have been the poorer. She produced, Eric says, a kind of folk music.

As a poet he considers she was even more talented, more sure, and quicker in expressing her ideas.

Eric admitted he never met her in an official capacity and endured no clashes of temperament such as one or two of his contemporaries have described. They respected one another, and in after years, when he thought of Eva Booth, he remembered her not so much as a General, an orator, a poet, or a musician, but as very much a woman – intriguing, talented, gracious, generous, demanding, human – and at heart, he felt – lonely.

FIVE

Eric the Exile

By the decade of the forties Eric Ball could have been said to have had the Army world at his feet.

In 1936 General Eva Booth had promoted the young Captain Eric Walter John Ball to the rank of adjutant – two years before it was due. Not that he himself used all of these names – he has often told the story of how he signed his very first pieces with his full name. 'Can't you find a few more?' Fred Hawkes had grumbled. Ever afterwards he had been 'Eric Ball' (or 'E.B.'). And it was after he had been threatened on the General's behalf by his 'superior' at Judd Street that his promotion would be withheld or postponed that this premature recognition of his service had been made by General Eva herself.

It was during the afternoon session of a series of councils for bandmasters, deputy bandmasters and YP band leaders of the British Territory that the General made the announcement. The reporter for *The Bandsman and Songster* wrote that '. . . the spontaneous and thunderous cheering which broke out when the General announced that Captain Eric Ball had been promoted to adjutant leaves no doubt in our minds as to his popularity amongst the bandmasters'.

But there were still further fields for him to conquer. In December 1940 'A programme of music entirely composed by *Major* Eric Ball attracted a crowd of more than 1,300 people to the Clapton Congress Hall', *The Bandsman and Songster* reported. Among the visitors 'from all parts of London and from places far beyond' was Eric's cousin, May Pyke, whose song, 'Service and sacrifice', was among those sung by the songster brigades from Harlesden, Regent Hall and Clapton Congress Hall. He conducted the massed songsters in 'Ah, then I knew' and 'The pilgrim song', and solo brigade items included 'Christ, my companion' and 'Enthusiasts'. Fred Grant, Grace Rolls, Isobel Stoker and Clifford Haines, all of them leading soloists of their day, provided accompaniments, vocal solos, monologues and trumpet solos respectively.

It is interesting to read *The British Bandsman*'s assessment of this programme:

> I was much struck with the perfection of blend as between band and voices, and doubt if such an effect has previously been achieved by such a combination of instruments and voices in Salvation Army circles. The conductor (Major Eric Ball, ARCM) demanded much of his forces and was rewarded by a magnificent response which oft-times reached an exhilarating height, and the large audience was not slow to demonstrate its appreciation.

By April 1942 he had been appointed Instructor of Rosehill (Salvation Army Assurance Society) Band. In May of that year Eric conducted Tottenham Citadel Band during the commissioning of cadets at the Royal Albert Hall. To the International Staff Band is usually given the privilege of providing the music at this annual occasion, but for some reason it went to Tottenham Citadel that year. The event was scarcely reported in the Army's press; pressure upon space due to wartime restrictions was probably the reason.

The next month Rosehill Band visited Luton Temple under Eric's leadership. Alfred Gilliard reported the visit in *The Musician*, commenting particularly on the conductor's invitation to the Sunday evening congregation to 'Sing all the songs you recognise', when introducing his selection 'Constant trust', and saying that, 'As a result voices provided an accompaniment to the melodies, and the linking and descriptive passages were better understood. It was a good example of making the "Sunday night selection" contribute to the main purpose of the meeting.'

The issue of *The Musician* dated 4 July 1942 contained the announcement that '. . . Colonel George Fuller has asked to be relieved of the bandmastership of the International Staff Band. The Chief of the Staff has acquiesced and appointed Major Eric Ball to be the colonel's successor . . . .'

The actual change-over of baton was made (according to Brindley Boon in *ISB*) on Saturday afternoon 19 September. Speaking on behalf of corps bandmasters, Bandmaster Albert Munn said that he had never heard the ISB in a 'shoddy' performance, and went on to express the hope that the new bandmaster would 'blend the sparkle of the SP&S Band with the broad tone and dignity of the ISB'.

Such an appointment could have been thought to be the very highest ambition for a relatively young man, but not for Eric Ball. Many times afterwards he said that the bandmastership of the ISB was not the height of his ambition: his highest aim was to emulate Christ.

Eric had already conducted the ISB in a broadcast. This had gone out on the Forces wavelength from 9.25 pm to 10 pm on Monday, 31 August. The programme included the march 'Spirit of victory', Eric's own suite, 'The pilgrim way', the selection, 'Memories of the masters', the *air varié*, 'The hardy Norseman'; and two unpublished pieces – the selection, 'Happy memories', and the march, 'Be of good cheer'. Then there was the band's first weekend campaign under its new bandmaster. This took place at Watford, the Saturday evening programme being given in Watford Town Hall. We are told that 'an innovation' in this programme was a song by the male chorus, directed by Lieut-Colonel Ernest Wellman.

By January of the next year Major Eric Ball, ARCM, bandmaster of the International Staff Band, had been appointed a member of the International Music Board, as successor to the late Colonel George Fuller. (The colonel had been promoted to Glory within weeks of handing over the baton to his successor.)

Two further innovations occurred in the programmes given as part of the International Staff Band's 'First London Week-end Campaign with Major Eric Ball' (*The Musician*, 3 February 1943). The Saturday programme was divided into three sections: Music from Russia, the United States of America, and Great Britain, the flags of these countries standing unfurled in front of the platform. 'Moments with Tchaikowsky' represented Russia, a new cornet solo, 'Memories' (John Allen) the USA, and 'Exodus' Great Britain. 'This is our Pilgrimage' was the theme of the Sunday afternoon programme. 'A.R.W.' (Arch Wiggins) commented that 'it is good to work on a definite line of procedure. Every item had relation to the truth that this is not our abiding place, that we are citizens of a Heavenly City, and are progressing daily toward that goal'.

When the band visited Upper Norwood on a Sunday in that month, Bandmaster Stewart Thompson commented quite frankly in *The Musician*, 6 March, that 'The band's response to the bandmaster's quick-changing modes of expression shows a great improvement since I heard it a few months ago. A better understanding between band and conductor is beginning to show itself. The best is yet to come.'

The next month the band was announced to conduct its first Manuscript Weekend at Regent Hall under Eric's direction on Saturday and Sunday 1 and 2 May. Before then it would make 'a tour of various camps', including the ATS

(women's corps) at Stoughton, Pinehurst Camp, Farnborough; and Boyce RAMC Barracks, Crookham, as well as giving a public festival in Guildford Cathedral, and leading a public salvation meeting at the Theatre Royal, Aldershot. The indefatigable 'A.R.W.' describes the tour in great detail, telling us, for example, that 'Major Eric Ball easily established contact with each of the band's audiences, both public and private, but only once did he venture a pianoforte solo . . . . The band's full-part and unison singing was as thrilling as its playing – exquisite at times – and made a most effective change from the instrumental items.'

The General (George Carpenter, Eva Booth's successor) presided over the Sunday afternoon programme given at Regent Hall. Wesley Evans, commenting in *The Musician*, 22 May 1943, says that, 'Major Ball had chosen a nice blend of

There are few pictures of Eric conducting the International Staff Band of The Salvation Army, and fewer still like this one, of him conducting before a military audience. This was probably taken at Aldershot in 1942.

well-known and new music, ranging from the deeply devotional selection by [Erik] Leidzén, 'The Saviour's name', to the lively and rather humorous march-medley, 'The Army on the march' (Herbert Mountain) . . . . All the soloists played with deep feeling and taste in the selection, while the subdued accompaniments were an object-lesson to the many visiting bandsmen present . . . . Major Ball not only played four short children's pianoforte pieces by Schumann, but gave illuminating comments on them and the composer.'

'I hope you noticed the spiritual as well as the musical appeal in the programme. If this is a sign of the portent of Salvation Army festivals, then we welcome it as such,' had been the words of the British Commissioner on the Saturday evening. 'A.R.W.' details the playing of 'The divine pursuit' (Bramwell Coles) in *The Musician* (29 May), adding the remark of a member of the congregation to the corps officer, 'I have been as much blessed as if I had attended a holiness meeting.' . . . 'Major Ball's hope that the second part of the programme would resolve into an act of worship, of seeking, and consecration, was thereby consummated.' Once again the singing of the male chorus is commented upon, 'A.R.W.' suggesting that it is 'likely to become proverbial'.

Two correspondents in a later issue of *The Musician*, one a one-time bandmaster of a St John's and a British Legion Band, and the other a salvationist serviceman who had walked 17 miles back to his camp after the Saturday festival, spoke glowingly in their letters of the impact the programmes had made.

'A.R.W.' – who else? – writing in *The Musician*, 5 June 1943, said: 'The International Staff Band continues to participate in unique experiences, the latest being its afternoon visit to one of the largest, if not *the* largest, military detention camps in the country . . . . The singing of "Abide with me" was something to be remembered by all who participated in this highly privileged event. Major Ball had asked the men to join in and to "Make it a link with all the best you know" and they did – with due sincerity and reverence . . . . In the morning the band had broadcast from the No 1 Studio of the BBC, and it was another unique experience for the writer to hear it play without a conductor during the balance test, and the piece was Bandmaster Marshall's arrangement of Schubert's "Unfinished" Symphony! Major Ball was listening-in with the engineers.'

The reporter of the band's programmes at Darlington comments on 'the trouble that Major Eric Ball took to explain the spiritual interpretation and message of each number . . . . The organ-like playing of "I think when I read" on the Sunday morning march to the citadel . . . .' 'A pre-OCTU [Officer Cadet Training Unit] camp, situated in the woodlands of Kent, was visited by the ISB for the purpose of providing cheer for the Troops', 'A.R.W.' reports in *The Musician* of 17 July.

And Eric was still composing.

Two settings of secular airs for Salvation Army purposes dating from this time are outstanding. Each bears out the later verdict of Eric Wilson, writing in *The Independent* newspaper, that '. . . even a short hymn setting was done to perfection'. For even though they were not originally conceived as hymns, they had taken on that character, by the employment of religious words, and by Eric Ball's exquisite arrangements.

'Praise him with psalms', for instance, uses the old Scottish tune, 'Turn ye to me'. Of his arrangement, Eric himself said, 'This beautiful Scottish air should be sung in a quiet, flowing style, not very emotionally, but in a manner perhaps inspired by the clear, cold strength of the mountains rather than the more personal beauty of southern valleys.' His arrangement of an Irish air, with the words entitled, 'The world so deceiving', was a great favourite with songster brigades for some 20 years, and deservedly so. It makes an effective contribution to a programme and to a gospel-type meeting.

The music of these two arrangements is reproduced in Appendices M and N.

Yet another of his songs from these years, this time for male voices, 'O fire of the Spirit', possibly written for Staff Band Chorus use, is most powerful. In the key of D minor it ends with a *tierce de Picardie* with the first tenors singing a ringing F sharp, approached from an F natural, this progression always being extremely effective, even if difficult to sing in tune! The F sharp is doubled at the octave in the divided first bass line. The song was used to great effect by the New York Staff Band Male Chorus in the late fifties–early sixties period.

Stanley Preece, a Salvation Army officer living in retirement in Canada, remembers the visit of the International Staff Band to Cardiff Stuart Hall Corps, where he was the corps officer, on 25 and 26 March 1944. 'This weekend with the band was the final weekend of the officership of Eric Ball,' he writes. 'We saw the band off back to London on the Monday morning of 27 March and on Wednesday 29 March we were informed in Cardiff that Eric was no longer an officer. The news answered for me, the host of the ISB visit, one or two questions. I recalled that during the whole of the visit of the ISB I could not get the leader of the band and the conductor together for the purpose of co-ordinating details.

Also, I had a real problem getting the conductor to talk to me about anything. He must have been under great stress. I have never forgotten the unusual strain of the weekend . . . '.

Little did the staff bandsmen realise, as they followed the sensitive yet demanding baton of their conductor that weekend, that they would not again play under his bandmastership. Within days of their return to London the leader broke the news that Major Eric Ball had resigned from Salvation Army officership. No reason was given' (*ISB*, Brindley Boon).

But it was widely rumoured that Major Eric Ball was experimenting in spiritualism.

It was on 6 April 1944 that the Chief of the Staff, Charles Baugh, acquainted the General's international commissioners with the news that he had received the resignation of Major Eric Ball as a Salvation Army officer. His announcement ran as follows:

For some time there have been fears that the outside interests of the major were wider than those of an Army officer should be. It became known that he was attending psychic meetings. Prolonged efforts were made to convince him that the practices of these meetings were far from helpful . . . . After allowing him full opportunity to consider his position it became necessary to ask him to choose between the Army and those things of which the Army disapproves, with the result already stated. His resignation has been accepted.

At the time of writing there is reason to believe that the separation of this comrade from us will take place with undiminished mutual esteem, as well as regret on our part.

Eric himself had written already to General Carpenter on 11 December 1943 in the following terms:

I feel it is time to let you know that I am sure that the path of psychic-spiritual unfoldment, about which you interviewed me, is one which I have been definitely led to tread.

Many years ago you spoke to me of the call of God, and since then I have been increasingly aware of his guidance and overruling in almost every phase of my life.

In this, its latest phase, I am more sure of that guidance than ever before, and have made up my mind that any latent psychic powers which have been given me shall be unfolded and used in the service of humanity, wherever and whenever possible.

I know this result of the interview will thus be a disappointment to you: but it helped me to an even clearer perspective of the whole matter; and I shall never cease to appreciate its value to me, as well as the value of our previous conversations.

God bless you.

Sincerely yours,

Eric Ball

The British Bandsman was quick to comment:

> The Salvation Army have suffered a severe blow in the retire-ment [*sic*] of Major Eric Ball, the accomplished director of The Salvation Army Staff Band. Eric is a fine composer and arranger for brass bands and we hope our bands will have the opportu-nity of performing some of his works.

And, in a later issue:

> . . . Eric is in the prime of life and will make a fine mark in any branch of music which he undertakes.

Clearly the brass band movement had 'an eye on the main chance'! And could it be blamed? He was obviously held in as high esteem there as in The Salvation Army.

Eric himself was to say later that with the benefit of hind-sight, he could see that perhaps his motives could have been somewhat mixed, but that whatever errors were made by him or anyone else, he could see the guiding hand that never fails.

He had apparently always been interested in the idea of the angelic presences and had warmed especially to General Evangeline Booth's description of seeing her father gazing from the battlements of Heaven, telling her 'Go on, Eva!' He had heard first-hand accounts of healings by the Army's early-day leader and song-writer, William Pearson. He was interested to hear of William Booth-Davey, Commandant Box, Hugh Redwood, and others who had similar interests. He had also been brought into touch with the London School of Mediumship. He had never had any doubts about angelic presences: it all came naturally to him. So he began to read and study with the School. He was asked to speak at one of their meetings, and did so – perhaps unwisely, as he him-self admitted, in view of the fact that he was a Salvation Army officer.

The blow finally fell when it became known that he was studying extra-sensory perception. It was viewed with disfavour – a fact which he afterwards said he perfectly understood. He had spoken at Caxton Hall, London, had played the piano for the School, and had given lectures on the spiritual basis of music – and all without official sanction. He was firmly informed that it would all have to stop.

His attitude at that time was that if he was invited to speak anywhere on the gospel as he understood it, he would do so – with the accent on the word *anywhere*. 'If I spoke at a spirit-ualist meeting I preached Christ – I never indulged in any of their practices,' he once declared. 'By the same rule, I would, if invited, preach Christ at a communist meeting – but I would not indulge in any of their practices. And I would preach in a brothel as well – if invited.'

But there was more to follow. After a weekend away with the ISB he would receive a note on the Tuesday saying, for example, 'The music board gave you permission to play such-and-such in the Saturday evening programme only. We hear that it was played in the "wind-up" [an occasional late Sunday evening musical 'extra' so beloved by salvationists on these occasions]. Why was that?' Or, 'In your broadcast last evening your programme included Schubert's "Serenade" – whereas the title we have is "A prayer". Why was this?' He would explain that he did not want the Army to appear foolish in including a title which Schubert manifestly did *not* write, so he gave the piece its correct Schubertian title.

Again, these things were part of the discipline under which he served, and though it would appear petty to the uninitiated it needs to be remembered that Eric was bandmaster of the International Staff Band – the band which provides the pace and the pattern for all other Salvation Army brass combinations.

Minor grievances though they were, these all added to the tension.

But the outcome of the larger issue was that he was told that he must not continue. A confrontation resulted with the Head of the Salvationist Publishing Supplies Ltd, John Lewis, and an interview followed with General Carpenter. At last he received a phone call from the Chief of the Staff, the General's right-hand person, who is responsible for the implementation of Salvation Army policy world-wide, asking what he had decided. He confirmed that he felt he could not give his word not to do this, that or the other.

'Then you'll have to finish, won't you?' was the Chief's reply.

Acting upon instructions John Lewis sent for him and asked, simply, 'How are we going to do this, Eric?' to which Eric replied, 'You mean you don't want to sack me?'

'Then you'll have to resign,' was Lewis's reply.

Eric did so.

On telling the story many years later to Brindley Boon for the latter's book *ISB*, he made it perfectly clear that in all of this he felt no bitterness. He could see that the Army's position was untenable. He had had a good time – particularly during General Eva's term of office – and he could not possibly imagine what sort of a life there could be for him outside of Headquarters. But he had made his decision. His leaders made further attempts to resolve the problem, but he felt he could not agree to let go the study of what he felt to be a further dimension of Christian experience. He realised that there was nothing else the Army could do but ask for his withdrawal.

Musician that he was, he must have been familiar with Haydn's oratorio, 'The Creation', and the final *recitative* sung by the archangel Uriel before Adam and Eve had been expelled from the Garden of Eden:

> O happy pair! and happy still might be
> If not misled by false conceit.
> Ye strive at more than granted is;
> And more desire to know, than know ye should.

'O happy pair! . . .' For upon Olive, too, the blow had fallen. It is an inflexible Salvation Army regulation that when a married officer resigns his or her commission, the spouse must resign too. She had to leave with him.

SIX

Eric and 'Elsa'

If, as has been said, Eric had 'the whole Army world at his feet', why did he throw it all away, resign, and go his own way – into a hard, harsh world; the unknown? Many have asked, but probably no one knows for sure.

Did Eric want to stretch his creative wings outside the constraints imposed by Salvation Army requirements? Salvation Army music is essentially functional, serving the needs of the organisation, and at the time of which we are thinking, the parameters were a great deal more narrow than they are now. Phil Catelinet certainly is of this opinion, and it will be remembered that he himself served as an officer for a period at the next desk as Eric in the Music Editorial Department. By the time Eric resigned, Phil had already done so.

But this was 1944 – the middle of the Second World War, which could have dragged on for many years. Eric knew that so long as he was an officer, with the status of a minister of religion, he was not liable for national service. As soon as he laid aside his Salvation Army rank and title he did make himself so liable. Besides, he had been exercising such a tremendous ministry among salvationists, musicians and non-musicians alike, that it seems the height of folly that he would want to cast that aside for an alternative career which, in the immediate future, would bring about the possibilities of danger on active service, a premature widowhood for his beloved Olive, and even if he survived the war, all the uncertainty that would follow.

Throughout his adult life Eric had a close relationship with his sister-in-law, Elsie Dorsett. She was seven years younger than Olive, and five years younger than Eric himself. For a number of years she was primary sergeant (a Sunday-school teacher working among very young children) at Southall I. He had his own pet name for her – 'Elsa'. And it was to 'Elsa' that he dedicated one of his most famous pieces, *'Resurgam'*.

He would obviously be deeply affected by her illness (tubercolosis) which led to her early death on 15 September 1942.

As has been seen in an earlier chapter, the Dorsett family was a very strong influence on Eric. It could be truly said that to be married to one member of such a powerful family was to be married to them all. Albert and Susan Dorsett were intensely proud of their son-in-law – he who was making such a name for himself in Salvation Army musical circles. They were an intensely devout family, and very committed to Army service.

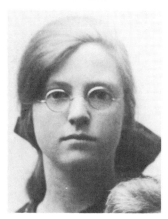

Elsie Dorsett — the 'Elsa' of 'Resurgam'.

A close friend of the Balls from this period says that Eric commenced attending spiritualist meetings round about the time of Elsie Dorsett's final illness. The writer of a programme note used in a broadcast performance of *Resurgam* soon after Eric's death said that it was dedicated to 'Elsa, the woman who brought him through a great crisis in his personal life.' Is it possible that he delved into spiritualism to try to find out the reason for her illness and premature 'entry into the Summerland' as her gravestone in Southall puts it?

For Christians, and for thoughtful Christians in particular, life is very much a quest, a seeking, whose end is hidden from them. They make their journey by faith; they make their decisions likewise. They *hope* their decisions are the right ones. At times their inner voices confirm that this is true. At others they find, when it is too late and usually with the benefit of hindsight, that those inner voices are mocking echoes of the truth.

For the creative person, particularly the writer, the poet, the composer, life is a hovering between two distinct worlds – that of the physical and that of the spirit. There are times when his feet stray dangerously close to the edge of the path and he is not fully aware of this – until it is too late to draw back. But he needs inspiration, or his creative instinct dies. He occasionally wonders where his creativity has come from. It is not always enough to wave his hand vaguely in circles in the air and say, equally vaguely, 'Oh, from – out there – somewhere'. He knows, too, that it is not enough to say 'It's all in my genes – or something'. He knows, even though it may be enormously difficult at times to convince his fellows, that he is directed by some force, some power, outside of himself.

The Christian creative person is totally convinced that his gift is of God – of the Holy Spirit. He must acknowledge this, or he denies the God he seeks to serve.

But is it always so? The moment a writer picks up his pen to write, he is vulnerable. He is open – to the *Holy* Spirit, or to some other spirit. Eric Ball himself said, on numerous occasions, in letters to friends, to students, in interviews, that he has not remembered much about the actual composition of a work; that just as novelists remember little of the actual writing of a book or certain passages in it, he has been used as the person through whom the Holy Spirit works.

In a letter to Stuart Frost, a young Salvation Army officer, and, with his parents, a close friend of Eric Ball for many years, Eric wrote on 11 May 1979, '. . . It was good of you to write in such generous terms re "The King of kings" . . . It is rated an "old" work now, I suppose: but it seems I was guided in choosing the tunes which it contains, and I can only thank God that it can be used as a channel for his power. St Francis's prayer comes to mind – "Lord, make me an instrument of thy peace." '

Spiritualism was very much the 'in thing' in the twenties and thirties. There are references to it in the novels of Agatha Christie and the Lord Peter Wimsey novels of Dorothy L. Sayers. Noel Coward's comedy *Blithe Spirit* is the classic example of a play on this subject.

Much of what is thought of as spiritualism is shrouded in mumbo-jumbo, of rapping on tables or walls, of speaking in strange voices, and so on. Much of this activity has been indulged in by the merely curious, and they have found afterwards, to their own cost, that it was ill-advised.

Just as some spiritualist activity is motivated by curiosity alone, and by fascination for the supernatural, for some it also has a much deeper intention. There are those who wish to convince themselves with regard to human survival of bodily death. There are others who, grieving the loss of loved ones and close friends, find a certain consolation in the belief that they are able to communicate with them. Still others want information about the future life.

All of this is amusing to some, and anathema to others, but is in any case merely an off-shoot of something which goes very much deeper.

But Eric's reason for going to a spiritualist meeting was, so he said, purely evangelical. He went to preach Christ. He once told a friend, 'My faith lifts me to a plane that enables me to be in constant touch with the Holy Spirit. There is, therefore, no need, and neither has there been a need, to interfere or take part in the practice of spiritualism. My work with those people was purely and simply gospel-based and evangelical.' He always said, too, that 'any spiritual gift is a *gift* – either you have it or you don't – and as such must be exercised.'

Eric himself testified afterwards to being drawn very early

in life to the more mystical side of religion. He remembered meeting, even as a boy, a woman who testified to having been healed 'by faith'. He said afterwards that he never sought this gift, but having discovered it, he felt he must develop it, as witness the letter he wrote to General George Carpenter and quoted in the previous chapter.

There are those who testify to physical healing through contact with Eric Ball. One such, living in Poole, says,

> Several years ago I was very ill, suffering from bronchitis and asthma, probably aggravated by my years as a prisoner of war. It has been published recently that many PoWs in the Far East are suffering from respiratory problems. I was so desperate one evening, being unable to breathe, that my daughter, without my knowledge, contacted Eric (she knowing of his ministry of healing), and asked him to visit me.
>
> Naturally I had been under medical care, but this had not proved very helpful. Typically, Eric came immediately. He prayed, and administered healing. He intimated that this problem was deep-seated and would require long-term ministration. Consequently, he came each week for three or four years, my wife acting as chauffeur during the whole of this time. If he was unwell, he would project his thoughts in my direction.
>
> I felt humbled to think that this great man should give his time, and use his God-given gift, for me, for I am such a very ordinary person, yet we felt it was a privilege for him to come into our home, and share this ministry with us. During this time my wife was supportive in every way. I cannot adequately describe those incredible hours we shared. Eric would come in and greet me, then sit down, and we would talk quietly about the corps, with which he was deeply concerned and very much involved. Suddenly he would look at his hands, and say, 'The Power is here; we can begin.' He would pray, and then lay his hands on me. As his hands came near me, I would feel a heat and a power.
>
> Afterwards he would thank God for being with us; then we would repeat together, 'I am one with Divine Love, and he is one with me', gradually decreasing to a whisper. He would then sit down, obviously spent. We felt the power of the Holy Spirit, being unaware of anything except the Lord's presence. We would sit in silence, not wanting to disturb the peace and the tranquillity which we felt. How long we would sit I don't know. I only know it was the most wonderful experience we have ever known.
>
> Before coming to know Eric, and being subjected to his ministry, I must admit to being rather sceptical, though my wife believed implicitly in this ministry. However, I am now leading a comparatively normal life, accomplishing tasks which would have been impossible before. It is a miracle.

Another friend of Eric's, living in Bournemouth, who

again wishes to remain anonymous, for the whole experience was too personal to reveal her identity, speaks of the intense pain of rheumatism in her fingers being considerably lessened when Eric had gently held her hands in his own, and prayed with her.

Gwen Barnett sustained injuries to her left wrist and to her left leg in quite separate accidents. On one occasion the pain in her wrist was excruciating. Eric held her hand in both of his own, and said a brief prayer. The pain immediately left her and has never returned. The stiffness is still there, but that she feels she can cope with. On another occasion, when the pain in her leg was very severe, she asked him if he would heal her. This time the result was different. The pain and the stiffness remained. 'It is as though God gave me a gift without my asking for it, but I should not have asked for a further cure, she says, philosophically.

Lynne Parker, of Poole, tells of sustaining a serious fall in July 1981, though not realising the gravity of her accident until some days later, when she began experiencing a dull pain in her left leg. By late September she had to seek medical advice, the pains by now becoming so distressing. The doctor prescibed physiotherapy and spinal injections which would deaden the pain, though the bone she had damaged in her spine would never heal.

Three months and three spinal injections later she was no better, and the wife of the then corps officer suggested some kind of spiritual healing. At first Lynne was more inclined to accept the pain she was suffering as some mysterious part of God's will for her, but in March the next year she entered the home of Eric and Olive Ball for the first time.

The hours spent there, quietly sitting in an atmosphere of peace and tranquillity she had never experienced before, became very precious to her. She writes as follows:

> Just sitting quietly, letting the Holy Spirit's presence fill the little music room, feeling God's love pour down upon me through the touch of Eric's hands as they trembled and warmed to such an intensity under God's influence and transferring his healing power to me was very real. Almost immediately I was able to return to a full and normal life.
>
> I continued to visit Eric twice a week for prayer and healing. He was so unhurried that I always felt that time was standing still for us. He seemed to be so interested in me and we would talk of our mutual love of music, which serious composers we favoured, and, of course, about my physical progress. There were a couple of times when I phoned Eric, in tears because I had had a relapse, but he would come to my home and gently explain that sometimes a healing experience comes in waves,

ebbing and flowing, each time getting stronger, and I found the pain gradually diminishing after each session.

In July of that year I went away for a fortnight's holiday, and Eric phoned to say he would be praying for me, particularly on the Thursday, as this was the day he set aside for prayer and meditation. It was with great amazement and joy that on that particular Thursday evening I realised that I had felt no pain at all on that day. And in the eight years that have elapsed since then, I have continued to feel no pain. I have been truly healed and am now a completely new person, enjoying a full and deep relationship with Jesus Christ.

Eric continued to keep me on his prayer list until he died, and never passed me in the Salvation Army hall without an encouraging word and a hug. I loved him deeply, respected him greatly, and will always thank God for him.

Even after my healing, when I returned to the hospital for what proved to be my final check-up, astounding the medical profession, I was advised to continue to treat my back with care, and not to consider having another child. Alison was born, without difficulty or defect, in March 1984, and we both continue to thrive.'

There are others, however, who found such contact at least disappointing or at worst uncomfortable. There are those who testify to receiving help through his meditation sessions, particularly those held when he was much older, even to being restored to the deep Christian experience which they had previously left behind.

Edit Smith, of Blackpool Citadel, remembers asking Eric,

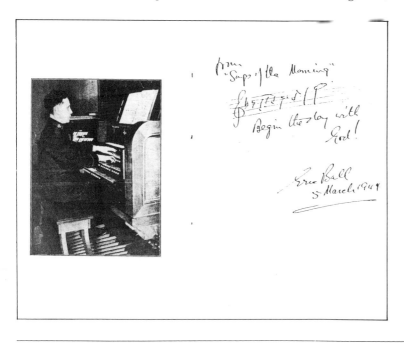

A page from Edit Smith's autograph book with the opening of 'Begin the day with God'.

many years ago, to write the opening bars of his favourite
item from his own music. He handed the book back to her,
with the page covered, saying, 'What is *your* favourite among
my pieces?' To her reply, 'The song, "Begin the day with
God",' he said, 'And here you are' – handing the book to her,
with the opening bars of that song inscribed in it. Geoffrey
Brand, who succeeded Eric as editor of *The British Bandsman*,
remembers Eric telling him that he *knew* instinctively that this
was the time to change to another career, and that he *knew*
equally instinctively that he, Geoffrey Brand, was the right
person for his replacement.

Eric testified later to thinking he might just perhaps have
seen a figure in his room. 'I was writing at my desk – a letter
or some such thing, certainly nothing about religion or
music – and I became aware of a Presence in the room. I
realised that if it were there it must be Him. The experience
nearly tore me apart.' Will J. Brand, the salvationist song-
writer and poet, had the same experience. It is interesting
that both men saw nothing of comfort in such a vision. 'To
me, it was like Gerontius, who wished to see his Lord, and
the Angel tells him,

> "Yes – for one moment thou shalt see thy Lord.
> One moment; but thou knowest not, my child,
> What thou dost ask; that sight of the Most Fair
> Will gladden thee, but it will pierce thee too . . ."'

Will Brand told me on one occasion. It is interesting that
neither thought they saw Jesus, their Saviour.

There is this story, too, about the parson's dog.

On one occasion Eric was conducting band practices in the
north of England, and he stayed in the parsonage of a certain
village. After supper he was shown to his room, and went to
bed. At around five o'clock the next morning he was woken
by snuffling sounds and a tugging at the blankets, to find a dog
in the room. Fond of animals he might be, but he felt, quite
rightly perhaps, that this was no time to receive the friendly
attentions of one. He fondled it and then told it to go back to
bed.

'I didn't know you had a dog in the house,' he told his host
at breakfast time.

'We haven't a dog,' his host replied, whereupon Eric
related his earlier-that-morning experience, describing the
appearance of the animal.

The parson went to a drawer and pulled out a photograph
of a dog. 'Is this the one?' he inquired. Eric said that it was.

'But this dog died five years ago,' his host replied.

During my research I heard this story three times, each

from an entirely separate source. The originator could only have been Eric himself.

Increasingly, the mystical writers, Julian of Norwich, Thomas à Kempis and the like, were ever at Eric's elbow. More and more Eric became a man of prayer; communion with the Unseen became more and more his goal. He often said that he could more easily commune with God when walking along the road than in the silence of his room. He would include a prayer in letters to friends: 'I am in touch with the Eternal, and the Eternal is in touch with me,' and recommend to them that they make it their prayer to realise that experience.

Grace Barrett, a salvationist living at the time of this incident in Wellington, New Zealand, remembers him conducting a songster workshop when songsters from the 10 corps in that division met. Under his baton they sang as never before; but his greatest contribution, she says, was when he sat at the piano and played, 'Turn your eyes upon Jesus'. They saw no man but Jesus only.

'Then Eric Ball recommended this simple prayer for our private devotions,' she writes:

O God
I give myself to thee
Body
Soul
And spirit
Thou dost rise within me
And manifest thyself
In my thinking
Speaking
And doing. Amen.

'I still use this prayer,' she adds.

And there appeared in his music from the fifties onwards, particularly that for bands, traces of this mysticism which was becoming the hallmark of his life.

In the *Festival Series Band Journal* for July 1954, there appeared the first composition by Eric Ball to be published by The Salvation Army for 10 years. I well remember, though a teenaged bandsman at the time, something of the stir it caused in Salvation Army circles. It was a meditation, 'Sanctuary', based upon one of his own songs for female voices, a setting of Albert Orsborn's words beginning, 'In the secret of thy presence'. There is an arc-shaped figure in the pianoforte accompaniment which gives this sense of mystery to the song, and it conveys this same sense of mystery in the band arrangement, sometimes as a straightforward accompanying figure, faithfully echoing its place in the original song, and sometimes playing an important role in the texture in the development section:

Key B flat

In 1942, the then *Ordinary Series Band Journal* had issued his meditation, 'The victory of love', based on his song 'Love stands the test', and his remarks which accompany the full score are significant: 'A general word of warning might not be out of place regarding the interpretation of this piece,' they say. 'In the first place note the title: 'The *Victory* of Love'. The contemplation of Divine Creative Love will surely not bring thoughts of mere sentimentality, and this music, inadequate though it may be, should not be allowed to suggest such thoughts. The term "Meditation" can also be misinterpreted: to meditate does not necessarily lead to purely passive thought, but sometimes gives opportunity for the inner voices to call the soul to creative activity.'

It is perhaps significant that this score appeared at about the time of Elsie Dorsett's death.

Four years after the appearance of 'Sanctuary' came 'Songs in exile', whose very title, when used in a spiritual sense, conveys an air of mysticism. An analysis of this work appears at Appendix I.

It was in 1968 that the tone poem, 'The eternal presence', was published in which the composer sought to capture 'moods evoked by reading Psalm 139:7–11':

> Whither shall I go from thy spirit? or whither shall I flee from thy presence?
> If I ascend up into heaven, thou art there: if I make my bed in hell, behold, thou art there.
> If I take the wings of the morning, and dwell in the uttermost parts of the sea;
> Even there shall thy hand lead me, and thy right hand shall hold me.
> If I say, Surely the darkness shall cover me; even the night shall be light about me. (*AV*)

The main theme is the hymn tune, 'Still, still with thee', which occurs hardly at all in full, but fragmentarily from the beginning. The note to the score (by Brian Bowen) is reproduced as part of an analysis of the music at Appendix J.

However, the piece which most of all conveys a sense of mysticism is '*Resurgam*'.

When he first started working on it, Eric would have had no conception of the impact this music was to make on the contesting world, and later on the wider circles of the brass band movement and the brass band world of The Salvation Army. 'It is certainly a teaser and will require a first-class band to overcome the technical difficulties. There are many traps waiting for the unwary or nervous player. The audience on 2 September is going to hold its breath many times before the judges' decision is announced,' wrote 'Lancastrian' in *The British Bandsman* on 5 August 1950. And the following week the composer wrote that 'This tone poem is not an attempt at propaganda work for any particular religious or other school of thought, or "ism". If it represents any ideas at all – however inadequately – such ideas are rooted in the very warp and woof of life itself, and the consideration of these is not only the prerogative of sects or societies.'

Frank Wright, the adjudicator at the contest at which it was first performed, called it 'an inspired piece of music . . . that touches the soul and it will, in my estimation, live as long as brass bands themselves survive.' *The British Bandsman* was to receive 'many letters' of praise for '*Resurgam*' and 'many [thought] that this and other original works for brass should be broadcast more often than at present'.

But to describe something of the 'programme' of this music one can do no better than reproduce the composer's own remarks contained in the full score published by The Salvation Army and these may be found as part of Appendix K.

I found it interesting to discover, when making my own detailed examination of the score of '*Resurgam*', that, almost at the end, there is tucked away a reference to the song, 'In the secret of thy presence'. The seeking soul has indeed found the way into the presence of the Lord he or she loves so much. I imagine that this was probably quite unintentional on the part of the composer, which makes it all the more fascinating.

Stories of the effect of '*Resurgam*' on its listeners are too many to relate, and anyone who has heard it or played it probably has his or her own. But without equal perhaps is the story of Cathy Post, a young American musician of great promise, who rehearsed the piece at the Star Lake Musicamp. The editor of the American *War Cry* wrote affectingly of her service in a tribute soon after her promotion to Glory:

> . . . Cathy Post excelled in her love for life and Salvation Army music.
> Testifying before a capacity audience at the New York Centennial Memorial Temple in February 1979, Cathy Post quoted Ralph Waldo Emerson: 'What lies behind us and what lies before us are tiny matters compared to what lies within us.'
> She went on to say, 'What lies in me is the strength and peace

and love of Jesus Christ. When I found out almost a year ago I had cancer, from that moment, my belief in him did not stop, but it kept on growing. His love for me and the love he has given in the people around me, my family and my friends, the love and support that I get from the band, is enough to last me my life. It's just amazing how the Lord gives you more than you can ever ask for.'

She concluded her testimony that night by quoting the verses of her favourite song which came to have deep meaning in her struggle with cancer, 'He giveth more grace'. Her own strength did fail 'ere the day is half done', for after a heroic struggle of more than four years, at the age of 22 she went to be with the Lord . . .

Lieut-Colonel Ditmer shared, 'She returned to the hospital where a myriad of visitors came to that room, which was in reality a sanctuary, an altar, a holy place. They came and went in a celebration of love, of life, of friendship, of spiritual awareness and devotion. Cathy knew where she was, and where she was going. In her final journey of the spirit, a beautiful smile became transfixed on her face which broke the gloom and sadness. It was as though she was singing once again, to them and for herself, "The joy of the Lord is my strength".'

Cathy's faith and witness were communicated through her music. In the summer of 1978 at Star Lake Musicamp she became deepened in her faith and very much moved by the playing of Eric Ball's 'Resurgam', meaning 'I shall rise again'. She wrote to Eric Ball after her deep experience with this piece of music. His reply among other things said, 'It seems to me that you have been given an insight into the real meaning of so-called "death" and resurrection. One could wish that more people would face this early in life rather than avoiding the matter until "some more convenient day".'

The funeral service was as she had planned it. It was appropriate that the congregation sang her favourite song, 'He giveth more grace' and that Montclair Band should play 'Resurgam'. It was also in keeping with Cathy's life and desire that the service was called 'A celebration of love'.

There are many to whom Eric's explorations into somewhat dangerous aspects of religious experience are a disappointment. But there is a sense in which they were, perhaps, a necessary part of the development of his personality. We have to accept him for what he was: a man of profound influence and intense spirituality.

But the question remains: could Eric Ball have written such incredible music without this tearing at his own heartstrings; this suffering at the loss of someone who was dear to him? Was his venturing into the unknown in this way inevitable if only because of this? We shall never know, until '. . . that bright, happy morning'.

SEVEN

Eric and ENSA

Norman Bearcroft 'thought the end of the world had come'.

He was in the sickbay of a military unit, an epidemic of German measles having swept the camp. Through a partly opened door he saw a newspaper placard. 'Army music-chief sacked', ran the legend. He hurriedly called for a newspaper and read for himself the brief account of the resignation of the man he had admired from childhood. He couldn't believe it.

Ray Steadman-Allen 'was shattered'. He too was serving King and country. He was on board ship in the Royal Navy when he saw the same newspaper account. He couldn't believe it either. His contacts with Eric Ball had been less frequent than Norman's. He had met him during his visits to Judd Street, and that had been all. But the effect was the same.

Albert Jakeway saw Eric, his erstwhile colleague, off at St Pancras Station – a stone's-throw from the office they had shared for so many years and in which they had enjoyed so many happy hours of fun, fellowship, and hard work. For him it was 'like attending his funeral'.

As the country was at war, Eric had to register for national service. His musical capabilities seemed to point him in a direction other than military combat. He had had his audition at the Drury Lane Theatre, and was *en route* for his first appearance in a concert party under the general auspices of ENSA – the Entertainments National Service Association. He was to appear in a show called 'Gaiety Revels' in which were four dancing girls, a soubrette and a violinist – far enough away from the kind of music he had hitherto been associated with! For him it was henceforth to be playing the piano for entertainers – tap-dancers, crooners, jazz bands and the like. Small wonder the auditioner summed him up with, 'You haven't got much style, have you?'

It was immediately after the outbreak of hostilities that theatre-producer Basil Dean was given the formidable task of initiating an entertainments division for the forces. Thus, on 11 September 1939, The Theatre Royal, Drury Lane, became the official headquarters for what was to become the largest of such organisations – ENSA, formed to provide 'entertainment for the armed forces and munition workers of a country at war'. In his book *The Theatre at War*, Basil Dean drily observes that, 'We had begun by calling ourselves the Actors' National Service Association (ANSA) [until] Leslie Henson had characteristically remarked that if we kept to ANSA we should be accused of knowing all the answers.'

The first ENSA concert had taken place at Pirbright Camp, Camberley, on 9 September 1939, and was organised by one Thorpe Bates. It was repeated at Old Dene Camp, Camberley, the next day. The following Sunday a party which included Beatrice Lillie, Helen Hill, Annette Mills and Jack Warner went to the Hurlingham Club for the Royal Army Service Corps (RASC). Harold Holt was to organise light classical concerts with some of his best artistes, and Jack Hylton soon went into action with his Bands Division at important military centres.

By the end of its first month ENSA had put on no fewer than 500 shows. At the end of two months the figure had mounted to 1492, and audiences had totalled 600,000. At any one time 700 artistes were 'on the books', and programmes covered dance bands, classical music, concert parties, variety, and straight plays, as well as one- or two-person shows that needed no theatre as such. Will Hay, for instance, spoke on his hobby, astronomy. Film shows and wrestling were also arranged, and sometimes as many as seven shows a day were given.

The names mentioned in the two preceding paragraphs, and those of others of similar 'star quality' who 'entertained the troops' under the auspices of ENSA, ensured that while the quip of 'Every Night Something Awful' might have been true, 'Every Night Something Excellent' also applied, even though sometimes the 'stage' might have consisted of little more than a plank across two beer crates!

In *The Greasepaint War* J.G. Hughes relates how a general announced that, 'Men, the Japanese have surrendered, and I'm now going to ask Miss Gracie Fields if she will sing "The Lord's Prayer". As the song began, men started taking their caps off and stood silently under the hot sun, heads bowed as each note carried across the jungle and over the lowered heads. "They seemed almost to have held their breath as I sang. It was the most privileged and cherished moment of

Eric develops the gift for improvisation for which he was so renowned.

my life. And for years afterwards I received letters from some of the boys who remembered my singing 'The Lord's Prayer' in Bourgainville'' ', Gracie's recollection runs.

The Adjutant-General (War Office) announced that ENSA would finish on 31 August 1946. The last performance by a star under its auspices took place in India, when Tommy Trinder played a garrison theatre there.

Some sources say that Eric looked back on his ENSA years with a degree of affection. He himself said that he met some wonderful people among stage-folk, with warm hearts and good minds. Some friends who were close to him say that he was always reluctant to speak of those days on the whole. Not that it was ever easy to persuade him to talk about his past – the future was always far more interesting to Eric Ball. But for many the very idea of such a superb, sensitive musician earning his living in this manner, with beer mats and ash trays around him, with the odd 'off-colour' joke the order of the day and the occasional betting slip changing hands among the clientele, is horror.

However, he did tell one story of how he apologised to an audience on one occasion that 'there wouldn't be any more Beethoven this evening . . .'. He had played a movement from a Beethoven sonata, and then announced 'I'll play a few choruses and perhaps you'd like to join in!' A large WAAF (Women's Auxiliary Air Force) officer on the front row boomed, 'Do you *have* to?' It seems safe to assume that 'more Beethoven' *was* played that evening – either before or after his selection of choruses!

Another of his popular solos at this time was Rubenstein's 'Melody in F' which he was later to arrange for brass.

Don Coppin, erstwhile member of The Salvation Army's Rosehill Band, remembers being called up for military service in August 1944. He had been 'very shocked to learn from the press that Eric had resigned his officership. In April 1945 I was at flying school at Woking, training to be a glider pilot. One evening an ENSA party gave us a concert and I was amazed to see Eric Ball at the piano, both accompanying other artistes and playing "solo". Although delighted to see him I was somewhat apprehensive about approaching him in view of his resignation etc. But when I did go to him after the concert he soon put me at ease with his usual sincerity and charm and even in that noisy RAF mess we were able to enjoy a period of quiet fellowship – a treasured memory over the years that followed.'

Eric himself said later that his life until then had been a very sheltered one. He had gone almost straight from school to work for The Salvation Army, and had never gone 'into the world'. His vision had been so narrow hitherto. Ray Steadman-Allen suggests that he needed to take 'a long, hard look at himself', and that these experiences enabled him to do so. It is perhaps a not inappropriate suggestion that by these means he broke the shell of the egg, and started to allow his personality to develop to its fullest degree.

Be all that as it may, in subsequent years he was able to draw on those ENSA experiences for Salvation Army purposes at least once, just as he probably used, during his ENSA years, that talent for improvisation he had developed in his earlier Salvation Army period.

Reports *The Musician* for 22 June 1963, 'Brother Eric Ball [he was by then known thus in Salvation Army circles], Songster Leader Sam Hooper and Bandmaster Ketteringham are names familiar to most salvationist musicians and especially to those associated with Hanwell Corps, of which they are all soldiers, but it is unlikely that together they have ever been associated with a home league programme.' The event was the National Home League Rally for that year, held in the Westminster Central Hall – the National Home League Secretary being that friend of Eric's from his Southall days, Ivy Memmott, by this time Mrs Mawby. 'On this occasion they all appeared – in an item entitled "Behind almost every woman . . .", presented by the Hanwell husbands. The two sectional leaders, having discussed the possibility of some fame in the home league, sadly left the platform when the songster leader declared he had heard he was to be overlooked for the position of home league singers leader in favour of Eric Ball (whose wife, incidentally, is responsible for that group)!

'They were succeeded by representative menfolk, who, with action and song, accompanied by Brother Ball, bemoaned their lot in having to attend to the chores on home league day. All ended happily with the "moaners" admitting delight that people new to the Army were attending meetings as a result of the home league ministry.'

The reporter makes no mention of the fact that Harry Read, then the corps officer at Hanwell, had written the lyrics of the song for the item, and that he had, 'in my innocence' he admits, used the music of a popular song of that year for one of the songs. Eric immediately told him, very kindly, that he could not do that because of copyright problems. To Harry's agonised 'then what am I going to do?' Eric promptly replied, 'Leave it to me; I'll write you another; it will be almost the same, but just sufficiently different to avoid accusations of plagiarism!'

It would be interesting to know just how long Eric's attachment with ENSA actually lasted. As early as 3 June 1944 (less than two months after his resignation from The Salvation Army), his professional 'card' was appearing in *The British Bandsman*:

ERIC BALL, ARCM
Composer, Conductor and Adjudicator
'Rosslyn', 200 Boston Road, London W7

But in the issue dated 24 February 1945, we read that 'Eric Ball was to have adjudicated at the Bristol contest but we understand, much to his disappointment, that ENSA could not release him. Eric's fine work in The Salvation Army and with its International Staff Band is well known.'

From this we learn two things: that he was serving with ENSA (the war was still on at this time), and that he was already taking on other professional engagements.

The second half of the forties was a difficult period for everyone, and those who lived through it will, like those who lived through the war years, have their own memories of the time. There were the problems of continuing austerity following the Second World War and of men and women returning to civilian life, with all the unsettling nature of readjustment. Thousands were disillusioned with what they found at home, and emigrated to various countries in the then British Empire. Food rationing continued in some form throughout these years. Eggs were a luxury, as were imported fruits such as bananas and oranges. The bitter winter of 1947, and a national fuel shortage which threatened to cause social and economic chaos, did nothing to help matters.

For Eric and Olive Ball there was the additional problem of finding accommodation. Salvation Army officers live in 'tied property' – a house or flat 'goes with the job'. It is quite possible, too, that, apart from his Salvation Army uniforms, he had hardly more than the proverbial 'rag to his back'. One friend remembers seeing him, around this time, leading a band practice wearing a pullover with a darn in it.

Kenneth Cook, bandmaster (retired) of Boscombe Salvation Army Band, was one who went to him for lessons in composition. 'It was late in 1945 – we discussed Mr Attlee's landslide victory in the polls the previous day.' Ken had known Eric for several years; he had himself been an employee as a boy at Judd Street and had collected messages from Eric.

Although Eric did not realise it, help was at hand.

Harry Mortimer had got to know him very well during his period as bandmaster of the International Staff Band. It was with some regret that Harry realised that the marvellous flow of music Eric had created and developed during his Judd Street years had now apparently come to an end. He felt that such a man was not to be wasted, and when Brighouse and Rastrick Band, one with which Harry had had close associations over the years, asked his opinion about a new conductor, he wholeheartedly recommended Eric Ball. Together with Fred Roberts, the band's solo cornet player and secretary, he approached Eric, who agreed to take the band on.

Despite the surprise expressed in many quarters, that a 'Salvation Army man' should take up such an appointment, he did so, quickly establishing himself as the best choice the band committee could have made.

But Eric's career with Brighouse and Rastrick Band deserves a separate chapter from this.

And what of his activities in The Salvation Army at this time?

They would appear to have been non-existent. For these

were, indeed, his 'wilderness years' with regard to the movement. It is difficult to understand why he was denied access to its platforms. But there were those who were eager to take and use him.

For instance, in *The British Bandsman*, 22 November 1947, we read that 'Brighouse and Rastrick Band are to give a concert in the Wesleyan Central Hall, Ashington, Northumberland on 30 November. This will be preceded by the usual evening service at which, by invitation of the minister, Eric Ball will be the preacher.'

As early as 17 November 1945 *The British Bandsman* announced that he had been appointed musical adviser to the paper, the editor saying that 'in Eric Ball I shall have a colleague and comrade who will give me valuable help in any work I may try to accomplish for the betterment and advancement of brass bands'.

It was a popular appointment, for the paper reported on 1 December that 'It is pleasing to us to receive so many letters of appreciation on the appointment of Eric Ball to our staff.' Eric's own reply to the invitation is worth quoting in full:

> I must thank Mr J. H. Iles for his very generous article on my appointment as musical adviser to R. Smith & Co, and *The British Bandsman*. To be counted a worthy successor to the men whose names he lists brings a sense of responsibility which demands to be taken very seriously. I feel sure the association will be a happy one, and look forward to some useful and constructive work for our bands.
>
> Mr Iles has allowed me a little space in which to pay tribute to my many former colleagues, in all parts of the world, with whom I worked in The Salvation Army. They will not mind if I single out the name of my old chief, Colonel F.G. Hawkes, now retired, under whose direction I worked during the years when he was pushing through against some odds – the reforms and expansion in Salvation Army music which have brought it to its present high standard. His integrity, selflessness and dedication to his work were beyond question; and his oft-repeated words – 'be mercilessly self-critical' – still ring in my consciousness. Of his work I may write at a later date, when considering the influence of Salvation Army music upon brass bands in general.
>
> To all my old colleagues I send greetings. *Perhaps, when the fog of misunderstanding and prejudice has blown away, we may in some way link again for the sake of our ideals in both life and art.*

The italics are mine. But 'fog of misunderstanding' there certainly was. Brindley Boon has told the story in his book *ISB* of how his old friend Alf Ringham had had to forbid Eric entry into his hall at Hendon, where Bandmaster Fred Cobb had invited him to conduct a band practice. Olive Straughan, a retired Salvation Army officer now living in Kent, but stationed, with her husband, at the corps at Acton at this time, remembers her husband 'getting his knuckles severely rapped by his divisional commander' for inviting Eric to chair a programme in his hall.

And Batley salvationists were 'ordered by their British Commissioner to cancel all arrangements for the concert to be given in the Gospel Hall by Brighouse and Rastrick. Everything was done according to Salvation Army regulations and no reason for the ban has so far been ascertained. However, the concert will take place under "outside" auspices and it is possible that the local Salvation Army band instrument scheme will benefit after all. *Eric Ball will be there to conduct.*'

The italics are again mine. This was obviously the reason for the ban. And it is interesting, in the light of this ban, to find him, in 1981, conducting, in a tribute festival at Huddersfield, CWS (Manchester) and Gainsborough (Salvation Army) Bands *together* in 'Resurgam'. On that occasion the Leeds Salvation Army timbrellists took part, as did Brighouse Salvation Army Band and salvationist Charles Dove of Stapleford Citadel. CWS (Manchester) played 'Journey into freedom'. By this time the exile had returned home.

But it must have come as a great comfort to the composer to read a letter from James Northey in *The British Bandsman* – a contribution to some ongoing correspondence about Salvation Army red shield (servicemen's) clubs forming their own bands – in which he tells of how Cairo Red Shield Band (perhaps the best-known of them all) had given a programme in Cairo's Cathedral Hall in which 'The old wells' was 'the high spot of the evening'.

As for Eric himself, he always spoke kindly of The Salvation Army, certainly in *The British Bandsman*. On 24 August 1944, for instance, he writes glowingly of experimentation by George Marshall in his scoring: trombones in five parts, baritones in three or four; horns and flugelhorns similarly divided.

And Eric's account of a typical scene in the Army's Regent Hall, in the west end of London, in its heyday is delightful:

> A few steps from Oxford Circus, in London, salvationists have an important centre known as Regent Hall, or, more familiarly, 'The Rink'. Since the very early days of the organisation this has been a meeting-place for visitors from the four corners of the earth, a setting for an ever-changing, colourful pageant of Salvation Army comings and goings. In this hall you may have heard important personalities speak, parsons and laymen preach; here witnessed the 'farewell' of missionaries, or their 'welcome home'; here you may have joined in a devotional service, sitting between a famous member of the diplomatic corps and a one-

time burglar; here seen a famous novelist – with flowing tie and
cloak – stand up and pray aloud; here rubbed shoulders with
sightseers and newsgatherers, with aristocrats and the unlovely
unwashed; here seen unhappy girls shepherded in at midnight
to receive help and advice; sights to make the tears start, sights to
cause a smile – all in an atmosphere of friendliness and welcome, with cups of tea never far away, and over all a brooding
sense of the Eternal . . .

The occasion to which his article refers is the retirement of
Bandmaster Herbert W. Twitchin, MBE, of that corps.

And on 14 June 1947 Eric paid warm tribute to the work of
the International Staff Band (this on the occasion of the
appointment of Bernard Adams as Staff Bandmaster): of the
difficulties of maintaining the right-quality personnel when
officer-members can be moved to the ends of the earth on
receiving a new appointment; of their prime duties of attending
'large' International Headquarters functions and presenting
new music to the International Music Board.

This latter reference to the Army received a warm reply
from Walter Rushton, the Leader (or executive officer) of the
Staff Band, who wrote, in the 28 June issue, 'I felt I would
like to write and say how much the spirit of it is appreciated,
and to thank you for your good wishes for the future of the
International Staff Band. The article has given much pleasure
to Major Bernard Adams and the members of the band; they
have happy memories of your leadership.'

Now, in the forties, Eric was taking the brass band movement by storm just as he had become the darling of The Salvation Army in the thirties.

On 10 March 1945 he was elected a vice-president of the
National Association of Brass Band Conductors (he had been
elected to membership on 2 December the previous year).
These honours had come to him within 12 months of his resignation from The Salvation Army. He adjudicated at a band
contest at Belle Vue in October 1945. By 24 November 1945
he was on the executive committee of the National Brass
Band Club. On 15 December he was an examiner (along
with Frank Wright) for the LGSM diploma (brass bands), at
which there were, apparently, two candidates, and at which
Hammersmith Borough Band gave valuable assistance. On
16 February *The British Bandsman* referred to 'another grand
show from Brighouse and Rastrick. "Morning rhapsody"
was played, and that delightful Mozart number [an excerpt
from the opera 'Don Giovanni'] so admirably arranged by
Eric Ball. The new original work "Free fantasy" composed
and conducted by Eric Ball gives promise of great things
from this mastermind.' This was following a BBC broadcast.

'Shut up, you two, I've come here especially to hear them play "Throw open wide your window," by Hans May, arranged by Eric Ball'.

These two cartoons of Eric are taken from Kenneth Cook's Miscellany, 'Oh, Listen to the Band', Hinrichsen, 1950, copyright *The Daily Herald*.

He was certainly not letting the grass grow under his feet.

And in 1954 he was awarded the Medal of the Worshipful Company of Musicians, being only the second person to be so honoured. Harry Mortimer had been the first in 1953.

It is interesting to recall the differing ways in which Eric Ball and Erik Leidzén resolved clashes with authority. Erik Leidzén had been bandmaster of the New York Staff Band in the 1930s when Eva Booth was National Commander for the United States of America, in addition to which he led the FET (Friday Night at the Temple) Band, a special ensemble to provide the music for a series of meetings held each week in New York. The meetings are still held, though the special band has ceased to function. In a public meeting the Commander asked the FET Band to play a chorus.

'That is not possible, Commander; we don't have the music,' Erik told her.

'But surely your bandsmen do not require music for a *chorus*?' Eva said, incredulously.

'On principle, I do not allow my bandsmen to improvise,' Erik told her, stubbornly.

The next day Eva sent for Erik. Erik tendered his resignation without further ado.

Obviously, there were faults on both sides. Eva Booth was quite right in one respect: the bandsmen could have improvised the required music, though Eva should not have taken them for granted and embarrassed Erik in public. Erik was wrong to have refused her request. In the spirit of the moment he could have given her the music she wanted. But he stood by his principle and refused.

Erik and Eric first met when Erik Leidzén visited London in 1934. He was announced to be present at the pre-bandsmen's councils festival to be held in the Queen's Hall, London, on 1 December of that year. Here, seven bands, including the SP&S Band, played some of the latest music by such composers as George Marshall, Bramwell Coles, Phil Catelinet, Albert Jakeway, Eric Ball, and Erik Leidzén himself.

In the event Eric handed the baton to Erik to conduct the SP&S Band in his own arrangement of 'Fling wide the gates' – originally a song by Eva Booth written in 1912 to honour the promotion to Glory of her father, William Booth. Erik Leidzén provided a critical report of the programme for *The Bandsman and Songster* of 15 December, in which he wrote, 'Moments with Tchaikowsky [played by the SP&S Band under Eric Ball] was a joy to me . . . I bow down with profound respect to this band and its master.' Of Erik's own contribution at the piano, Herbert Twitchin wrote, 'Bandmaster Leidzén . . . revealed the fact that he has a beautiful touch and is an artist of fingering and technique.'

Erik and Eric maintained a friendship which lasted until the promotion to Glory of the former in December 1962. Mainly this was through letters, a number of which have been preserved in The Salvation Army's New York archives. They present a picture of a very warm relationship. ('They think in counterpoint,' Erik Leidzén's wife, Maria, once said.)

But in 1955 Eric Ball arranged for his friend to visit Europe and attend the Belle Vue band contest in September of that year – allowing for a visit to Sweden, Erik's homeland, which he had not seen for many years.

During the visit a programme was given in his honour at Regent Hall by the International Staff Band. The hall was packed to capacity; a coach-load from Margate, a family from Bristol and a party from Birmingham helping to make it so. It was during this programme that he spoke his oft-quoted words that his desire had always been 'to serve the present age – not to flabbergast or bamboozle it – my calling to fulfil'. Earlier in the day the Chief of the Staff presided over a private reception given to him by the ISB, in which Erik replied to the 'undeserved' things which had been said of him, telling the bandsmen that it had never been in his mind to outdo another composer, but that he had always striven to reach beyond the technical to the hearts and minds of the people.

Erik and Maria Leidzén, with, centre, Sam Hooper, during their visit to London in 1955.

Jesus can save little children

A reception given to Erik and Maria Leidzén at Hanwell Corps during their visit to London in 1955. Seated are, left to right, Sam Hooper, John Hunt, Eric, Lieut-Colonel (DC) Badley, Erik and Maria Leidzén, Mrs Lieut-Col Badley, Olive Straughan (wife of the corps officer, who is standing far left, Maisie Wiggins (Ringham), Marjorie Ringham, Connie Clark is standing behind and between Erik and Maria. Olive's absence from the picture is due probably to the death of her father a few days before.

Although the correspondence between Erik and Eric was a fairly regular one, this letter, from Maria Leidzén to Eric and Olive, following the visit, sums up the warmth and charm of the relationship:

Dear Olive and Eric,
    We received your letter this morning and have already read it twice. Need I say with the greatest interest? How many pleasant memories flood our minds and hearts!! If I should write to you every time your names are mentioned as we recall a year ago you would be swamped with letters. As it is I am sure you must *feel* how often you are in our thoughts, and always with love and gratitude for the privilege of living in your home and really getting to know you.
    As we on our walks through Central Park pass a chestnut tree, we never fail to say to each other, 'Ealing Common', and there is a certain warmth in the voices and a glow in the eyes as we look back and remember.
    It took me a long time to get order in our scrap-books, but it was such a pleasant task. I have three large volumes in which I have the pictures and mementoes from our trip placed in the correct order, so we can re-live the experience over and over again at will, then I have my diary which I am ever so glad that I kept up so regularly, for it is a great help as a reminder as we had so many wonderful days to recall and it is so easy to get mixed up.
    Some day maybe you will come over here and I can show you 'my etchings' – read scrap-books.
    When the lilacs were in bloom around here, we recalled your

huge bushes in the back garden, and we often speak of how there were *always* fresh flowers placed on the dresser in our room (*your* room which you so kindly placed at our disposal for such a length of time). And the pleasant evenings in front of the fire, with a cup of tea in our hands, when we came home and were so full of all the wonders we had seen, it was good to have such interested listeners.

Whenever a British film is showing here we go to see it, if only to look at the – to us – now so familiar places. The other day we saw Saint Albans and naturally we recalled the day we were with you and Harold and Edith [Eric's brother and sister-in-law], or when we see the Thames we remember so many pleasant trips on that lovely river. Everything is so indelibly etched in our minds and hearts and we are deeply grateful for it all.

I know Erik will write and answer your letter, but I wanted to have a few words myself to include when he does, and I must take the opportunity of using the typewriter when he isn't needing it. Just now he is working on some arrangement so I have a chance to have the machine . . .

Much love to you both and please give our regards to Mrs Dorsett and Miss Pegg.

Lovingly,

Maria

('Miss Pegg' was an elderly lady 'in reduced circumstances' – a friend of Eric and Olive for many years, who came to live with them until she became so frail as to require full-time nursing attention and then entered a nursing home.)

A letter from Eric to Erik is, on the whole, much more 'down to earth':

Both Maria and yourself have been much in our thoughts this year: passing through Ealing Common, with the trees in various stages of bud, leaf, and now autumn colour: at Belle Vue, where you were very much remembered by many: and even last evening, when television featured some dirt-track motor-cycle racing! And at Edinburgh, and so on, and so on. The weather has not been so kind this year as it was in '55 – there has been persistent rain – but it seems rather better now, and perhaps we shall get an Indian summer . . .

I have had forwarded to you by surface mail a full score of the piece ['Festival music'], which has something of the influence of hearing so much Mozart this year. It is, as they say, 'after Mozart' – a long way after. In the same envelope you should find part of an issue of *Radio Times*, by which you will see that one movement of one of your suites for strings was broadcast. It was the finale, and so far as I could tell, they played it quite well, although one felt that its conciseness would have been more effective following at least one other contrasted movement by the same composer. However, it was heard, and I believe our friend Geoff Brand was responsible for its inclusion.

There is little or no out-of-the-ordinary news. I have done one or two – or a few more – SA jobs, including some rehearsals with the very good Norwich Citadel Band, spending a good deal of time on the trombone concert[in]o, and enjoying it very much indeed: they have a most efficient and musical soloist. Hendon want me to do something similar with them, and especially mention, 'Where flowers never fade' [Erik Leidzén], which I shall look forward to with great interest. 'Dixie Rhapsody' had another 'airing' in August, by Ransome & Marles . . .

We are all well here. Maud Pegg sends her kind regards to you both. Olive's mother is well, but perhaps rather more frail.

It is Sunday evening: Olive has gone to the meeting, and I watch while she prays! She sends her love to Maria, and will write to her soon, she says.

> *Au revoir*
>> As ever,
>>> Eric.

An excerpt from Erik Leidzén's reply (of 30 September 1956) shows the high professional regard in which he held the Englishman with the similar Christian name:

The references to the chestnuts on Ealing Common, Belle Vue, and Edinburgh were appreciated by us both. We have re-lived those delightful days over and over again, not least on the anniversary of each happening.

Which brings me to your 'Festival music'. I played it through carefully last night and think you are too modest in ascribing its predominant flavour to the influence of Mozart. You may have been prodded and lifted by him these last few months, but you have certainly written your own music. I am certain the bands have taken to your suite with unusual fervour. It is a difficult piece. (I wonder how they will negotiate some of the trills.) But the music will 'pay off' very soon in rehearsal and delight the players. I predict it will be a far more popular (in the best sense) number than my 'Sinfonietta' could ever hope to be in a hundred years. Looking back on that venture I marvel at my own presumption in accepting the challenge. And even more so at your intrepidity in programming it *twice* on the Embankment last summer. But thanks in any case . . .

Have not heard from ***** since I left London. He used to write twice a month or so, but I fear his corns still smart where I stepped on them. ('Brothers, we are treading where the saints have trod!')

And another:

Your crack about it possibly being a bad sign that 'Festival music' was popular is something I cannot go along with. Your music has always had more to it than the kind which becomes – in the bad sense of the word – popular. The fallow patches you mention are a proof of this. It is only the writer who really

CARL LAWTON PRESENTS

SIX EDAC CONCERTS

CENTRAL HALL, WESTMINSTER S.W.1.

EDAC concerts are presented for a purpose. At a convenient time, and in the middle of the week, they give you, especially the young men and women, a wide range of music.

It will be performed by :

A FAMOUS ORCHESTRA	The London Symphony Orchestra (Leader, George Stratton)
THREE FAMOUS ARTISTES	Leon Goossens (*Oboe*) Dennis Brain (*Horn*) George Stratton (*Violin*)
THREE NEW ARTISTES	Nancy Lockwood (*Soprano*) Sheila Randell (*Pianoforte*) Penelope Simms (*Violoncello*)
A NEW CONDUCTOR	Eric Ball
AT PRICES YOU CAN AFFORD	925 reserved seats at 3/- 776 ,, ,, ,, 4/- 431 ,, ,, ,, 5/- 477 unreserved seats at 2/-

The complete programme, which is subject to alteration, is given overleaf

empties himself into his work who must wait while the batteries are being discharged. The shallower writer keeps on spouting his diluted gruel with no noticeable inconvenience to himself and little or no profit to others.

Early in 1948 Eric made his one-and-only venture into the world of orchestral conducting.

Some group or body calling itself 'Education and Action for Leisure' gave six 'EDAC' concerts at Westminster Central Hall. The leaflet proclaims, 'A famous orchestra, The London Symphony Orchestra (Leader, George Stratton); three famous artistes, Leon Goossens, oboe, Dennis Brain, horn, George Stratton, violin; three new artistes, Nancy Lockwood, soprano, Sheila Randell, pianoforte, Penelope Simms, violoncello; a new conductor, Eric Ball'.

The British Bandsman went to great lengths to advertise the event, including a handbill with each copy of its 21 February issue in which it made its initial mention of the concerts, and urging as many of the banding fraternity as could attend to do so. Six concerts were given, and in the event Eric himself

Above left: Leaflet advertising the series of concerts Eric conducted with the London Symphony Orchestra in 1948.

Above: Photo of Eric which appeared on programmes around this time

conducted only five, suffering from nervous exhaustion and needing to stand down for the other. Blyth Major, a former Salvation Army bandmaster at Coventry City Corps, took up the baton at short notice for this one. Frank Wright conducted (presumably at Eric's invitation) his own *Preludio Marziale* in the 22 April concert.

Robert Simpson 'remembers to this day' the 'most beautiful performance of Beethoven's Fourth Symphony', and a correspondent to *The British Bandsman* says that ' . . . He [Eric] seemed in his element, and as much at home with the strings as with the brass. Congratulations on a fine performance.'

Alas, the organisation known as EDAC seems to have 'nose-dived', as have the 'three new artistes'! No more seems to have been heard of any of them. Even for Eric the venture was not to be repeated – much against his will apparently. Robert Simpson says that 'with typical modesty he [Eric] said he felt a bit intimidated by the thought of the orchestra: that he didn't know enough about the strings. But he knew far more than some . . . who have made big names while the orchestra literally carries them!' The orchestra leader said afterwards that Eric did 'a fine, detailed rehearsal' of the John Ireland 'London' overture, the last item in the first concert, though the *Times* critic was not so kind; of this concert he mentioned Eric's brass band background and spoke of his 'military beat' – an unnecessary and cheap remark.

Throughout his life Eric Ball realised his lack of 'background'. To be a self-taught musician is to no one's discredit, but he knew that a good musical education would have been very much to his advantage. He never had the opportunity to develop his vocabulary, orally, literally or musically. The fact that he achieved so much is a minor miracle; what he would have achieved with the advantages of education and 'background' one can only speculate upon.

And what of Olive all this time?

She was, in modern parlance, quietly 'doing her own thing'. There is a reference in *The British Bandsman* to her receiving 'an ovation' for 'Coronation March' from *Le Prophète*. She was apparently 'chairing' a programme at the Clapton Congress Hall at which Albert Jakeway was the guest conductor, and Southall, Hendon and Croydon Citadel bands were taking part. This was in March 1946. In November of that year she appeared as a soloist in a programme arranged by Gurney Doe and Norland Castle Band. Again Albert Jakeway was the guest conductor in a programme made up entirely of his own music. Olive's solos were 'Joyous heart' – a taxing *coluratura* number, and 'On wings of prayer', which is more reflective by nature.

A CAROL FANTASY FOR STRINGS — *Eric Ball*

This 'Carol Fantasy' is possibly Eric's only excursion into the world of composition for orchestra. It was afterwards rescored for brass and published by The Salvation Army.

Gwen Barnett, now living in Poole, but at that time living in Wealdstone, north London, remembers inviting her to be the speaker at her home league. 'She was an excellent speaker who drew people to hear her – in the home league particularly. She was in considerable demand at these meetings.' It is an oft-referred-to fact that she remained a hardworking salvationist in the corps at Hanwell, where she was deputy songster leader to Sam Hooper for a number of years; she was his sergeant (assistant), too, for a time, and also home league singers' (women's group choir) leader. Connie Clark, who was Eric's secretary for a long time when he was editor of *The British Bandsman*, writes equally warmly of Olive as she does of Eric:

> I heard that the editor wanted a secretary, and although I was living at home in Oxford then, I decided to apply. To my surprise I got the job. It was hard work, of course, but I loved it. Eric was always so kind. And Olive – she was a gem. Being new to London and only recently having left home, I found it hard to settle down at first, and I must admit I wondered whether I ought to go back to Oxford. Eric suggested I link up at Hanwell Corps. He introduced me to Olive, who, he said, would 'keep an eye on me'; I did so, and am still a member of Hanwell Corps today.

Olive was a more-than-competent pianist, who could 'pick up' a chorus immediately – such a boon for a Salvation Army meeting leader, and a gift which is sometimes taken for granted by them, until they are not able to find it. She would testify, too, in the meetings, and in conversation, of the love of God in her life.

But she seldom if ever went with Eric to contesting and other band occasions, in the early years at least. Possibly she felt it was 'un-Salvation Army'. She was always fiercely loyal to the Christian movement which had nourished her both musically and spiritually through the years, just as she was always fiercely loyal to her husband, but it could have been that she felt that Eric had somehow betrayed his trust when he resigned his officership and took a more secular direction.

She often accompanied him on his Salvation Army 'errands', however, gently supporting him in his chairmanship roles and so on. No praise can be too high for her for the spirit in which she accepted this, or for the hours of sacrifice she made when he was working, whether in his study, in the rehearsal room, or during his more public work. On one occasion she said that she often heard one bar of music played in varied forms quite 50 times, always hearing the music her husband composed before the score was written, and that, although she could not write music she keenly appreciated it. And she often accompanied him when he went to music schools, at home and in other countries.

Eric was becoming an international figure in brass band circles, with an influence which only time itself will fully evaluate.

EIGHT

Eric the Interpreter

The issue of *BB** bearing the date 12 May 1945 congratulated Brighouse and Rastrick Band in obtaining the services of Eric Ball as its professional musical director. 'Eric Ball made a great name for himself when in control of The Salvation Army International [Staff] Band,' it said. And the next week it commented that 'Eric Ball has already got busy with Brighouse and on VE2 day had a great success at Leeds. They are visiting Cornwall and our West Country lads will be glad to give them a welcome. It is hoped Eric Ball will be with them. Salvation Army bandsmen will be particularly glad to meet Eric.' On 11 August the band was announced as being at Caerphilly on 7, 8, 9 and 10 August, the event being reported in *BB* on 25 August.

The Brighouse and Rastrick Temperence Band commenced operations in 1860 as a brass and reed band, changing to all-brass in 1881, and dropping the adjective 'Temperence' from its name in 1928. In its early days, every intending member was required to 'sign the pledge', buy his own uniform, and pay his subscription of sixpence a week. It would be difficult to evaluate what financial sacrifice that entailed. The band remains completely independent; a local committee of bandsmen and supporters determines its affairs and accepts responsibility for its destiny.

The story has often been told of how, on his first being approached, Eric consulted his diary 'to make sure I'm free next Wednesday' – even though at that time his diary was woefully empty. Yes, he was free. And afterwards, was he free the next Wednesday? Yes he was, he said, pretending to consult it again.

'And what about the standard of the band?' the secretary asked.

* Throughout this chapter *The British Bandsman* is referred to by its initials, *BB*.)

'Well, pretty good on the whole. But there's a second horn [or was it a second baritone, or second trombone – who wants to be identified all these years later?] I'm not too happy about.'

By the next Wednesday the second horn (or second baritone or second trombone) had been replaced. Such was the remorseless will of the band committee in those days, and such was the influence, whether he liked it or not, of Eric Walter John Ball.

He quickly established himself. On 13 October a massed band concert was given at Huddersfield Town Hall, organised by Brighouse and Rastrick, and was 'a brilliant success' according to *BB*. Bands taking part were Grimethorpe Colliery and Wingates Temperence, as well as the hosts, Brighouse. Eric Ball conducted the massed bands. And on 1 December that year the band held its annual dinner at the Royal Hotel, Brighouse. A company of over 80 attended and congratulated the band on its success at the *Daily Herald* Contest. It had come fourth, with 169 points. The president said that the band was fast approaching the top rung of the ladder.

By 8 February 1947 *BB* was commenting that 'Brighouse are full of engagements [it had already said that the band was to visit London 'for a whole week'] and are maintaining the great reputation they have won. Their playing of the classics raises great enthusiasm from their packed audiences, and everywhere Eric Ball conducts he gets a fine reception.' Later that year 'Brighouse and Rastrick with Eric Ball played to great crowds. Our Scotch friends are very enthusiastic on their playing and the same goes for the other places they have visited. We owe them our warm thanks for so well upholding the prestige and dignity of brass bands and in this they are doing us a fine service. They are now in Eastbourne [where a later report says the band 'raised a furore'], and then go to Coventry and follow with a fortnight in London' (*BB*, 26 July 1947). At the end of that year 'the massed bands of Brighouse, City of Coventry and Manchester CWS Band, under Eric Ball, put up a fine show at the Town Hall, Huddersfield, and the local press were full of praises for the performances. Special mention was made of the massed performance of "Divertimento", which is proving to be very popular with brass bands' (*BB*, 27 December 1947).

By early 1948 Harry Jenkins had been appointed bandmaster of Brighouse and Rastrick, Eric continuing as proessional teacher.

Eric's major triumph with Brighouse occurred in 1946, when, in October, it won the National Championship at the

Royal Albert Hall. The band received 'a wonderful reception on its arrival home . . . All traffic for a time was stopped and the enthusiasm was great . . . Eric Ball received a great ovation' (*BB* 26 October). And, according to Geoffrey Brand, in *Brass Bands in the 20th Century*, '. . . their success was national news and the media descended on Brighouse. Fox Movietime News made a film of the band marching in triumph from the station into the town centre for a civic reception. The film was shown in all cinemas contracted with Fox Movietime News, so that even in 1946 Brighouse were receiving star treatment.'

It will be noted that this result came only months after his taking the band, only in the second year of the National Championship's being resumed after the Second World War, and a mere 18 months after severing his link with The Salvation Army.

Eddie Noble, at the time of writing the treasurer of Brighouse and Rastrick Band, remembers an incident when Eric was conducting a rehearsal:

Brighouse and Rastrick, with conductor and trophy, in 1946.

It was the rehearsal immediately prior to the National Contest the following Saturday. At six o'clock Brighouse Salvation Army Band held its open-air meeting just below our bandroom. On

Adjudicators' remarks on the performance of 'Oliver Cromwell' by Brighouse and Rastrick Band, first prizewinners in the National Championship, 1946. 'A most impressive performance' said Henry Geehl. '. . . is obviously led by a musician,' wrote Frank Wright.

Oliver Cromwell

Adjudicators' Remarks on the "Daily Herald" National Brass Band Championship Saturday 19th October, 1946. Held at the Royal Albert Hall, London.

Draw no. 13.

A fine and impressive start. Fine tonal variety. Congratulate the cornets on the 'flutter tongue' bars. Good climax. The start of the Allegro should be 'ff' in leading instruments. Poor balance in horns after 8. Too much sf. in trombones from Lento. A finely played Andante section. Intonation slightly off at 13. Good muted bars. An excellent climax to the Fugue at 20. Most impressive from 22. The Allegro beautifully played. Excellent from here to the end.

A most impressive performance.

Points awarded 192.   Henry Geehl.

- -

Splendid soprano in opening bars - and band is very good. Euphonium is not quite up to the mark on page 4 (high Ab). Otherwise a splendid movement. Allegro. this is marked pp - you are playing it at least mf. Balance is bad on page 15 - the solo and 1st horns are too soft for the flugel. The accents by trombones are overdone - a pity: this spoils the general effect. Still the band has a good tone: and is obviously led by a musician. The muted effects on page 24 were very fine.
The work at times is most impressive. The effect before 28 was the best so far. A most impressive section. Work proceeds at a very good level - I have nothing but praise for this work. The final section, too was well done.
There were, however, some lapses, but these were not really serious faults considered as a whole.

Points awarded 192.   Frank Wright.

- -

Good start, tuneful and pleasing, forte a bit big else all goes well. Euphonium out, but good playing, (flut. well done). A good band here, and good playing. 12/8 Heavy start. Some good playing, why alter the tempo and pay more attention to marks. 8. good euphonium, much good playing 9 onwards. Lento, good basses, troms not tuneful.
Andante. Good soloists, and band render good support, little faults in intonation here and there. A pleasing rendering on the whole. Muted section very good.
Fugue, good start is made, and all goes along nicely. Troms. not tuneful, but there is certainly some good playing, pleasing in every way. 22. Very good, but why modell. again, playing good all the way, and generally good style. 27, intonation out, 28 all is nice and pleasing and some character is displayed. 31, nicely done, onwards all is good and pleasing, and a good finish is made to a real good show.

Points awarded 192.   J.A. Greenwood.

- -

hearing the sound of its music, Mr Ball just put his baton down and walked across the bandroom. He opened the window, and said, 'Gentlemen, the Lord is with us.' Hushed silence descended for about half an hour. As the Salvation Army band marched away Mr Ball responded with these words, 'That was a blessing for everyone.'

In his book *On Brass*, Harry Mortimer tells us, 'his [Eric's] immediate repayment to me [for 'putting him in the way of' Brighouse and Rastrick Band in the first instance] was to beat one of my bands into second place at the National in 1946 . . . Although my bands were to win the National in the following three years, the sweetest revenge came in 1950 at Belle Vue. By now Eric had moved to CWS Manchester, and the test-piece for that year was his own composition, 'Resurgam'. Whilst I won the contest with the Fairey Band, Eric only managed fourth place. The first to offer his sincere congratulations, he did something which confirmed, if such confirmation was needed, my opinion that he was the most noble of friends and the least conceited of musicians, avowing that I understood the piece better than he did, and found more depth in it than he had imagined.'

Thus, where there could have been animosity and, possibly, a deep rift, their warm friendship was only interrupted by Eric's death in 1989.

But as has so often been commented upon, that 'least conceitedness' was a hallmark of his character. 'One of our

A striking studio portait of Eric taken in the early 1950s.

readers wonders why Eric Ball was not introduced to the great Belle Vue audience (this after his "Salute to freedom" had been played). It was his personal desire not to be and he had to leave early for another appointment. In his short speech, J. Henry Iles paid tribute to his brilliant work, saying, '. . . Eric Ball is as modest as he is clever' (*BB* 21 September 1946).

This 'least conceitedness' was always an integral part of his character. There have been those who have stated that Eric was always aware of his influence, and that is probably right. But that is quite a different thing from being conceited. On one occasion he suggested that 'The brass band movement still awaits its *own* Beethoven, its *own* Elgar, its own genius', not realising that in the eyes of many he was rapidly attaining this status himself.

And this 'least conceitedness', gratefully, never left him. In 1975, when he was almost at the pinnacle of his popularity, he attended an appreciation programme at High Wycombe, appearing, as usual, as composer, conductor, compère and accompanist, and earned for himself a seven-minute ovation. He told his audience, 'I'll go back to my desk at home and look at the bust of Beethoven who glowers down at me when I'm working!' Probably the best way of all of getting himself and his achievements into some sort of perspective!

Two more stories which typify Eric's attitude to life, and which really belong to a later chapter, can also be related at this point. Here is John Winnard of Bolton:

> Eric had just been the recipient of the Baton of Honour at the Royal Albert Hall, and had been acclaimed by the vast crowd assembled there. My wife and I had enjoyed a marvellous evening and were on our way to our hotel. We were travelling by tube and sitting close to us was Eric. None of the passengers would have been aware that just an hour previously he had been cheered to the echo in the Royal Albert Hall. I couldn't resist speaking to him, and although he had not the slightest idea of who I was he gave me the impression I was the one man he wanted to meet.

And Peter Millest, a cousin-once-removed of Eric's, has this to say:

> I invited Eric to lead a weekend of meetings at Scunthorpe in 1983. He stayed with my father for the weekend as my son, David, was quite small and I thought he might be too boisterous for Eric. But Eric left his impression on him. A few weeks later I put on a tape cassette while David and I were in the car. I told him the music was written by Eric Ball and asked him if he could remember him.
>
> 'Yes Daddy – that was the man with the white hair who was at Grandma's. He reminds me of Jesus.'

Eric Ball with his contest-winning CWS Manchester Band.

What a remark from a two-year-old! He still remembers Eric in that way.

Perhaps one of Eric's greatest triumphs in the championship stakes occurred at Belle Vue in September 1948, when the results read as follows:

CWS Manchester (Eric Ball) 192 points
Fairey Aviation (Harry Mortimer) 189 points
Carlton Main Frickley (Eric Ball) 186 points.

To have gained two out of the top three places 'can't be bad' as they say! The comment column in the 11 September issue of *BB* spoke of it as 'a special triumph for Eric Ball'.

For by now other bands were sitting up and taking notice. The 3 November 1945 issue of *BB* had commented that 'Eric Ball has had some interesting rehearsals with the de Haviland Works Band and hopes to conduct them in [Themes from] Beethoven's Fifth Symphony on 11 November.' By 16 March of the next year he had been appointed professional teacher of the Bradford Victoria Prize Band. By January 1948 Manchester CWS were said to be 'on the warpath . . . and with Eric Ball in frequent attendance they should go far.' This prophecy was soon fulfilled, as the preceding paragraph shows.

On 28 February 1947 Hoo Silver Band was announced to be playing, under Eric, 'Themes from Beethoven's Fifth

Symphony', 'Four preludes' and a new march, 'Men of Kent'. He was announced to be guest conductor of Highfield Modern School Band on 9 October of that year, having already, on 10 July, appeared as guest conductor at a concert in connection with the Brighton Festival, when 'the historic Dome of Brighton' was said to have been 'crowded out . . . and there was some good playing under Eric Ball'. By August 1948 Carlton Main Frickley had engaged him, with the result we have already seen.

Eric's regular conducting schedule at this time (1950) leaves one breathless, realising that he was contributing to *BB*, editing for R. Smith & Co, composing, teaching and adjudicating, and accepting public speaking engagements. He was conducting Manchester CWS in London from 16–22 June and in Derby on 25 June; he was at Brighouse (with Brighouse presumably) on 27 July; on tour in Scotland (Glasgow, Aberdeen, Edinburgh) with Manchester CWS in August; and at Huddersfield Town Hall with Brighouse, Ransome and Marles, and the Colne Valley Male Voice Choir on 14 October. He was at Rushden (Park Road Baptist Church) on 26 October; the Albert Hall, Manchester, with CWS Manchester on 28 November; and at the Central Hall, Chatham, with Hoo Silver, on 2 December. He was by now approaching 50, and was probably at the height of his powers, creatively speaking. It will be recalled that 1950 was the year of '*Resurgam*'.

Early the following year (28 January) he was announced to visit Camborne where, in the afternoon, he would address an interchurch meeting at which Camborne would play, and in the evening he would be present at a concert with Camborne Band, with Doris Coles as soloist. He was given a generous welcome, and conducted his own 'Morning rhapsody'. In the event, Doris Coles was ill, and Pauline Holman stood in for her. Eric spoke highly of the organisation of the event, in which he himself appeared, as he so often had done before, and so often did afterwards, as conductor, composer, speaker and pianist.

Again he pursued his relentless round of activity: at Halifax on 8 February with CWS Manchester and Manchester Male Voice Choir and Isobel Baillie; at Dorchester on 12 February with Dunrovia Silver; at Coventry Central Hall on 22 March with City of Coventry, massed choirs and Millicent Phillips. On Sunday 24 February he was at The Salvation Army's Regent Hall to take the chair (more of which anon), and on 19 May he chaired a programme at Southall Citadel, also conducting a couple of items. He was there at Don Osgood's request to help a Salvation Army missionary officer in India. On 27 May he was announced to lecture for the National Association of Brass Band Conductors at its West of England Centre on, 'The band as a musical team', with Woodfalls Band in attendance. He was to conduct massed band concerts for the then London County Council in Finsbury Park, before taking CWS Manchester on a tour of Switzerland in June.

At this time he worked from his base in west London. His days of 'journeyings oft' were over – so far as houses were concerned, for he and Olive stayed at Rathgar Avenue, Hanwell, until they moved to Dorset many years later. He never owned a car, so that he was always dependent upon public transport to get to his engagements, and had to travel to Yorkshire, Lancashire and Warwickshire to rehearse his bands. He would not, naturally, do that every week, but would certainly want to immediately prior to an engagement.

But what sort of conductor, what manner of interpreter, was he? His reputation was sufficient to cause Crawley Town band to journey to London in July 1951 to hear 'an authoritative performance' of 'Indian summer' by CWS (Manchester) band, conducted by the composer. Later, the band took first prize at the Brighton contest with this piece.

On the subject of interpretation, Eric himself wrote:

The Balls' house in Rathgar Avenue, on the borders of Hanwell and Ealing.

Brighouse and Rastrick photographed with Eric Ball in 1950.

Again and again it must be repeated that the printed score is not a blue-print. We call it music – but that is incorrect. It is a series of symbols describing musical ideas, as the written word describes only in a measure the ideas of poet and philosopher . . . Just as in reading poetry or great literature you seek for the idea enshrined in the words, so you must do in reading and interpreting music (*BB* 25 March 1950).

Robert Simpson says that 'he was a gentle, sensitive man, graceful in his nature. This came out in his movements, specially when he conducted . . . He was much loved by players, not only because he was a musician they could trust, but because he was a natural gentleman, and always considerate. He had a rich feeling for music and could convey it to the players naturally and effortlessly . . . I wish I'd seen more of him – our paths didn't cross often, but my impressions of him in boyhood have never faded . . . One of the happiest personal memories I have is of him conducting 'Energy' with the massed bands at the Albert Hall in 1970. Once again I could see him as I saw him as a boy in the old days, full of the same graceful authority that held me riveted when I was 10 years old. Not to be forgotten – ever. They say our earliest formative experiences stay longest with us, and this is still for me a vivid example of that.'

There are those who say that Eric was economical in his movements, letting the music unfold by itself and speak in its own language. There are others, Geoffrey Brand among them, who wonder whether he was a little *too* modest in gesture – a little bit *too* unself-assertive. 'Yer've got ter be able ter lowse yer temper ter to get the best owt o't men,' he says, imitating the northern brass bandsmen who loved Eric Ball so much.

It could well have been in defence of this criticism that Eric wrote an article in *BB* entitled 'On losing one's temper', which is worth reproducing in full here:

The average bandsman is, perhaps, rarely tempted in this matter – at least in regard to his band duties; but the poor bandmaster is often sorely tried, especially in rehearsal!

Of course, he must *never* lose control of his temper: that is an unalterable rule. He may, perhaps, be allowed, as Paul puts it, to 'be angry and sin not'. What he must be careful of is the cause or motive of his anger.

If a bandsman is careless or wilfully wrong-headed in his treatment of some lovely music, then he must expect to be trounced for his short-comings. 'It is the music that matters,' and a conductor may well be angry if a bandsman treats it as if he 'couldn't care less'.

If, however, the bandmaster's anger is inspired by a more per-

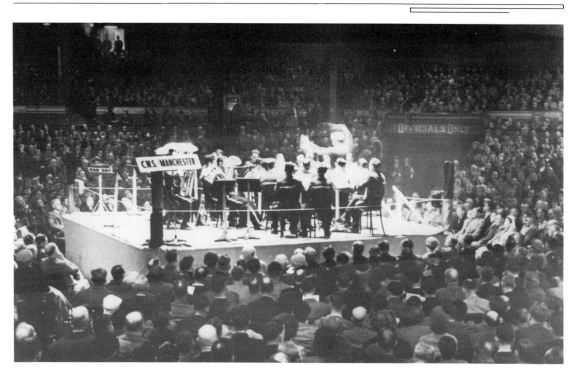

Eric conducting CWS
Manchester Band in a
contest-winning performance.

sonal point of view – as for instance when a bandsman is thought to be purposely awkward or contentious thereby threatening discipline and exhibiting prejudice against a person – then the same anger is more dangerous and less excusable, for the simple reason that it concerns *self* and not music-making.

Of course, a successful conductor cannot always be calm and patient. I know of one who sometimes *pretends* to be very angry, thereby shaking up the rehearsal to very good effect. Some bandsmen, of course, do not reckon to have had a decent rehearsal unless they have been well and truly 'told off'!

Here is another of my favourite parables from the works of Sri Ramakrishna, a 19th-century Hindu sage. During his journeyings, a holy man came to a village where the inhabitants were all in a state of fear because of the activities of a great serpent which lived near the one road in and out. The holy man visited the serpent, dealt with him about his sins, and left him very meek and mild. Returning some years later, the sage met the serpent again, now very battered and bruised and sorry for himself. 'Sir,' he cried, 'since you converted me I have received nothing but bad treatment from the villagers. They are afraid no longer, and take advantage of my meekness.' Then said the holy man, 'Good serpent, when I told you not to harm these people, I did not suggest that you should not sometimes hiss a little!'

But so much of criticism, professional and otherwise, is merely opinion. Geoffrey Brand himself once suggested five criteria for a successful conductor:

1. A profound knowledge of the music;
2. An inate communication with the players (or singers as the case may be);
3. A possession of energy – emotional, spiritual and physical;
4. A total sincerity on the rostrum;
5. An ability to make people perform.

Possibly the last of these is the most important quality of all. But if one feels that Eric Ball possessed all these then he was on the way to being what one could call 'a good conductor'.

And all the time he was composing and arranging, not only marches and items from the classics and other run-of-the-mill material, but that marvellous series of test pieces in which he excelled – test pieces which, besides putting their players on their mettle, were packed with memorable tunes for the ordinary listener, and with thoughtful, considered development for the critic. Perhaps this instinct for a memorable tune was his greatest gift and surely a legacy from his Salvation Army days when he was a composer of songs as well as of band music.

His earliest essay in the direction of test pieces would appear to have been his tone poem, 'Thanksgiving', used in the National Festival Area Contest, held at the Friends' Meeting House, Euston Road, on 16 February 1946, and of which it was said that 'a glance . . . will give pleasure and satisfaction to junior bands which are contesting on it'. 'Divertimento' quickly followed, and was used for fourth-section bands in the 1947 area contests. But most important of his first group, possibly, was 'Akhnaton' – a powerful and deeply felt portrait of an ancient Egyptian priest/pharaoh.

Eric was probably finding it a considerable relief to be able to throw off the yoke of restriction which his Salvation Army composing had forced him to wear, due to its very limited (at that time) boundaries and essentially functional character. At the same time, he always said that he found it exceedingly difficult to write abstract music. Given a picture or a concrete idea, he could usually go ahead and work out the germinal thoughts such a picture or idea started up in his mind.

When working for The Salvation Army, he always needed to have a 'recognisable' Salvation Army tune within the fabric of the music – that was, and still is, one of the unwritten rules, even though the rule is not so rigidly enforced these days. Many composers, Eric among them, got around this by writing songs which were then published, and working them into their more extended works. His 'Songs of the morning' is a case in point; had he not had this suite in his mind, those two charming songs 'Welcome, happy morning', and the delectable 'Begin the day with God' would possibly never have been written at all. And the lives of many salvationists would have been the poorer as a result.

Such apparent 'flouting' of the rules might appear risible to the uninitiated, but on the whole it seems to work. One is sad when, occasionally, both song and extended brass composition are unpopular (Erik Leidzén's meditation 'Where flowers never fade' is an example – neither the song nor the brass band number ever became part of the repertoire), but one is grateful when it does work.

It is interesting, however, to find that many of his test pieces are as profound, as spiritual, as philosophical, as anything he wrote for The Salvation Army. Even 'Morning rhapsody', which commences, he tells us, with a section which is 'rather dark in colour, representing, perhaps, the grey light of dawn, before the sun is up . . . [until] there is a sudden burst of sheer brilliance – the sun has risen! – and a little later the trumpets of the dawn call us to the day's duties, while a sinister, *feroce* figure reminds us that there may also be evil influences to fight . . .' But the music ends with '. . . the *molto moderato* (figure 11) [which] reminds us of the serious purpose of our day of life; and the final *molto lento, trionfale* of our glorious destiny, the ecstatic sunrise to which we all, consciously or unconsciously, look forward.' (*BB* 4 December 1948)

He suggests, for instance, that 'Divertimento' should be taken *cum grano salis* – with a grain of salt – with its 'March of the Serious Young Men':

its 'Interlude – The Passing Years':

and its 'Dance of the Happy Old Gentlemen':

All would seem to be tongue in cheek. And yet he tells us in the next paragraph that 'There may be those who believe that it is the old gentlemen who are serious and the young men who wish to dance, but who can tell?' (*BB* 28 December 1948). So although he calls it 'a piece of unashamedly "light" music', it has perhaps a strain of profundity aching to express itself such as is to be found quite often in the slow movements of the *divertimenti* or *concerti* of Mozart himself.

In Eric's music, then, there is no essential difference between that which he wrote for The Salvation Army and that which he wrote for contesting bands. Each is full of singable, lovely tunes, and while the former has recognisable hymn tunes overtly or covertly woven into the texture, they are developed in the same way as the themes in his secular music, with contrast and conflict, sunshine and shade, broad sweep or majestic utterance and delicate patterning to give the desired effect.

Eric was not alone in this. Many of the great composers would use and re-use material, transferring it from 'secular' to 'sacred' use and sometimes back again with complete freedom. Handel, for instance, based three of his best-known choruses in 'Messiah' ('He shall purify', 'For unto us a child is born' and 'All we like sheep') on three of a series of Italian duets for two sopranos which he had published only a year or two previously. Then, a year or two later, he used two of his 'Messiah' choruses ('And the glory of the Lord' and 'Lift up your heads') as the basis for two movements in *concerti* for two groups of wind bands and strings. And very fine they sound in that form!

Handel's great contemporary, Bach, did the same thing. Many of the movements from his Christmas Oratorio and his Mass in B minor either originated in or were re-used in cantatas or orchestral works of a greatly differing character from those in which we are accustomed to hear them. While it comes initially as a bit of a shock to hear familiar music in an unfamiliar guise in this way, we very soon find that the music sounds quite 'right' in each context if we listen to it without prejudice.

With Mozart, too, we find similar things happening. An aria like, for example, 'Per pietà', sung by Dorabella, one of the lovers in *Cosi fan Tutte*, that most elegant of comic operas, sounds, with its horn *obbligato*, exactly like a movement from one of the mature piano concertos, movements which Mozart used to give vent to some of his deepest and most profound thoughts.

This makes us think afresh our ideas about inspiration and where musical ideas come from; whether we have the Christian idea of a God who inspires music or the the idea of a basic 'creative spirit' which breathes into our nostrils the breath of creative influence.

For it is surely 'Akhnaton' which, as has been observed, stands out among these early test pieces as having the deepest philosophical undertones, and is thus the most characteristic of Eric's music as a whole. Akhaton himself was one of the pharaohs – Amen-hotep IV – who changed his name to Akhnaton, and whose wife was the famous Nefertiti, whose bust in the British Museum has been a criterion for female beauty down the years.

In a programme note for the piece the composer tells us that Akhnaton, who was born into 'an age ridden with the grossest polytheism, superstition and barbarism, evolved and taught by precept and example a philosophy which in purity and spiritual perception has rarely been surpassed in world history. A lover of peace, the arts, and of mankind, he was a man born "before his time", and at his death at an early age, the priests of the old gods destroyed almost everything that might perpetuate his teaching. The music sets out not to describe any particular events, but to illustrate something of this conflict of ideas and ideals: while the last section was written in the spirit of one of the great psalms of Akhnaton.'

Elsewhere, Eric tells us that the coda to the piece, which 'is quite short, includes details of balance, rhythm and expression, which need careful attention. Although brilliant in general effect, the prevailing mood of exaltation becomes darkened a little, as if suggesting the frustration and apparent failure of Akhnaton's life and work. But he – like One even greater – only seemed to fail: his teaching and example live on' (*BB* 18 January 1947).

Thus, Eric has only partially thrown off his Salvation Army mantle. He himself suggested, perhaps merely because others had already done so, that this work might be looked upon as a companion-piece to his own earlier tone poem 'Exodus' but my own feeling is that it could more properly be considered a companion piece to 'The King of kings'. It is for the reader to decide whether that is a valid opinion or not. An analysis of this piece appears at Appendix L.

'Akhnaton' received a warm welcome from players and critics alike. *BB* (1 February 1947) suggested that it is 'full of beautiful contrasts and mixed harmony, and is very fascinating to both players and listeners.' A correspondent was to suggest (5 April), 'What a fine and scholarly "test" is "Akhnaton". We can all feel proud that it was written by a bandsman born and bred. The work of Eric Ball will live for many a long day and his further creations will be looked forward to with great interest . . . The happy thing about Eric's work is that both players and listeners are pleased.'

On one occasion Eric even received a message from 'Four Kentish fans' after he had instructed Hoo Silver Band in the background of 'Akhnaton' before a contest:

> O Isis, Osiris, smile down on Akhnaton,
> May Hoo be the victors 'neath Eric Ball's baton.

Not everyone regarded him with such idealistic vision. A correspondent to *BB* castigated 'the composer' of 'Quartet for four tubas' on having written very poor-quality music. Two other correspondents immediately rushed to Eric's defence, and Eric himself published a note saying that the item was merely a piece of light music, and not to be taken seriously, whereupon the original correspondent came back with 'a most dignified apology' (though hardly an unqualified one), saying that he still didn't want to hear the quartet.

But another important facet of the work of Eric the interpreter needs to be considered – that of the adjudicator.

Eric himself left some of his thoughts on this subject in a short series in *BB* in February and March 1950, suggesting that the responsibility of adjudicating at a contest should not be undertaken lightly: the amount of effort in planning and rehearsal put in by each competing band, the expense involved for a band to be present, the high hopes with which they inevitably attend, should cause him to realise that the person whom they trust to judge between them must be a musician both of efficiency and of integrity. 'Here is no place for the mere experimentalist or seeker after novel experience, or for the person who wishes to give an impression of superiority above his fellows, but rather for one who is concerned with progress in the art of brass band music, and who by his judgments and criticisms sincerely tries to encourage that progress.' A worthy aim indeed, and one which Eric himself impressively fulfilled.

But he went on to suggest that an adjudicator's technical equipment should be wide in its scope, and of a high standard: that he must know a good deal about instrumental technique – such seemingly simple things as how to produce a note, for instance; the recognition of correct balance and blend; what type of passage-work lies most (and, for that matter, least) easily 'under the players' fingers'; he must be able to define the varying degrees of fine tone; he must be constantly sensitive to poor tuning and intonation. All these mean that he has, in fact, to be aurally sensitive to a marked degree.

An adjudicator, in his opinion, should be able to *read*

'*Daily Herald*' *Brass Band
Contests*, Harry Mortimer, Sir
Malcolm Sargent, Frank Wright
and Eric Ball at the 1955 Finals.

music, and he defines this as not merely a single line of notation, but a full score, which should be as an open book to
him. In this way he is able to judge the general effect of the
music, so that any band which plays 'number one' in the
contest may receive as fair a hearing as all the others which
come along afterwards. To be able to 'hear' the music before
he can judge an appearance of it is not an advantage, especially in 'own choice' contests, where the adjudicator may
meet new and unfamiliar works.

Eric Ball believed that the adjudicator must *know* the music
as distinct from merely being able to *read* it – the latter ability
perhaps denoting a somewhat superficial knowledge. The
form and construction of the music must be familiar: its
varying idioms; the interpretation of 'period' music; the varying styles of the romantic and classical schools; orchestral,
choral, operatic, chamber music – all these, with their own
separate subtleties and nuances must be familiar to him as
types.

But most of all Eric Ball thought that an adjudicator should be a man of unquestioned integrity. Without this his musical attainments would count for very little. 'In adjudicating, there are so many subtle temptations to mental laziness,' he wrote. To listen, as sometimes one must, to some 25 or 30 bands and give every one equal attention is no easy task. He cannot even ease off when the opening bars proclaim a band which is very poor, for that band may at any moment improve, and its position in the general summing-up has to be ascertained and marks awarded.

He wrote much more on the subject of interpretation. But the foregoing is perhaps sufficient to indicate just how seriously he saw his task. All those who sat under his judgments on contesting occasions will have their own opinions as to how he met up to his own criteria.

NINE

Eric the communicator

As has already been mentioned, Eric joined the staff of *BB**
on a part-time basis in November 1948. Since March of the
next year his contribution to the paper had been a considerable
one.

BB (not for many years did it, in common with many other
newspapers and magazines, drop the definite article from its
title) was founded in 1887 by Sam Cope. Its first issue, as a
monthly magazine, was dated September of that year, and it
cost 2d. Sam Cope was a writer, a performer on several
instruments, and a conductor, being associated with choral
and orchestral societies, and with military and brass bands.

It will be interesting to musical readers of this book that of
the other eight musical journals published at that time, only
two, the *Musical Times* and *Musical Opinion*, have survived –
which says something for the staying power of *BB* and for the
loyalty of its readership. It is also of interest that in that same
year the gramophone was invented; that a patent was taken
out for the first disc, coated with lamp-black – the first record
company being founded on 14 July 1887; and that Heinrich
Hertz first produced radio waves.

In the centenary issue, the present editor, Peter Wilson,
paid tribute to some of his predecessors: 'Founder, Sam
Cope – refined, idealistic yet courageous; John Henry Iles –
flamboyant, powerful, larger than life; Herbert Whiteley –
modest, erudite, tireless in his crusade for better music and
higher standards; Eric Ball – diplomatic, deeply spiritual, the
finest musician of them all.'

Eric himself recalled, in that same centenary issue, the
'three small second- and third-floor offices, in a building
adjacent to our giant newspaper neighbours in Fleet Street

---

* Throughout this chapter *The British Bandsman* is again referred to by its
  initials, *BB*.)

[which] housed *The British Bandsman* and R. Smith and Co Ltd, band music publishers.' He tells us that 'the great John Henry Iles was the editor and I was able to be of some service to him, in an advisory capacity [a typically modest self-assessment], for a short time before his death. His son, Mr Eric Iles, offered me the editor's chair, and so began an interesting and rewarding period in my life.

'It was not a particularly arduous task in those days, so long as we adhered to the regular times and dates for the delivery of material to the printers, for proof-reading and the final make-up of the pages. Nor was it for me a full-time job. There were concerts and contests to attend, and new music to write, plus editorial work for R. Smith & Co . . . 210 Strand was an address easy enough to find. Visitors came from here, there and everywhere, some from overseas. Invariably friendly, keen on the band movement – which was now recovering from the stress of years of war – they sometimes discussed various problems – administrative, musical, personal and even spiritual.'

As one studies the life and career of Eric, it becomes clear that had he never lifted a baton or written a note of music, he would, through his public and written work, have been a great communicator. So far as his public ministry is concerned, little is left to us. Fortunately, so far as his written work goes, the opposite is true: far more has survived than can ever be reproduced in a book of this size. Much of what he wrote was not meant for posterity, but always it is carefully constructed, and shaped with care and skill.

But as far back as 1934 Eric was contributing regularly to The Salvation Army's press. Not for nothing had he listed ' "composition" (essays)' as one of the things he was good at at school.

In the first issue of *The Bandsman and Songster* of that year we find 'a new and useful series by a well-known Army composer' being announced – 'Letters to a musical friend'. Addressed to 'Dear John' (a name generally assumed to be that of his friend, John Hunt), he begins, after the expected New Year salutations have been expressed:

> It seems to me that more than ever we must try to improve our standard of musicianship. People are getting used to good, well-played music via radio and gramophone, and *anything* simply will not do in our present-day service for God. Ignorance and incapacity are more than ever likely to repel than to attract.

From week to week we find him giving advice on such matters as leading a songster brigade, dealing with criticism, persevering with composition, plagiarism, and so on. Of par-

ticular interest, nearly 60 years on, are his comments about
'the three latest Army gramophone records':

> As to the actual job of recording, about which you request
> some details, it is, of course, very interesting and instructive . . .
>
> With the band, each recording session has differed in a
> marked degree. Each has been preceded by intensive rehearsal,
> in which the special demands of the microphone have been
> considered. At the recording studio it is not possible to place the
> band in the usual festival formation. All players face the 'mike',
> but the band has never been placed in exactly the same position
> twice running. Solo cornets are generally in the front row; horns
> and basses being also to the fore, although this varies according
> to the type of music to be recorded, and is dependent upon the
> rhythmic effect required etc. Trombones are often placed
> behind the rest of the band, but are sometimes raised above its
> level. Baritones are put rather well back. Euphoniums cause the
> most trouble, they being difficult to record satisfactorily. It
> seems that their tone does not suit the mike, being liable to
> blasting; they are therefore given a back seat. Percussion
> instruments are not encouraged, except for special effects . . .
>
> Once the balance has been proved satisfactory, by repeated
> tests, a test record is made, and 'played back' to the band for
> criticism. Possibly another change of position will be necessary,
> or an unsatisfactory passage may need a little rehearsal, but at
> length the word is given to make a 'Master'. One hears the
> warning buzz for 'Get ready!' and a second buzz for 'Silence!'
> There is a tense moment or two; one observes the glow of a red
> lamp, and then the band starts. Absolute silence is maintained
> throughout and until the lamp goes out. Two of these 'Masters'
> are made, one of which, it is hoped, will eventually be found
> suitable for general release . . .
>
> Recording is just as intriguing for vocalists – the turning
> slightly away for high notes; the bending slightly forward for low
> ones; the difficulty with consonants that do not record well, the
> placing of accompanying instruments, etc, all being matters for
> absolute concentration. Songster brigades, also, sing in varied
> formations, and when the band is to accompany them complica-
> tions are added.

This was before the days of stereo, and of work being
recorded on tape, to say nothing of analogue and digital
techniques, let alone compact discs.

And on 30 March 1946 *BB* announced that Eric would
commence a series of 'Letters to a Musical Friend', the next
issue presenting the first of these. 'My dear John' it commenced. Is there a feeling of *déjà vu* – a 'haven't-we-been-
here-before about this'? Never mind:

> So at last you are 'demobbed' and back with the old band
> again! I am glad to know that you are happily settled once more,

and particularly interested in your decision to play a 'secondary' part, at least for the time being. Please do not let that phrase 'for the time being' loom too largely in your mental horizon. Frankly, my dear old friend and pupil, you were not a star soloist *before* your call-up, although you did some very good work as leader of your cornet team; but I should be glad to hear that you are dedicating your not inconsiderable musicianship to some part less showy but of equal musical importance. If you get a chance, why not a baritone? Your deft touch should be useful there, and I should think you would hardly try to make the instrument sound like a thin euphonium, as so many do.

Do you remember reading about ***** in the dance band business, who was described as 'the best second trumpet in London'? Remember also Will *****, my second trombone player, who was the real *leader* of the section, although never the soloist. Oh, for more of his kind!

So my first letter has become a homily. 'Twill not always be so! By the way, do not expect the old band to be quite the same as before; speaking from memory, I sincerely hope it has improved!!

Thus, the formula is similar to the previous, and the same kinds of subjects are dealt with: criticism, true *pp* playing, type of baton, applause, and so on.

The last of these shows Eric's sense of humour coming through:

> . . . A very good rule is to sit down *before* the applause ceases. It is most embarrassing to find oneself in the middle of a bow and to suddenly realise that no one is clapping at all. The only thing to do then is to bend still lower and pretend to tie up your shoelace as if you didn't care what the audience thought . . .
>
> I once heard a terrible violinist in a cinema concert. At the end of her act the organist commenced his filling-up music; he got a cheer; the violinist thought it was for her and came back to give an encore. Three times this happened, until the audience was quite convulsed with laughter . . .
>
> It could even be a thought to have printed at the bottom of your programmes the legend 'Please do *not* applaud – we know we're good!'

But his 'letter' of 8 May 1948 has deeper undertones. Should John accept an application from a salvationist who wants to join his band?

After showing great understanding of the dilemma the applicant finds himself in of wanting to be true to his essential ideals, whilst wanting to stretch his musical wings, written obviously from his own experience (was this to explain the essentials of Salvation Army banding to non-salvationist readers?) he says, 'If he can honestly come to your band with his spiritual and musical ideals undimmed, he will probably become one of your greatest assets; but do not be surprised if he decides to stay where he is!'

These letters continued for several years; first weekly, then monthly, then occasionally, until they disappeared altogether. But they served a very useful purpose in the thought-provoking advice given and ideas expressed, and some deserve to be preserved in a more permanent form.

The issue of *BB* dated 2 June 1951 announced the death of John Henry Iles, the editor, and that of 9 June announced Eric to be giving the address at his memorial service at St Sepulchre's Holborn Viaduct (that most musical of churches), the next day. In the same issue Eric paid tribute to Iles, saying that 'to me he gave great encouragement at a very trying time'. His item covered more than two columns, and ended with the familiar quotation from the Book of Wisdom always associated with '*Resurgam*' – 'In the eyes of the foolish they seemed to have died; but they are in peace'. When Iles's secretary, Frances Bantin, read the lesson at the memorial service, she was said to have been the first woman in the 1,000-year history of that church to undertake such a duty.

It was on 23 June that Eric was announced as taking over the editorial chair. His reception on taking up that appointment, and the opinion of the present editor, have been commented upon already. His own contributions to the newspaper are likely to be the stuff of which history is made. So much of quality is there in just a few words, however, that a group of short quotations could suffice to indicate what he was able to give to a periodical, and other examples find their places in other parts of this book:

Jealousy cannot really hurt you if in your own heart you have yourself conquered jealousy. . . .

Study for yourself the scores of Beethoven and his famous notebooks and see how much literally grew out of a very little. Many can string together a few tunes and call it composition, but few can create an involved work of art out of a few short phrases, as can the symphonists. . . .

Too often the keen young enthusiast fritters his time away when a little expert guidance would help him achieve more in five minutes than he might do in as many hours. Too often the conductor tires his men in rehearsal because he has not planned what he will do and use his time economically. . . .

The true artist, like the saint, will feel 'So much to do, so little time to do it', and this sense of urgency, plus that 'divine dissatisfaction' which is always with him, will best help him to avoid wasted time and effort. . . .

In the re-creation of great music there is no place for selfishness or insincerity: the players must be taught and encouraged to play together, as one. . . .

Let others plan their own lives. The artist, the mystic, the true philosopher, know their lives to be planned for them by hidden, unconquerable Spiritual Powers. . . .

But from time to time he gives very practical advice, such as here, on the subject of compèring:

Do not lecture (much less preach at) your audience.
Do not talk down to your hearers – treat them as at least on the same level as yourself.
In speaking of the music tell how it appeals to you and not what the theorists say about it.
Speak naturally as in ordinary conversation, yet make your voice heard.
Speak too little rather than too much.

Any who heard him compère a programme, either of Salvation Army music, or in the concert hall, will have their own remembrances of how he came up to his own expectations of other people in his own performances.

So far as his own public speaking is concerned, probably all that is available for future generations – thanks to the art of the recording engineers – belongs to his later years. By this time his voice, always soft and gently-toned, was failing and tremulous, and can thus portray little of the power he must have had in younger days to hold an audience. Besides, one needs to have seen the man: the upright, slight figure; the twinkle in the eye; the shock of greying, later white, hair; the familiar jut of the hands in the jacket pockets: all these proclaim, if proclamation were necessary, that one does not need to be 10 feet tall to captivate an audience.

Derek Dolling, a Salvation Army officer, and erstwhile corps officer at Enfield, recalls having Eric preside over a Saturday evening programme at his corps, and prevailing upon him to lead the meetings the next day – or one of them at least. Eric showed some diffidence, saying that the date was Mother's Day, and that he might not be the best person in the world for that particular feast. 'Well, we'll accommodate that somehow,' Derek told him. 'Eric led the finest Mother's Day morning meeting I have ever been in,' he says. 'He took as his theme "Love consists in the letting go." It was wonderful.'

My own memory of him leading a Sunday morning meeting concerns an occasion some years ago. His theme then was that much-neglected miracle of the changing of the water into wine. 'Composers write their notes which are like the empty water-pots,' he said. 'Musicians fill them to the brim with their interpretation, which on its own is merely water – and then God turns it into wine – something far richer than it ever could be on its own.'

One of the earliest occasions we have on record of him as a public speaker after he had left the officer-ranks of The Salvation Army is when he appeared as 'the well-known conductor, composer and authority on brass band music' at the Gloucester Music Club in February 1950. *BB* for 15 April reprinted some comments from a local newspaper:

Working-editor Eric Ball preparing one of his famous 'pieces' for *The British Bandsman* in 1961. 'Snapped' by Connie Clark.

> A common criticism of brass bands is that they are too loud. Mr Eric Ball . . . disagreed with this view. Brass bands, he said, need be no louder than an orchestra. The band should be good enough to play *pianissimo*. Many people suffered from the over-amplification of music in a cinema without complaint. With the assistance of the City of Gloucester Band, Mr Ball demonstrated the functions of the various instruments. He did not agree that there was lack of tone colour contrast in a brass band. The same might be said of a string orchestra or a choir, as the instruments or voices would be of one 'family'.

During the evening Eric conducted the band in various classical arrangements, mostly his own, 'A Handelian suite' by Denis Wright, and 'A moorside suite' by Gustav Holst.

And in 1958 Eric spoke on 'The art of the composer' at the National Association of Brass Band Conductors' AGM, saying that 'The compere should act as a bridge between audience and band . . . most definitely a "funny man" is not what is wanted . . .' The next day the association held its morning service at Regent Hall, Eric leading. The service was said to have been 'a season of rich spiritual content'.

Connie Clark has her own memories of him in the editor's role:

> We were always under pressure to keep a rigid timetable. As well as being editor, Eric was the professional conductor of more than one championship band, travelling extensively, rehearsing, conducting, adjudicating and lecturing. He carried out many overseas engagements too – some tours lasting a few weeks or longer. He was also composing and arranging music at the same time, sometimes working into the early hours of the morning. It was amazing the amount of work he could pack in.
>
> Whatever pressure he was under, however difficult and sometimes unjust some situations were, Eric had great patience and inner strength and serenity that helped everyone. One was always aware of his sincere Christian spirit. However busy he might be, he was always courteous, always making time for all who phoned or called unexpectedly.
>
> Eric influenced and enouraged many people in all walks of life. A well-known chairman and director of several companies, who was also a JP, told me more than once that however many problems he had in his business affairs (and there were times when he felt overwhelmed by his responsibilities, especially those as a JP), to spend a while in the company of, and in con-

Eric and Olive in relaxed mood.

versation with, Eric Ball, helped him to get his priorities into the right order. He was able to talk with, and to confide in, Eric, in a way that he couldn't with anyone else. Eric always revealed to him an extra dimension to life that renewed him in spirit and enabled him to go on with his work.

Eric had a great sense of humour. I remember the occasion when I had bought some navy-blue gloves to wear with my uniform. One particular Sunday they were 'taken' by mistake. At the *BB* office I was complaining to Eric that my gloves had not been returned to me. Eric said that maybe the person who had taken them needed them more than I did. 'But it's still stealing!' I said. With a twinkle in his eyes, Eric replied, with an arm upraised in William Booth style, 'Hallelujah! Sinners are still coming to the Army!'

Violet Brand, too, has memories of Eric during this period:

Like many whose roots are firmly embedded in The Salvation Army, I had known Eric through his music, his reputation and his performances, for many years. But it was not until the early months of 1967 that I grew to know him as a person – a teacher, a manager, and a negotiator – with a delightful sense of humour and an empathy with people from all backgrounds, whether he agreed with their opinions or not.

The opportunity came because we [that is her husband, Geoffrey, and she] were taking over *BB* and R. Smith & Co. *Someone* had to be initiated into the weekly routine of editing. I was the person delegated to undertake the task. Having spent my previous working life as a teacher, I knew nothing about running a weekly paper and managing its output. This was the ignoramus that Eric Ball agreed to take on and educate.

I shall never forget his qualities as a teacher, helping me to understand the pure mechanics of editing, 'pasting-up' and organising advertisements. But beyond that it was the way he handled the contributions from all over the country, understanding the 'politics' of local situations, and relationships, that impressed me. Editing became much more than cutting items down to size!

Outside the *British Bandsman* office, The Strand, in 1967. With Eric are Connie Clark (left), with Doris Coles and John Hunt (right). The young man (centre) has not been identified.

His relationships with the staff were excellent – no wonder they loved him dearly and thoroughly enjoyed working with him. There was no 'distance' between himself and them.

One telephone call that took place during March 1967 stands out clearly in my memory. I had never realised that Eric could be so firm. A discussion took place with the Chairman of Bandsman's Press and R. Smith & Co, concerning a meeting of directors which was shortly to take place, to finalise the sale of the companies. One director had not been informed and the announcement due to be made at that meeting was to be quite a shock to him. I stood up to leave the room as the telephone discussion developed, but Eric motioned to me to sit down again. 'It'll give me strength!' he whispered.

He then proceeded to insist that the news be broken to the other director before the scheduled meeting. There was obvious reluctance from the Chairman, but Eric was *very* firm. His hand trembled as he held the phone, but he continued to urge that the honourable thing should be done. He won the day!

Peter Wilson the present editor, has his own opinion of Eric as editor of the journal, and that has already been mentioned. His son, Eric (named after 'our Eric'), writing in *The Independent* newspaper shortly after the composer's death, said '. . . he invested the paper with some of the most wisely conceived editorial pieces in its long history . . .' and reading some of Eric Ball's 'Comment' columns and other pieces, one sees this assessment to be a realistic one.

By 13 April 1963 Eric had given up the editor's chair, remaining as 'music adviser' when Alfred Mackler took over from him. The paper immediately had a new, brighter 'look' about it. Better-quality news-print helped in achieving this, as did fresher, snappier use of type-faces. Far more photographs were henceforth to appear. But gone were those 'wisely conceived pieces' – until Eric returned as editor on 11 April the following year.

In 1967 a further change of editor was announced, this time to Geoffrey Brand. Eric was never to return to the 'chair' again – in a full-time capacity that is; he was 'to concentrate on musical work and other of his special interests' the official announcement of the change of editor stated. But he did later on take up his office temporarily at times when need arose. Frank Wright commented a few weeks later (15 April), '. . . Immensely knowledgable, tactful and *kindly*, Mr Ball's calm, wise counsel will be missed'. He was to return later to provide a further short series of columns, and even as late as 1982 (when he was 80 years of age) wrote a Christmas message for the paper.

But soon after relinquishing his editorial chair to Geoffrey Brand, on 29 April, Eric and Olive were announced to be

Eric Ball with Peter Wilson, Conductors' Workshop, Carberry Tower, Scotland, 1963.

touring the United States – 'an all-Salvation Army tour' from 3 May to 11 June. Those 'special interests' had to be served, and serve them he did, as a communicator-extraordinary, wherever he went.

However, it is basically as a musician that we are considering him, and if we ask ourselves the question, 'Did (or does) his music communicate?' the answer must be a very resounding 'yes'.

This is most certainly so of his test pieces – a field where one might not expect to find communication a top priority. But always his music had style and purpose, and one feels always that Eric wants to communicate with his players, his adjudicators, and, most of all perhaps, with his audiences. Given a contest, where it is necessary for adjudicators and audiences to listen to anything up to 25 or more performances one after the other, with scarcely a break between them, the music must communicate to be successful.

Four *BB* editors: Left to right;
Geoffrey Brand, Eric Ball, Alfred
Mackler, Peter Wilson.

Take his 'English country scenes' for instance, published by Novello in their 'Paxton Music' imprint in 1971. Eric himself provides a programme note, telling us that his suite is in a somewhat nostalgic mood, and is divided into the usual three movements. The first of these, 'Stately home', begins in serious tones and then continues with a minuet, which is formal, and even, maybe, old-fashioned. Then 'Quiet river', which flows peacefully along, though observing the life going on around it and on it and in it the whole time. Thirdly there is a 'Garden party' movement, subtitled *'Humoresque'*. This, he says, is 'suitably gay but quite decorous, of course. There are a few "gossipy" cross-rhythms. To end there is a reminder of where we are – at the stately home!' Thus he observes a classical model with a simple recapitulation at the end, but with most successful results for all concerned.

We see this again, in his 'Rhapsody on American gospel songs', written originally for the Chicago Staff Band of The Salvation Army, and intended for publication by the Army. The Army released it when Eric rang Ray Steadman-Allen, the then Head of the International Music Editorial Department, 'in a bit of a panic' to use Ray's own words, saying that he needed a test piece 'in double-quick time and I haven't an idea in my head at the moment.'

The 'fine Methodist tune "Sagina" . . . heard in the first part (and more completely towards the end) is a good example of a species of hymn melody sadly neglected at present', Eric tells us, again in his own admirable programme note. He goes on to use 'I will sing of my Redeemer' and 'Shall we gather at the river' before 'Amazing grace' appears (it had been top of the 'hit parade' for months and would be known by countless younger listeners and players to whom the other three tunes possibly would not communicate). The whole adds up to a tuneful 'selection' of melodies in a very traditional Salvation Army fashion, yet threaded together in the style of an overture to a musical, and in a way in which audiences would be quickly humming under their breath as they listened.

Occasionally Eric explored greater depths than these in his test pieces, as we have already observed in 'Resurgam'.

His 'Journey into freedom', for instance, voted after his

At the *British Bandsman* Centenary Dinner, 1987; Left to right: John Iles, Doris Iles, widow of Eric Iles, Eric Ball, Connie Clark, Muriel Jakeway.

death as the most popular of any test piece in the current repertoire, was said by the composer to have been based upon John Wesley's hymn-translation 'O Love who formedst me to wear the image of thy Godhead here . . .'. The piece is conceived in one complete movement, divided into six short sections, played without a break.

In its *Moderato e feroce* first section, an atmosphere is evoked of materialism, rigid, unyielding, and enslaving, machine-like and merciless in its forcefulness. Music of protest, of revolt, follows, in an *Alla marcia*, though variable in its moods, a combination of high resolve, bravado and fearfulness. Then the initial mood returns, though if anything even more rigid and harsh by now, with ejaculatory sub-themes being brought into the overall texture of the music, and dynamics stepped up to heighten the tension of the new mood.

Then the 'hero of the story' seeks escape through human love, in an *Andante con espressione* theme in which various instruments add their hopeful voices. In the fifth section, an *Allegro scherzando*, high spirits would seem to offer some kind of relief if only for a short time, before the 'love theme' returns, transformed and purified in an *Andante cantabile* ending. Thus, ideal love, and a contemplation of The Eternal, bring, finally, inner freedom.

And again, 'Sinfonietta' (subtitled 'The wayfarer') would appear to be based upon the Bible story of the prodigal son. The first movement, entitled 'Adventure', commences with an *Andante semplice* introduction of eight bars, which could be said to depict home comforts and tranquillity of lifestyle, before an *Allegro marcato* changes the mood to one of cheerful waving of goodbyes to home and kindred. A baritone solo (how frequently Eric wrote or used beguiling tunes for the baritone, so often neglected by composers until he rescued it!) is marked *Gaiamente* and continues the carefree mood. This is soon taken up by the more robust euphonium, with charming 'embroidery' from the flugelhorn, and then a countertheme is brazened out by the trombones. Both of these themes are now used in counterpoint, to depict a conflict of moods – the prodigal is perhaps more determined than happy on his journey – before the *gaiamente* theme is sung by the flugelhorn with great confidence.

But this confidence is short-lived. A movement called 'Exile' follows, with a brilliant *cadenza*-like passage for soprano cornet – the prodigal is 'wasting his substance . . . .'. An *Andante* theme of great beauty is then introduced as a horn solo where the exile is obviously thinking of home. But again, conflict is introduced with a florid passage marked *Poco animato* for cornet and flugelhorn, before the wayfarer decides to 'arise and go to my father . . .'. So is introduced a theme of chorale-like gravity which the composer develops into a *passacaglia* with variations, the theme striding along, mainly in octaves, by the basses, though not always, for at length other instruments take it up. His step lightens in a *Quasi scherzo* passage where the original theme of the movement is all but lost, before an *Andante trionfale e sostenuto* passage triumphantly brings the wayfarer back home to his family once again.

It is difficult to think of these as being only test pieces. Each one is a legitimate 'concert item' in its own right, deserving to be remembered as music which communicates at its own individual level of experience.

TEN

Eric the Ambassador

It has been suggested that, following his resignation from The Salvation Army, Eric Ball became one of the finest ambassadors of music.

But as far back as 14 August 1937 *The Bandsman and Songster* contained the announcement that 'Adjutant Eric Ball, ARCM, leaves for the USA and Canada on 20 August. He will give practical demonstrations and lectures to salvationist-musicians in those countries, who have long been looking forward to seeing and hearing him. The adjutant will comment on his travels especially for *The Bandsman and Songster*.'

That same newspaper tells us, on 11 September, that '. . . Adjutant Eric Ball is now having his first experience of . . . the generous hospitality and heartiness of our salvationist-musicians in the United States of America. [Having] arrived safely . . . [he] was immediately rushed from New York to the Star Lake Band Camp, some 40 miles distant . . . [where] hundreds of campers gave the adjutant a breath-taking reception. In the darkness which enshrouded the camp entrance, he passed hundreds of cheering youths to the place where a 100-piece band gave musical greetings. One can imagine the thrill given to the bandsmen-campers as the adjutant later led this splendid combination through the "Torchbearers" march.'

Following his visit to Star Lake he was at numerous other centres before crossing over to Canada.

Among these, probably the most interesting was his visit to Washington, where he '. . . not only maintained, but enhanced, his reputation as a musician, and left upon the crowd a remarkable impression of his ability as a pianist' (*The Bandsman and Songster*, 30 October 1937). 'Arriving on the Friday, his first introduction was a band rehearsal, and this was followed by an interesting touch of American life . . . . The adjutant was present at the "Constitution Day" speech by President Roosevelt, and was privileged to see 20,000 Americans in the beautiful setting of an outdoor auditorium, receive the president in their vociferous manner. This was followed on the Saturday morning by an introduction to the United States Army band stationed in the national capital. The adjutant was received as an honoured guest, and certain numbers were dedicated to him as a Salvation Army musician. From a musical standpoint, the high spot of the weekend was when he stepped on to the conductor's stand during a national broadcast and directed the United States Navy Band of 80 players in a march composed by Lieutenant Benter, the director of the band.'

On the Sunday afternoon Eric visited the Walter Reed Hospital, 'a huge military medical centre, wherein are housed from 3,000 to 4,000 incapacitated men, and in the bandstand of a wonderful open-air auditorium . . . conducted the band in numbers chosen to suit the occasion. The evening meeting gave the large audience a still further glimpse of this many-sided officer, for, turning aside from the music, he devoted himself to a spiritual appeal. The Monday morning will never be erased from the minds of the officers who gathered to hear his presentation of the international spirit. At 10.45 that night he was a very weary, but nevertheless happy, young man, on a huge transcontinental aeroplane bound for the city of Miami, 1,500 miles away.'

To mark his return, a welcome-home meeting was arranged by Phil Catelinet. This took place at Regent Hall on 20 November, and was given by the SP&S and Upper Norwood Bands, and Southall Citadel Songsters. Sam Hooper was there to sing 'The door sergeant', and in an 'All-Ball' programme 'Sound out the proclamation' and 'Songs of the morning' were included. 'None surely were more proud or more thrilled at the reception he received in the heart of London than were his mother and his wife, who were on the platform and to whom, as he himself remarked, he "owes so much", ' *The Bandsman and Songster* reported.

For that newspaper he recorded his impressions which appeared at almost weekly intervals (about eight of them) in the middle of the next year.

'One or two things must be borne clearly in mind as a background to the scene,' he wrote. 'The USA has no brass band cult as we have in England, where it is part of our national life; so that this form of music expression has there to overcome the handicap of being unique and not particularly to the public taste. The "military band" is immensely popular. . . . Numbers of high schools and colleges have bands of more than 100 players – some as many as 250 players

– of both sexes, an influence in education which is already having an effect on young salvationists, and through them on Army musical outlook. . . . Another point to be taken into account is that vast distances separate most of our Army bands, so that they can rarely indulge in united festivals, with their frank incentive to improved performance. Many of these bands work away year in and year out, faithfully and well, with no chance of comparing their own playing with any other brass band at all. . . . The loss sustained by not hearing other brass bands – and so being tempted to imitate them – is not an insuperable difficulty, if one's mind is alive to the inspiration of such remarkable orchestral and choral performances as can be heard in America, especially via the radio – if the listener is critical in his choice! . . .'

He went on to speak highly of the New York and Chicago Staff Bands, working as he did on 'Streams in the desert' and 'Sound out the proclamation' with the first of these, and 'Songs of the morning' with the second. He wrote equally rapturously of bands at Cambridge (Mass), Detroit, and Flint, saying, among other things, how 'well' the last of these looked, 'with its six sousaphones being lifted together, and with its dressing and deportment on parade, where the men wore scarlet-lined capes. I enjoyed all this immensely!'

But 'smaller bands of four, five, six or a few more players' did not escape his notice, and he pays tribute to their loyalty and patience. 'Hampered by the lack of suitably arranged music, practising hymn-tune after hymn-tune, working away in almost complete isolation year in and year out, they are among the Army's musicians to whom we should give a *special* thought and prayer,' was his comment. '. . . and what useful players many of the girls make! In nearly all bands . . . they take an important place, and some of them are first-class players; cornets and horns suit them admirably, but they are not limited to the smaller instruments. I heard a lassie-captain in West Palm Beach play effectively on a sousaphone!'

Nor did his reports speak only of the brass bands he found, but 'special congress brigades' in New York and Chicago. The New Jersey Divisional Songsters apparently 'brought the house down' with 'Travel along in the sunshine'. Vocal soloists 'were very good, especially those who featured the "evangelist"-type of singing'. He found time for 'the private enjoyment of some classical arias' with R. Gifford [a Salvation Army officer], 'a first-class tenor'. He heard quartets with guitar accompaniment at West Palm Beach, and the costumed North Carolina Mountain Missioners in 'songs of "hill-billy" type, with a proper cowboy nasal accent'; the Territorial Salvation Singers, led by S.E. Cox, in a new song by him, 'This one

Reading left to right: Dr Frank Simon, Director of the Armco Band, Cincinnati Conservatory Band and Past President of the Bandmasters Association of America. Adjutant Eric Ball, Mr Ernest N. Glover, Assistant Director of the Armed Band and Cincinnati Conservatory Band. Picture shows Dr Simon welcoming Eric to Cincinnati.

thing I know'; and the string ensemble from Tulsa, Oklahoma, which reached 'a very commendable standard of rendition' having ten mandolines, divided into two parts, ten guitars, divided into two, and sometimes three, parts, bass viol, bells and chimes, two accordians, a clarinet, and percussion. Memories of his own Southall Orchestra were surely evoked!

As examples of bands and songster brigades in Canada he commented particularly favourably on Dovercourt, Earlscourt, Hamilton Temple, East Toronto, Montreal Citadel and Winnipeg Citadel Bands. Many of these played his own compositions – Winnipeg's interpretation of 'Exodus' being 'as near to my own idea as I hope to hear'. The 'finest choral work I heard [in Canada] was that of the special Congress choir in Toronto', though he saw he had 'a special note in my diary about Songster Leader Horwood's brigade at London,

Olive pictured with Senior-Major and Mrs Arthur West of Pittsburgh Temple Corps, USA in 1954. While on one of her many visits to the USA with Eric, she was principal speaker at a Mother's Day meeting.

Ontario'. He wrote much more, before saying 'All these memories, and a thousand more unrecorded, are pleasant to dwell upon. . . . I shall treasure the memory of the many intimate contacts, and of the private as well as public joys which they gave me. In both countries I received more than I could ever hope to give of blessing and inspiration. To all my comrades there, a thousand thanks. Adieu!'

This was the one and only such visit he paid as an officer of The Salvation Army. The war and his resignation prevented a repetition. But he was often to be there on subsequent occasions in a private capacity, in the interests of the brass band movement as a whole, and as an honoured guest at Salvation Army music camps. He made very many friends, especially in the United States, many of whom 'thank God for every remembrance' of him.

One engaging story reaches us from the unwritten annals of the United States Central Music Institute, and probably every student there who sat under his influence would have his or her own story to tell. Space allows just the account of George Aren of Dearborn Heights Corps in Michigan to be related of how in the early 1960s he and his wife Dorothy celebrated their wedding anniversary while at the Institute. One can imagine all kinds of 'high jinks' accompanying any such celebration, and this particular year all the married couples, including Eric and Olive, autographed a *rolling pin* for George and Dorothy. George is thus of the opinion that he and his wife are probably the only people in the world possessing a rolling pin autographed by Eric and Olive Ball, a claim which is hardly likely to be contested!

Of his visit in 1979 to the United States Central Music Institute, for instance, it was said later that 'As the days passed . . . all who came into contact with [Eric] Ball were amazed at this 75-year-old's vitality, awed by his musical insight, made to feel at ease with his warm blue eyes and charmed by his

A certificate presented to Olive at Star Lake Musicamp — not meant to be taken too seriously one would imagine.

A rare picture of Olive wielding the baton — this time in the Toronto Spring Festival, 1 May 1954.

wit . . .' Of the Wonderland Band's performance of 'The Kingdom triumphant' Eric himself said, 'I am very pleased with this band – the way they've worked on this. They play with great maturity in this piece. It's difficult to do. But it's been a joy to play with them. It's good to serve the Lord together: for me, an old man, and all these young people. Well, "even so, come quickly, Lord Jesus", to us all.'

Soon after severing his official link with The Salvation Army, Eric was reported to have visited Belfast on 2 March 1946. The occasion was a massed concert for the Northern Ireland Brass Band League. 'This was, we hoped and believed, the beginning of a new period of achievement for Irish bands. Keenly interested and enthusiastic, they feel rather cut off from the main stream of brass band music-making,' the *British Bandsman* said.

Early in 1952 he was in Australia. The Australian *War Cry* for 16 February 1952 mentions 'A musical feast presided over by Commissioner Joshua James, who introduced the well-known composer'. Interestingly, a column 'filler' announces that 'Commissioner Joshua James will conduct the Service of Remembrance to King George VI, at Rockdale, on Sunday 17 February at 7 pm,' and one immediately recalls the pall of grief which descended over the whole Commonwealth at the death of the much-loved monarch.

The Musician (Australia) tells us that, 'Unfortunately he arrived in the city in rather poor physical condition following the arduous travel from winter through the tropics to humid heat conditions' (failing to mention that he was suffering from 'one of his famous colds' as well), 'but he was able to participate in the festival at Sydney Congress Hall when Rockdale, Petersham and Dulwich Hill Bands took part, assisted by the Rockdale Songster Brigade. . . . Bandsmen from Rockdale, Dulwich Hill and Petersham journeyed to Rose Bay flying base to bid him Godspeed on his flight to New Zealand. As the launch left the pontoon for the flying boat resting on the calm waters of the Harbour, bandsmen played and sang "God be with you till we meet again". We were left with an inspiring memory of Eric Ball.'

His visit to New Zealand, and his contacts with contesting and Salvation Army bands, were covered in *The British Bandsman*, in a series of articles, far too detailed to reproduce here in its entirety. But a taste is included:

> It does not take very long for a visitor from Great Britain to feel very much at home in New Zealand. The beauty of the country, so varied and colourful, the warm friendliness of the people, their love for all that is best in the British tradition: these quickly offset any feeling of being in a strange country, and there is certainly no sense of 'foreign-ness', such as one can feel in

Eric, with the well-known Danforth Songster Brigade and its leader, Eric Sharp.

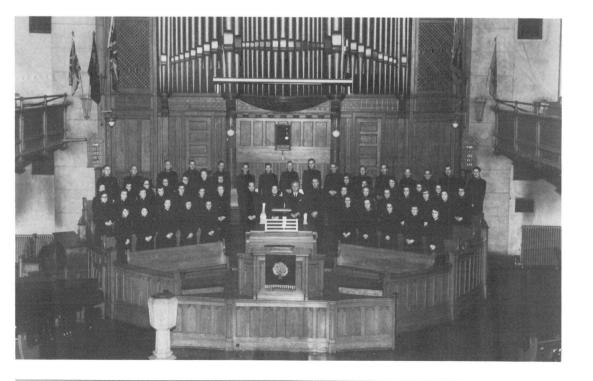

some European countries . . . and even at times in the USA.

Amongst the most distinctive of British traditions in New Zealand is the real love of brass band music evidenced in every part of the country: indeed, it is in some ways appreciated even more widely than here in Britain, for almost all classes of the community take a great interest in their bands; and at the contest it was particularly noticeable that the audiences were made up not only of 'fans' but of the general public, who were glad to have the opportunity of hearing and seeing what was going on. . . .

The newspaper reporting this year was, I thought, excellent, both in regard to space and matter. Their reports were objective and serious; there was none of the 'big blow' type of publicity from which we have too often suffered here in Britain. Photographs, the latest results, and comments by both adjudicator and music critics were given daily, in both morning and evening papers, with a care for correct detail and the dignity of the brass band movement, which showed a real understanding of its significance as an important part of the cultural life of the nation. . . .

In September of that year, Eric was received in the City Chambers, Edinburgh, by the Lord Provost, where he delivered greetings from the Mayor of Dunedin, where he had conducted massed bands on Accession Day, 6 February.

Also in 1952, Eric compered a programme at the South Street Mission, Hammersmith, and conducted massed items there by four mission bands. On the Sunday evening he conducted the special service arranged in connection with Hammersmith Mission Band's weekend. Again, as on a previous occasion, he was willing to go anywhere to preach Jesus Christ.

In February 1955 he was back in Australia again, *The Courier*, Ballarat, Vic, headlining, 'Civic Recognition for Famous Musician', and reporting the introductory remarks made by The Salvation Army's divisional commander for Western Victoria, who spoke of Eric as being 'a great writer and arranger of salvationist music. His creative genius has gone beyond our limits. The high order of his accomplishments has brought him world acclaim and honour. The highest circles of music have honoured him. He has conducted the London Symphony Orchestra, and received a silver medal for outstanding services to brass bands from the Worshipful Company of Musicians, London.'

Replying to this and other eulogistic speeches, Eric said, among other things, that 'Wherever I find brass bands there is a keenness and excitement about the music they make. Some people say there is a declension, but I do not see it in my travels. Radio and television take people's attention. For the good of their souls they must turn back to music. They must make music together in their homes and communities. And with choirs and bands they must make music for themselves.'

As well as hearing his music (including 'Songs of the morning', 'Constant trust' and 'The old wells') played to packed halls, Eric again gave one of his piano improvisations, 'linking up some of the solo items' in one programme, 'and the atmosphere created was indeed soul-stirring'. He also addressed a congregation in 'the delightful Hawthorn Town Hall', where he counselled the large congregation, 'Pray for the participants, send out your love to them . . .'.

Arthur Linnett, Leader of the Melbourne Staff Band, contributed to *The Musician* (Australia) a number of quotes from Eric's public remarks, which are significant:

> There are other things for a musician to do in a corps as well as singing and playing.
> We are Christians *all* the time, but musicians only a *little* of the time.
> Remember, as musicians you are sensitive beings, you are channels.
> It has always been my deep desire to practise the presence of God.

Eric was later to write in the Australian *Musician*:

> . . . It is quite impossible for me to express in any way my deep feelings of gratitude to God, and to my many friends in Australia, for the blessing and inspiration received whilst touring there earlier this year. . . . I hope you are already going on to greater things with a more complete dedication; with the grace of self-criticism; and with the one shining purpose that all shall be for his glory, we cannot fail to make an impact upon the world for the Kingdom's sake.

Dean Goffin, composer of 'Rhapsody in brass' and other pieces. Eric and he 'were great pals' affirms Marjorie Goffin

Following this visit, Eric was again in New Zealand, where his professional work of adjudicating band contests coincided with the annual territorial congress of that year. Of this event, Marjorie Goffin, widow of Dean Goffin, the much-loved composer of Salvation Army and other band music, has the following enchanting story to tell:

> It was the era of 'short back and sides' hair cuts, and Eric had lovely white hair. My two small daughters were in the gallery at the festival and one said, 'Hasn't Mr Ball got long hair?'
> 'Yes,' replied the other. 'But I think it's a wig!'
> Dean told Eric this and jokingly suggested he either got a hair cut or bought a violin! Eric enjoyed the joke. He and Dean were great pals and Dean had great admiration for his music.

Even when he was on holiday in Switzerland in June, 1950, he was attending the rehearsal of Berne Town Band. The

Eric Ball (third from right) with representatives of the Timaru (New Zealand) Salvation Army during his visit to the city on March 14, 1955. From left: Mr E. S. Chrisholm (bandmaster of the Timaru Salvation Army), Mr Granville Hawkey, Colonel H. G. Wallace (secretary for Salvation Army bands in New Zealand), Mrs Grant, Eric, Captain A. Grant (officer in charge, Timaru) and Mr Frank Smith (musical director of the Timaru Municipal Band, and late Fairey Aviation Works Band, England).

conductor there arranged a reception for him by influential people in the district. Eric was 'very appreciative' of this (*The British Bandsman*, 24 June 1950). His connection with Switzerland was destined to be a long and very happy one.

It was in 1948 that Karl Voegelin, of Switzerland, finding he had numerous young converts in his church, and wanting to find some way of harnessing their energies, formed his Scripture Union Brass Band. A former Salvation Army officer, he used the same instrumentation as was used in British Salvation Army brass bands. Finding a lack of suitable music, he decided, in 1951, to contact Eric Ball, to enquire if he would provide suitable arrangements and original music. It was a contact with far-reaching results.

Eric was immediately very helpful, and in the years that followed, he provided a 'library' of more than 50 items for the band.

The band developed successfully, and other groups of a similar nature were formed all over the country. A certain amount of criticism was made of the occasionally lively march rhythms played by the band, and it was said by some that 'spiritual music should surely sound different from non-spiritual music'. The conductor replied that 'there is no specifically "Christian" music, only music which is mainly played at Christian events, or which is accompanied by words conveying a Christian message. Music can be used for sacred or secular purposes; the decisive factors are not rhythm, volume, or instrumentation, but the inner attitude of the musicians and listeners. It was always the band's aim, in the spirit of John Sebastian Bach, to be able to write *"Soli Deo gloria* – to God alone be the glory" at the end of each performance.' Eric would have concurred with this view.

Karl Voegelin felt the need for better instruction, and so asked Eric if he would visit Switzerland and give his men some sort of specialised training such as he himself could not give. Thus, on 11 October 1961, Eric arrived, with Olive, in Thayngen, where 35 bandsmen were waiting for him in the free evangelical chapel at which Karl was the preacher. A busy daily programme ensued, with morning prayers preceding

Eric with members of the *Bibellesbunde Blasorchester* (Scripture Union Band) in Berne, Switzerland. Karl Vogelin, the 'father' of the Swiss Church bands, is to the right of the flag.

everything else each day, a short Bible address from Eric, rehearsals, and discussions. These activities culminated in some fine concerts over the weekend in Winterthur, and in the beautiful church in Schaffhausen.

The exercise was repeated in 1966 in Berne, where the bandmaster of the Scripture Union Band in that town, Heinz Jakob, invited Eric to conduct a week of training at Gwatt, in Thun. A group from Eastern Switzerland joined them, resulting in 35 players who practised hard for a series of succesful concerts in Berne, Thun and Burgdorf. Good work was done, and good congregations attended the performances. Olive was there again, as were Karl Vogelin and his wife.

Eric paid further visits in 1971 and 1974, the first of these being to Thayngen, where almost two days were spent in a studio in Zurich producing a long-playing record, and where concerts were given in Mannedorf and Wetzikon. On the second occasion a holiday home, beautifully situated in the hills of Aeschi, was the scene for hard but enjoyable work. There were moments of leisure, too, and time for every bandsman to have conversation with the English visitor, whose friendliness and warmth, coupled with his sense of humour, made him a friend to each of them. This time Eric conducted concerts in the churches of Aeschi, Langenthal, Langnau and Berne. The bandsmen also formed a male voice choir which Eric conducted, with arrangements specially written for them.

Throughout the sixties and seventies more brass bands were being formed in the Free Evangelical Church in Switzerland. For its jubilee celebrations in 1979 the Bernese group asked Eric to spend another week in Aeschi.

From 17 to 27 May of that year Eric worked hard with the band and a series of memorable concerts was presented in Berne, Thun, Bill and Langnau. In 1959 the *Bibellesebund Musik* (Scripture Union Band) from Thayngen, Switzerland, visited Geisweid Free Evangelical Church, Germany, under Karl Vogelin's direction. Inspired by Karl Vogelin's band, Karl-Heinz Schnell, the choirmaster in Geisweid, decided that it would be an asset for the Free Evangelical Church in Geisweid to have a brass band for use in the church services. Some instruments were obtained and Eric wrote some music for training purposes. He set about the task of teaching this small group and progress was made.

Knowing something already of the influence of Eric Ball in the development of brass bands in Switzerland, Karl-Heinz Schnell obtained some of the music being used in Switzerland and decided to invite Eric to Geisweid to give the band

While staying with Karl-Heinz Schnell, Eric and Olive presented him with a recording by the Virtuosi Brass Band, conducted by Eric.

more expert tuition than he himself could, and to partake in concerts at the weekend. Eric not only taught the music, but in a very special way imparted spiritual values to the playing in the services and concerts. Subsequently many programmes given by the band contained much of the music composed or arranged by Eric.

Karl Voegelin's band went from Thygen-Wilchingen to campaign in Geisweid in Germany, where a brass band was soon formed under the leadership of Heinz Schnell. Progress was quickly made, and Eric was once again pressed into service to conduct concerts, where his compositions were frequently used.

Eric was invited, with Olive, to Switzerland on six separate occasions, to conduct rehearsals and concerts, and to take part in the Sunday services. They became firm favourites with the congregation as well as with the band.

It was in 1973 that Portsmouth Citadel Band, while on its second tour of Germany, visited Siegen and Geisweid. At that time, Lloyd Bates, the deputy bandmaster, was a guest, with Bandmaster Harold Nobes, of the Schnell family in Geisweid. As a result of this Lloyd was invited to return to Geisweid, partly to develop industrial and academic contacts, and partly to rehearse the local church band for concerts. Eric had already suggested that it would be a great help if an 'English sound' could be developed in the band, and intimated that Lloyd Bates would be useful.

Thus started the connection whereby Eric and Lloyd visited Germany together, for Lloyd was invited to accompany Eric and Olive on a number of occasions. Eric dearly wished to make a 'biblical seventh' visit to Germany, but it was not to be. He made only six visits: on the last two occasions on which he was invited he was unable to travel due to ill-health. Eric expressed his sadness at not completing his cycle of seven visits on the very Sunday before his death. Lloyd Bates visited him in the nursing home that day and Eric mentioned the wonderful times he had enjoyed in that country and sent his good wishes to all his friends there.

Eric was always extremely pleased when he noted the continuing progress of Geisweid Band year by year, and composed special music for it, to supplement the music being used from Switzerland and from some Salvation Army sources.

Lloyd Bates speaks warmly of the wonderful memories he has of taking part in many concerts with Eric, and of the privilege which was his of having Eric accompany him at the piano in such numbers as 'Clear skies', 'Jubilate', 'Haydn's Trumpet Concerto', 'Someone cares', and numerous hymn tunes. Eric was always insistent that 'slow melody' solos were very important, and hymn tunes were always used in his concerts. What recollections Lloyd has of 'Beautiful Christ', 'Sing a hymn to Jesus', 'What a friend we have in Jesus', and the like, with Eric at the piano!

On one occasion there was no piano in the building, only an electronic keyboard of, in Lloyd's opinion at least, limited capabilities. 'Surely you're not going to play that!' Lloyd said.

'Lloyd, these people have come to hear us play "Clear skies", and "Clear skies" they are going to hear,' was Eric's reply. And 'Clear skies' they did hear, Eric working as hard at that as anything else, to make the pianoforte accompaniment sound as effective on the instrument as he possibly could. 'He was a wonderful accompanist,' Lloyd confirms, in the way that so many others did before him. 'As he got older, and his hands were becoming more and more troubled with arthritis, he would deftly change an awkward chord here and there – though I defy anyone listening to know the difference!'

It amused Lloyd in later visits to be mistaken by complete strangers *in the street* for Eric Ball. 'It seems that any white-haired Englishman *must* be Eric Ball!' he chuckles.

It is interesting, too, to find that this high regard the Swiss had for Eric repaid itself. In October 1959 a Swiss band which called itself the *Ensemble Romand d'Instruments de Cuivre* visited this country – its name being taken from the letters of Eric's Christian name!

When he was on tour in Switzerland with Manchester CWS

Lloyd Bates plays with the Geiseid *Blasorchester* in a concert in Geisweid Church in 1976. Eric conducts.

Olive called this picture 'Consternation'. It recalls the occasion when Eric was presented with an electronic keyboard on which to accompany Lloyd Bate's cornet solos whilst in Germany. Eric is seated; Lloyd is immediately behind him (the likeness between them will be seen), and Karl-Heinz Schnell is at the far right.

Band in June 1951, a local newspaper reporter stated that 'Eric Ball . . . has eliminated all heaviness from the brass. With the assurance of a sleep-walker his musicians play the most exacting trills and heaviest intonations. No wonder that this group has carried away prizes in national band contests!'

He was often on the continent adjudicating continental championships. In July 1974, for instance, he was at Kerkrade, Holland, for the World Music Festival. Camborne and William Davis Construction Group Bands obtained 'distinction' ratings. It is stated that the football World Cup caused the festival to close down temporarily!

The first visit (on Salvation Army business that is) that Eric paid to Sweden was in 1959. He was on a visit to Copenhagen, where he was conducting Copenhagen Temple and Malmö (Sweden) Bands, and salvationist Bertil Hanssen, of Sweden, invited him, with Olive, to Limhamn. Olive conducted 'Star Lake' (as she quite often did on visits like these); other items by Eric included 'Torchbearers' and the rarely-performed tone poem based on Eva Booth's song, 'Streams in the desert'. Eric conducted Phil Catelinet's *air varié*, 'A sunbeam', and the bandmaster's fourteen-year-old nephew Tornjie Hansen played the classic cornet solo, 'I love him better every day'.

This was just part of a long connection with Scandinavia which stretched back to Eric's earliest days in the Music Editorial Department at Judd Street. He had studied the scores of Klaus Østby, the so-called 'Father of Norwegian Salvation Army music', considering his music to be at least 50 years ahead of its time. For Swedish Salvation Army bands he composed a 'Rhapsody on themes by Klaus Østby', though it has not to date been published in Britain. In 1910 Østby had composed a 'Passacaglia' – a form completely unknown in Salvation Army music at that time, though used by Eric in his *air varié* 'The old wells'. Perhaps somewhat academic in content it would probably not be acceptable today in Salvation Army circles. A festival overture, '*Fest*', a festival march, 'To the land of glory' and a meditation on the hymn tune 'Princethorpe' are all compositions of his which appear in the Swedish *Band Journal*.

Tornjie Hansen has a deep love of the music of Eric Ball, saying that it contained the 'message of love' which was so needed in the 1930s, with the imminence, though no one knew it at the time, of the conflict of the Second World War. He writes of a visit Eric made to Sweden in 1978:

> Eric Ball is for all Army musicians and others interested in Salvation Army music a well-known and highly respected name. . . .
> It was with great joy and expectation therefore that Bertil

Andersson, head of the music department for Sweden, and I went to Arlanda (Stockholm) Airport to welcome him to Sweden, on a sunny day in May.

Regrettably this visit had to be rather short, from Friday to Sunday only, because nowadays Eric Ball doesn't want to be away from home for longer periods of time. Thus he was able to visit two centres only, Stockholm and Jönköping. . . . On Friday night a gathering for bandsmen was arranged at Stockholm 7 Corps. The intention was to provide an opportunity for the bandsmen to meet the man and the preacher through his musical and verbal ministry. He answered the questions raised about his music and his role as a composer willingly and in detail. His piece 'Constant trust' became a sermon in itself as he rehearsed it and commented with the thoughts and emotions expressed in the music. Stockholm 7 Band stood for a fine interpretation and William Larson [a retired Swedish Salvation Army officer with strong British connections] assisted with a translation marked with alertness and efficiency. This evening was indeed a spiritual experience.

On the Saturday morning we went to Solberga Hospital to see Mrs Carin Lydahl, sister of Erik Leidzén, a patient there, too weak to lift her head. For me, to be permitted to listen to their conversation was an hour in Heaven.

It was a busy programme that had been prepared for the weekend, but in spite of his age, Eric Ball accomplished it all with inspiration and efficiency. The Saturday evening musical festival was preceded by three hours of rehearsal with three bands taking part – Vasa, Södertalje and Stockholm 7. The programme featured music by the visiting composer: 'The old wells', 'Songs of the morning' and 'Resurgam' were given, and the three bands united for 'Torchbearers' and 'Safe in the arms of Jesus'.

Eric Ball expressed his delight to be able to hear his songs, 'Begin the day with God' and 'In the secret of thy presence', beautifully rendered by Gunilla Brunnberg and the vocal group of Stockholm Temple respectively. Lars-Gunnar Bjorkland and Anders Ljungberg played 'Clear skies' and 'Swiss melodies'.

Jönköping Corps hosted us on the Sunday. This was a great occasion for the bandsmen, all of whom did their best, and the whole gathering was mingled with determination and the gentle humour characteristic of Eric Ball when at work.

Later in the afternoon the rehearsals continued in the Jönköping Corps hall with the brass band and the stringband. Eric rehearsed the stringband in two songs. Surely this was the very first time he had stood in front of a stringband! He was glad to do so and emphasised to me several times how important it is that different styles and genres are given space and are preserved within the Army's music-making. 'Why do we not give more room for woodwind and string ensembles, for example?'

Eric Ball led the corps band in 'Sound out the proclamation' and 'Songs in exile', and Bertil Berg in 'Swiss melodies'.

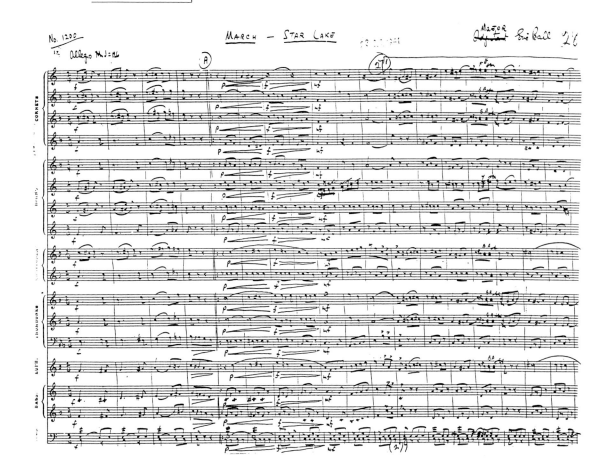

The opening of Eric's march 'Star Lake'. A good example of his musical penmanship, neatness in which is an obvious requirement for a music editor. Interesting too are the note of his change in rank and how his signature changed little over the years.

I believe that all who were permitted to listen to and to see Eric Ball, to converse with him and to share fellowship with him, thank God for it all, and for Eric Ball and his music.

And from *The Musician* for 10 November 1979 comes this report of a visit to Denmark:

For months Copenhagen Temple Band (Stanley Hansen) had looked forward to the visit of Brother Eric Ball for its band weekend.

Immediately following his arrival on the Thursday evening, Brother Ball met the band for a two-hour practice. This was the first time that many of the bandsmen had met the composer whose music they had often played. . . . Brother Ball was energetic and inspiring and . . . the bandsmen will never forget not only the musical impact of his visit but also the deepened spiritual insight he gave them.

When Eric Ball entered the fine Temple hall he was greeted by the strains of his world-famous march, 'Star Lake'. The ensuing programme . . . included many of the composer's most well-known pieces. 'Constant trust' and 'Songs in exile' . . . brought particular blessing. Eric Ball impressed everyone when, at the piano, he improvised on three melodies chosen by different people. This item, perhaps, received the longest applause of all. Brother Ball went on to explain the background of some of his music and, in that way, gave it new dimension.

On Saturday afternoon a further practice, which included the Temple String Band, was held in preparation for the evening festival to be given in Copenhagen Cathedral. This lovely building . . . is famous for Thorvaldsen's sculptures of Christ and the apostles. . . . All the music played by the band was by Eric Ball and among the items rendered were 'Torchbearers' and 'A warrior's reward'. Among other highlights . . . were Erik Silfverberg's playing of the cornet solo, 'Clear skies' and the inspiring singing by the string band of such pieces as 'In the secret of thy presence' . . . and a special vocal arrangement of the march, 'Star Lake'.

The climax of the evening was, unquestionably, the selection, 'The King of kings', and the impact of this famous piece was not only enhanced by the band's fine playing under the composer's

Eric conducts the Copenhagen Temple Band in the cathedral in 1979. Thorvaldsen's statue of the Saviour (which The Salvation Army's *Musician* report mentions) can clearly be seen.

Eric and Olive share a quiet moment at the piano at Los Angeles Congress Hall, May or June, 1967.

leadership but also by the inspiring sight of Thorvaldsen's gigantic statue of Christ in front of which the band was seated.

As the band played, every eye could see the outstretched, beckoning hands of the Saviour and read the inscription, 'Come unto me'.

But no account of Eric's activities in Scandinavia would be complete without reference to his work with Solna Brass.

Solna Brass commenced in the late 1960s with a group of students in the Stockholm Municipal Music School and keen local salvationists who met together for deeper study of their art.

When the band visited Great Britain in 1972 Eric conducted it in a recording of 'Resurgam' in the Church of St Giles, Cripplegate, a most moving occasion for all who took part. Eric himself said afterwards that '. . . Very quickly I found that not only had the bandsmen sufficient technical skill to deal with the music, but that there was also an emotional and even spiritual response. There was also a great sense of friendliness and Christian fellowship . . .'.

He said that he would like to write something new for the band, but could not promise to do this for some time to come, having already promised to write much new music for bands in New Zealand, Switzerland, Germany, Holland, the USA and in Britain. This reference will show something of the worldwide demand there was still for new music by him. He was, by now, 68.

In January 1975 Eric visited Sweden to conduct the band in a concert in Stockholm, arriving on Thursday, 30 January, rehearsing in the evening, and on the Friday, the Saturday and the Sunday, conducting the concert on the Sunday, and returning to England on the Monday, 3 February. He regretted not being able to stay in Sweden for a longer time. This was because he had so many engagements in Britain, as well as appointments in the USA. Again, one marvels at the number of appointments this by now 71-year-old was able to undertake.

An unexpected place, perhaps, for Eric's influence to be felt is Japan, but it is a fact that his name is not unknown in that country. Towards the end of Eric's life R. Smith & Co received a request for an arrangement of 'Resurgam' to be made for wind band, using the military-band style of scoring. Eric set to work on this, but was unable to complete it, due to the state of his health. His friend Geoffrey Brand completed the work for him. It is an engaging thought that Japanese wind bands are playing music associated with the words and idea, 'I will rise again'!

And another example of Eric's 'ambassadorial' influence is contained in the fact that when Grace Barrett, a retired Salvation Army officer, born in New Zealand, and married to an Englishman, joined the local garden club in New South Wales, Australia, she and her husband were immediately welcomed most warmly by a most charming English lady. Why? Because they were salvationists, and because Eric Ball and his wife had been her neighbours in Bournemouth; for this English lady every salvationist wore a halo!

Eric Walter John Ball was a figure on the world music stage and a legend in his own lifetime. But everywhere he went he was an ambassador for Christ, not only through his platform and his publications, but by his very presence.

ELEVEN

Eric the Encourager

The mud-fish lives in mud but is not soiled by it. The sea-gull lives in water but shakes off, with a slight flutter, all water from its wings. Likewise mayst thou live in the world, untarnished, unstained, O son of man! – Ramakrishna, quoted by E.B.

'He had this marvellous knack of making everyone feel "special" – as if they really mattered!'

This remark can be attributed to everyone and no one; I heard it so often from so many people that this 'marvellous knack' seems to have been just one more hallmark of the character of Eric Ball.

'He conducted a band practice at Staines Salvation Army Corps, where I was a bandsman. That evening I had transferred from the trombone section to the baritone section, and felt somewhat insecure. I apologised to him at the end of the rehearsal for my poor performance. He was most encouraging in his comments, and helpful in his advice.' So writes Jim Dalloy, a member of the band reserve at Worthing.

But long before this, on 10 September 1926 he had written an appreciative letter to the bandmaster at Croydon I, after the National Musical Festivals held at Alexandra Palace on Saturday 4 September:

I feel that I would like to thank you and your band for the splendid performance of 'A Soldier's Experience' on Saturday last at the Alexandra Palace.

You will readily understand that a composer appreciates deeply a good rendition of his own work, especially as so many times he is called upon to hear it indifferently performed.

Your rendering of the piece was very near to what was intended throughout, and when allowances have been made for what may be called 'conductor's licence' in the matter of *tempi* and general interpretation, it may be said that the performance was all that could be wished for.

This must have meant a good deal of hard work on the part of

To the bandmaster of Croydon I,
after the National Musical
Festivals held at Alexandra Palace
in September, 1926.

21 Beachcroft Avenue,
Southall, Middx.
10th September 1926.

Dear Adjutant,

I feel that I would like ~~you~~ to thank you and your band for the splendid performance of "A Soldier's Experience" on Sunday last at the Alexandra Palace.

You will readily understand that a composer appreciates deeply ~~the~~ a good rendition of his own work, ~~and~~ especially as so many times he is called upon to hear it indifferently performed.

Your rendering of the piece was very near to what was intended throughout, and when allowances have been made for what may be called "Conductor's licence" in the matter of tempi & general interpretation, it may be said that the performance was all that could be wished for.

This must have meant a good deal of hard work on the part of yourself and the men, but you have the gratification of knowing that you have achieved a musical triumph, and I would again like to thank every individual man concerned.

Sincerely yours,
Eric Ball.

Adjt. Searle.

yourself and the men, but you have the gratification of knowing that you have achieved a musical triumph, and I would again like to thank every individual man concerned.

Stories like that one abound through the years, both so far as bands and so far as individuals are concerned. E.W. Tadd, of Chichester, writes:

> Just before Christmas, 1971, the Chichester City Band, under its conductor, Robert Ayling, was out carolling in the Stockbridge area of Chichester. A woman came along, and explained to the conductor that some time previously she had composed a Christmas carol for a BBC competition and had gained a prize for it. The carol, entitled 'See for Yourself', she was willing for the band to use, if we could get it arranged for brass band.
>
> In June the next year, I visited Canada with the National Brass Band Club, Black Dyke Mills, Manchester CWS, Fairey, and GUS (Footwear) Bands, with Eric Ball, Geoffrey Brand and Harry Mortimer. While we were waiting in the departure lounge at Manchester Airport I happened to get into conversation with Eric, and mentioned the carol, which I had with me. He confided to me that it probably 'wouldn't make the charts', but that he would make an arrangement for us. He refused to accept a fee for this.

When Trevor Walmsley was appointed conductor of the Brighouse and Rastrick Band in 1956, Eric was still visiting the band to rehearse for contests. The band would rehearse all day on the Sunday, and then Trevor would take him home for a meal before driving him to Leeds to catch the night sleeper home to London. Trevor was thus privileged to spend many hours talking with him, and getting to know the man and the musician.

Eric always insisted that, whilst he had rehearsed the band, Trevor Walmsley should lead them on to the contest platform, so that, if there was any public acclaim to be received, Trevor should receive his share. This, he said, was a tremendous encouragement to a young conductor with his first top-class band, and illustrated the measure of his unselfishness, his generosity, and his desire to help a newcomer. Mr Walmsley was always grateful to him.

'I don't think Eric was the best teacher in the universe – of composition I mean,' Kenneth Cook said over the coffee cups. 'Composition is a gift from heaven – and if you don't have it, you don't have it. On the other hand, if you showed the slightest flair, he would encourage you to the nth degree. When I first commenced studying with him he gave me a little Christmas poem by Christina Rossetti, called 'The shepherds had an angel' with the suggestion that I prepare a setting for it. I did so, and submitted it on his further suggestion to the

Music Editorial Department of The Salvation Army at Judd Street, and it was subsequently published. This put me on the path to a career of composition which I am still pursuing.'

In the same way, Robert Simpson writes most generously of 'a man for whom I always had deep affection and respect, a fine musician and a generous person. I remember when I was a lad of about 14 or 15 travelling with him in a train (I think it was to Oxford for some reason I don't recall) and talking with him about all sorts of music – classical music particularly, of which he had a very wide knowledge and a fine appreciation – he was very encouraging to me, though at that time there seemed to be no chance of my taking up music as a profession, since my parents wanted me to be a doctor. . . .

'I showed him a few of my teenage attempts at composition, done without any formal training at all, and he made all sorts of kind but pointed criticisms that set me thinking much more positively about what I was trying to do. . . . He was one of the first people who ever made me feel I wasn't an idiot in wanting to be a musician! For that I'll always be grateful to him. . . . I saw him very little in the next decades – in fact I had another long conversation with him only in 1970, when 'Energy' (which was dedicated to him) was going to be the test piece at the Royal Albert Hall. Then we had lunch together and talked over old times and music in general – like a continuation of the train conversation, as if nothing had interrupted it.'

Over and over again Eric would receive letters from students, working on theses for degrees, essays for 'A' level music, lowly junior school projects, and asking for information about himself, his music, his life-style, etc. These were coming in to him almost up until the time of his death, and must at times have been irksome, especially when he was busy with other matters, in indifferent health, or concerned about the health of his beloved Olive, but always they were dealt with courteously and promptly. This one, originating in Holland, is typical (the original letter being reproduced as it was, 'broken English' and all):

> For my education I must make a report. I play in a Band off the Salvation Army and it seems me a good idea to make a report off the Brass Bands and the musik.
>
> I have already two composers asked and I get some information: Capt. R. Redhead – Canadian Staff Band and Roy Newsome.
>
> But it is not enough for my report, that is whay I ask you. I hope you have some time for me to answer the questions.
>
> 1   How do you come to compose.
> 2   How did you learn it.

3   How do you compose.
4   Can you give me an example off your own stile off compos-
    ing, just a little piece so I can put it in as example in my
    report
5   What is your oppinion off the Brass Band musik
6   How do you see the future for the Brass Bands an the musik
7   Have you some information off the beginning off the Brass
    Bands. Here in Holland there is so little to find of the his-
    tory.
8   Have you some other things for me or things that you will
    say.
9   Can I get a photo off you?

I hope not that I'f bin impudent.

I look forwart to your letter an if you are interested in a copy
off my report I be happy to send it to you. There is a chance that
I make another report in Englisch.

I wish yo good luck with your beautifull compositions, and I
look foreward to your letter.

Your sincerely

* * * * *

To which Eric's reply, as follows, is typical:

Dear * * * * *

Thank you for your letter. I am interested to know that you
are a salvationist and also a musician. Now I will try to answer
some of your questions.

1 & 2: When a boy of about 11 years of age, I learnt to play a
brass instrument, and commenced pianoforte lessons. Later I
became interested in church music, and studied organ and theory
of music with church organists. Later I 'taught myself' with the
aid of lessons from a correspondence college. (If you can obtain
from The Salvation Army a copy of *The Musician*, published here,
for 21 October, you will find some information about my career.
I regret I have no spare copy to send you.)

3: Music is like language. Just as you or I would write a letter
with *words*, so in composition we use *sounds*, organised like language. Training and experience help; we consider ideas in our
minds and use our physical brains to express them. But actually
the process is too difficult to describe.

4: I enclose part of the first movement of '*Resurgam*' in manuscript. *Resurgam* in Latin means 'I shall rise again'. Salvation
Army and concert bands play this work.

5 & 6: There is a long list of music published for brass bands,
most of it in England, although these are also published in Holland, Switzerland, Scandinavia. New composers are now writing
interesting compositions, both for concert bands and for The
Salvation Army. It is almost certain that brass bands will continue to develop for many years to come.

7: Brass bands in Great Britain became popular 100 or more

years ago (like The Salvation Army). Working people learned to play in their spare time; and the brass instruments invented by Adolphe Sax in France and manufactured in many countries supplied the players with saxhorns, tubas, etc, which were not too difficult to play. In Britain, competitions were organised – contests are like sport with music!

I hope these few words will help you in your report.

There is a book on brass bands to be published later this year. I expect there will be an announcement in *The British Bandsman* or some other paper.

Now I wish you good success with your report.

Yours sincerely

Eric Ball

Eric in the early 1950s.

It will be noticed that he deals with all points of the letter except for two. His usual modesty will not allow him to send a photograph, and perhaps even his patience was a little strained at the type of report this student might have produced!

Among Eric's other interests so far as young people were concerned were the National Youth Brass Band and the National School Band Association.

As early as January 1951 we find references in *The British Bandsman* to the formation of the National Youth Brass Band and to Eric's activities with it. Kenneth Cook had much to do with its formation, which apparently originated in a 'brass band holiday course', sponsored by the No 1 Area of the National Association of Brass Band Conductors and Hinrichsen Concert Direction. Clifford Barratt, Gurney Doe, Phil Catelinet, Roy Budden, and Ken himself, were the auditioners. At 11.30 am on 1 January 1951, the band ('the first brass band to be formed in this half-century' *The British Bandsman* confidently claimed) played its first tune, 'Brother James' Air'. The afternoon was apparently spent in sight-reading new music, some in manuscript, some in proof, and some straight from the press. But in each case the music was being performed by the players for the first time.

Harry Mortimer was a guest at one of the sessions, and 'excitement mounted as Eric Ball arrived [on Friday 5 January] to take the morning's rehearsal', and soon the four-day-old band was getting to grips with 'Divertimento'. The next day the band gave the first broadcast performance of Eric's march 'Sure and Stedfast', written for the Boys' Brigade, whose motto forms the title of the piece. Throughout his life, Eric Ball was a strong supporter of the band, appealing for funds in his 'comment' column, and attending its concerts and summer schools from time to time.

He was a member of the advisory council of the National School Band Association from its earliest days, when it was known as the National School Brass Band Association, the word 'Brass' being removed from its title when its activities became wider than the previous one would have suggested. He lectured at the first residential course held by the association at Worcester in 1958 ('and what a success he was!' comments Charles Sweby, the president at the time of writing).

Vincent Smith (a member of the association and editor of its magazine) has written of Eric's activities with it:

> At the time of his passing he was one of our vice-presidents. Prior to that he was for many years a member of the advisory

council. In this capacity he freely gave his services as guest conductor at a number of massed band festivals organised by the
Association. I know that former committee members who have
been associated with [us] for many years will speak with affection
of the help and encouragement he gave our movement in its
earliest days. . . . He . . . proved to be one of the main links and
builders of bridges between two diverse aspects of the brass
band world. . . . NSBA is proud to have been associated with a
man who was able to combine eminence and esteem with
humanity and humility.

One of the association's main activities over the years has
been the massed band festival at which guest conductors
have agreed to conduct without fees. Eric Ball conducted
such festivals at Darlington (1960), Bristol (Colston Hall)
(1964), Stoke-on-Trent (1966) and Harlow (1968). These festivals brought together not only full school bands, but small
delegations of players who enjoyed the thrill of playing in a
large group.

When the association prepared a graded list of suitable
music for school bands in 1965, Eric gave much valuable
advice.

In addition to the continued support Eric gave to the association he was also a frequent guest at events arranged by
individual member-bands. For instance, he spent three days
at the Peter Symonds School (Winchester) at a joint event
arranged with the Rotheram High School (Luton) Band.
Charles Sweby, to whom I am grateful for this information,
was Head of Music at the Rotheram High School.

It was not only at 'national level' that Eric had the needs of
youth bands to the fore in his thinking. A typical announcement in *BB* (10 January 1969) says that he is to be at Fowey
for the Cornwall Youth Brass Band. And in the 15 March
issue he is reported as having conducted (as president)
Netteswell (Harlow) Youth Band in a concert of his own
music, including 'Swiss festival music', 'In Switzerland',
'Indian summer', and, in the second half, 'Three songs without words', 'Rhapsody on negro spirituals', and the first performance of the overture, 'Homeward'. Of the players, he
said afterwards, 'They are children in age, but musically
adults.'

Vincent Smith also remembers playing under Eric's direction with The Salvation Army's Red Shield Band in the late
1950s. 'Formed of salvationist-members of the guards bands
and RAF Central Band, it was the first English Salvation
Army Band (so far as I am aware) to play in concert pitch,
and to include French horns instead of tenor horns', he
writes. 'We gave regular programmes and although there was

a number of guest conductors, the two most frequently used were Dean Goffin and Eric Ball.'

This is another example of the ability Eric had to communicate with the young!

Eric always had the needs of smaller bands very much to the forefront of his thinking. 'It may surprise some to learn that the writing of easy but effective music of quality is at least as difficult a task as that of producing something technically demanding, and that a composer worth his salt puts as much of himself into his "little" pieces as he does into more ambitious works,' he once wrote. He wrote a test piece for the Youth Section of the brass band championship in 1970, the bicentenary of the birth of Beethoven, to encourage not only higher standards of performance from bands in this section, but a study of Beethoven's music. The subject of the piece, 'Youth salutes a Master', is a bass line from the *scherzo* from the piano sonata Op 2 No 3. The piece continues with a solemn fanfare, reminiscent of Beethoven's fifth symphony (the 'Fate knocks at the door' theme), and with references to the final phrases of the same composer's 'Creation's hymn' at the end.

An interesting event in which Eric took part, which shows very much this sense of being an encourager, was a 'play-in' arranged for Salvation Army bands, at Regent Hall. The delegates, armed with their instruments, came not only from London, but from places as far apart as Bridgwater in Somerset and Felixstowe in Suffolk. Other instructors included Eddie Gregson, Maisie (Wiggins) Ringham, Barrie Perrins and Michael Barrett, the last-named deputising for Will Overton. Eddie Gregson discussed with the delegates the piano in its relationship to the brass band, with Regent Hall Band in attendance (having that morning appeared in the Lord Mayor's Show) to illuminate his points.

Then Eric took over, thoroughly rehearsing them all in an *Ordinary Series* selection and a meditation out of the *Festival Series*. One visitor from Teynham said, 'I've never seen Eric Ball, or even a *Festival Series* selection before, and tomorrow I shall be one of a band of five at the open-air meeting.' For Eric, this was probably tribute enough, and that word alone would have made it worth his while to take part.

Bob Getz, an American salvationist, and for many years bandmaster at Cambridge (Massachusetts) Corps, tells of how at one time his band was a very difficult group to handle, but very talented. In 1975 Bob invited Eric to visit his corps and lead a retreat for the band, telling him first of some of the difficulties he was experiencing. Eric said he understood, and agreed to accept the invitation.

The banner speaks for itself. Always a friend of young musicians, Eric was a popular figure at music schools held by The Salvation Army or other bodies at home and overseas. This one was in the USA.

The meditation he shared with the band was profoundly moving and had a lasting effect on everyone. The ripple effect of that visit was being felt 15 years afterwards.

One specific personal ministry Eric undertook was with a solo horn player – a brilliant man and instrumentalist. He had a serious and not-so-hidden problem with drugs and alcohol. Faced with the prospect of even being in the presence of the English visitor, he went on a 'binge' and never arrived at the retreat. Eric wrote him a beautiful, non-judgmental letter of hope in the Lord. The effect of this gesture on Eric's part is still felt by those who know and love this man – who is now on his feet in life and living in the love of Jesus. The absence of this player left the next young man in line to take his place, for which he was not at all prepared, and he was quite intimidated by Eric's presence. Eric understood immediately, and quietly put the man at total ease, and released from him the best performance of his life up till then.

In similar vein comes a story from Newfoundland of a music camp Eric conducted for Corner Brook Temple and Grand Falls Citadel Bands during the summer of 1960. The Corner Brook Temple Band had just passed through a most difficult experience and the need for something very special to help rebuild its morale was most urgent. This was the reason for the request for Eric to visit Newfoundland, and a training clinic of some four or five days' duration was arranged.

Eric flew into Gander, and from there in a single-engined floatplane to the camp site, in an idyllic spot. Despite the limited abilities of the members of the two bands and the awkward acoustics of a spartan assembly hall, Eric, with great patience, taught and rehearsed the groups. He quickly assessed their level of competence, requiring the very best of which they were capable, but always careful not to press them beyond their limits.

As we have seen, Eric was a great encourager of young people, particularly young musicians, but even more particularly of young Christians. An important aspect of this was his association with the Boys' Brigade which spanned the years. When the Boys' Brigade Brass Band Association, formed in 1985, held a National Contest in 1987 in Eastleigh, he went along as a guest, listening to a number of the competing bands, including the massed band finale, when all competing bands joined forces to play a number of pieces, including 'Sure and Stedfast'.

Not for nothing was he a constant visitor, year in and year out, at The Salvation Army's summer schools of music, in

Britain and America in particular. The young people loved him, and he loved them in return, as did Olive. Peter Millest, for instance, remembers him at Tylney Hall in 1975, and again at Cobham Hall in 1978 and 1979. 'The whole school would sit for hours and listen or rehearse, not feeling any hardship, only complaining when the session had to end. One always felt the presence of the Master when Eric Ball spoke; he could turn a rehearsal into a holiness meeting, just by saying a few words,' he writes.

One particularly touching story in this connection concerns the National School (held annually at Cobham Hall) at which Eric was always an honoured guest, taking rehearsals, master classes, and Bible study sessions. He was to have been there in the last summer of his life, but had to decline the invitation with great disappointment. Perhaps even he realised that by now he was nearing the end of his earthly journey; certainly he had become very frail and by this time was under medical supervision. When the students heard that their adored 'master' would be unable to be with them this year, they all of them signed a card and sent it to him. Stan and Mary Randell, his friends in Bournemouth, with whom he was staying, realised that he was very quiet this par-

Eric seen in familiar pose at a Salvation Army bandmasters' refresher course at Sunbury, 1980. He was often a guest at these events.

ticular afternoon, and on knocking on his door, found that
he was praying for all of the members of the session – indi-
vidually by name.

But often Eric's encouragement would be aimed at, and
felt at, a much deeper, personal level. In one of his 'Letters to
John', for instance, he wrote:

> If one is a musician he is a musician *all the time*, at rehearsals,
> at concerts, at contests, and even in his spare moments. His
> ideals and selfless service to his art are never in doubt, and he
> gives the best he possibly can on every occasion.

And again:

> Put one of your well-worn, even hackneyed, pieces on the
> stand and 'take it to pieces', reading it critically as would a proof-
> reader and you might find the result highly interesting and
> educative; strong light may even be thrown upon bad habits in
> playing, hard to eradicate.

And again:

> In the re-creation of great music there is no place for self-
> ishness or insincerity; the players must be taught and encour-
> aged to play together, as one. . . . We have in many of our bands
> shining examples of the type of player who submerges his whole
> personality for the good of the whole and any successful conductor
> will tell you that his heart warms as much at the sound of a well-
> played third cornet passage as it does when a soloist brings off a
> difficult passage.

As Peter Wilson has said, 'Eric always wanted to point people
to a higher realm of experience, whether it be in playing, in
listening, or in living.' On one occasion Eric wrote that he
self-consciously tried to give every player something interesting, citing an example in a little *Triumph Series* piece, 'World-
wide witness', in which the second cornets have the tune
because 'it is easy' in his own words. He said on that same
occasion that he liked to look at a score and say, 'Now, has he
got anything else to play? . . . Why should a player be
expected to sit through a rehearsal with almost nothing to
play?'

On another occasion he wrote, '. . . *make* a little time *every*
day to dedicate [yourself] to that to which calls you – good
health, spiritual development, or your music making: perhaps all three!' On another, 'To be a true amateur is to pursue one's art for the love of it, with no thought of material
reward: and the best professionals approach their work in the
same spirit.'

And following an adjudication in Exeter, he said:

> You have had to interpret compositions which are rather off

the beaten track as far as brass band music is concerned. We in the brass band movement are still only at the gateway of music and there is much yet for us to do; but if you will add these special pieces to your repertoire and constantly add music of the same standard – rehearsing it thoroughly and playing it well – there is no doubt that you can take an increasingly important part in the artistic life of our country.

These remarks were later printed in *The British Bandsman* and Eric was taken to task for what some felt were churlish remarks. He replied thus:

It is something to have reached the gateway of music and to have peeped inside the city! But we must remember that we have obvious limitations in technique, tone colour and musical effect generally. We can admit, of course, that a few of our finest bands have gone ahead of the mass – in some cases a long way ahead. Unfortunately, these are heard by comparatively few of the listening public, whose main impressions of the brass band are received from the hundreds of 'local bands' which form the solid backbone of the movement, and from the many and varied Salvation Army bands. It is those who are still at the 'gateway of music', and those whom I would wish to call to increased effort towards technical improvement, and a greater appreciation of what is loosely termed 'good music'. I believe in what has been called 'the renaissance of the brass band' as one of the more healthy signs of our times; but may we be saved from becoming complacently self-deluded.

His 'Comment' column in *The British Bandsman* was full of encouragement to bandsmen to improve their musical knowledge. On one occasion for instance he suggested a library in every bandroom, containing books on brass bands, biographies and autobiographies of great composers, musical criticism, books on choral and orchestral matters, novels with a musical background, magazines such as *Musical Times*, *Musical Opinion*, etc, brass band and orchestral scores

Eric Ball always wanted to share his love of 'classical' music with others, and partly for this reason he made numerous arrangements of the classics. In July 1969 he is announced as having arranged Debussy's pianoforte piece. 'The golliwog's cakewalk' for bands. The reviewer, in *BB*, adds the wry comment, 'It's a pity the French markings weren't translated into English; after all, it isn't every brass band conductor that understands *tres net et tres sec*!'

So far as pointing people 'to a higher realm of experience in . . . living' is concerned, a story told by George Church is typical. George and Joy Church are British-born officers who served for many years in the United States, and were at the same time friends of Eric and Olive Ball.

In the spring of 1989 George had the privilege of purchasing for The Salvation Army a most beautiful camp 9,000 feet up in the mountains of Colorado. He named it 'High Peak' after Eric's test piece of that title and used the four sections of that piece as four points in a message at the opening ceremony. In his last letter to George Church, dated within six months of his passing, Eric expressed the hope that George and his wife might 'both have more than one High Peak in your spiritual and social-evangelical journey in the coming years: and may you be constantly aware of our Lord's presence.'

To the end of his life Eric was encouraging smaller, or less well-known bands in their endeavours. Typical of him is an exchange of correspondence with a band secretary who must, for the sake of everyone, remain anonymous.

In June, 1986, the secretary wrote to Eric, thanking him for 'a short fanfare' he had written for his band, and asking what his fee would be. Eric replied, saying that he would charge them a certain sum, giving the band exclusive rights to use it, but retaining publishing rights, in case he wanted to incorporate it into a more extended piece.

Later, the treasurer had to write to Eric to say that the band was running at a loss, the sponsorship it had previously enjoyed having been withdrawn, so that even the modest sum he was asking was beyond the band's means at that time. The band was willing to return the music immediately if he wished to have it for use elsewhere. Eric replied, saying that he quite understood the problem of finance, being only too pleased that there were still bands like his who 'soldiered on' in spite of difficulties, and telling the band to accept the score as a gift with his compliments. That was typical of him.

To this the secretary replied, expressing his gratitude, and telling Eric a little more about the band's circumstances. He wondered whether he would care to become the band's president; this would involve him in no official duties, but would encourage the membership in its endeavours. Eric replied, saying that he was loath to accept such things 'because now I can do little to help'. (He was by now turned 80 years of age.) 'However,' Eric continued, 'if the committee so wish, I will be honoured to accept and will look forward to hearing news of the band from time to time.'

Back came a further letter. How would Eric wish to see his name on the band's letter-head? Eric replied, 'I must let you know that I would prefer the plain "Eric Ball", but if you think it would help, then add OBE. It could be followed by ARCM – I *earned* that many years ago: the OBE just happened!'

I found this exchange of correspondence particularly engaging and typical of all I had read and heard of Eric Ball.

In a quite different context he wrote to Doris Rendell, a salvationist song-writer of many years' standing: 'I often think that we musicians get more credit than we deserve, especially when it comes to song-writing. The poets are so often our inspiration: we rely on them!'

Another, and a more subtle, way in which Eric was an *encourager* needs to be explored.

Not for nothing did he often use the phrase, particularly in correspondence, that we are 'instruments of God's peace'. These words form part of the well-known prayer of St Francis, which Eric himself set to music for Salvation Army purposes. But the clue and the connection lie in the fact that Francis believed most firmly that all of life was one: that all living things are inter-dependent each on the other, all of them are dependent upon God, and that they are thus linked together in some mysterious way.

For this reason Eric was a convinced vegetarian. He could not bear to think of any animal being killed merely for food, and certainly not for sport. Not that he would ever dream of embarrassing anyone with his views, particularly when, as so often happened, he was being entertained for a meal. He would usually say something like, 'Just a little meat only for me, please,' and somehow contrive not to consume most of it without apparently leaving too much on his plate – rather like the lady in E.H. Benson's novels who, having something she did not like on her plate, hid it underneath the fork when the plate was taken away. When he got to the office after a weekend away, or on the morning after attending a dinner, he would give a rueful reply to inquirers as to how he dealt with the meat or poultry course, 'Well, I had to disobey regulations I'm afraid – only very slightly though!'

But this deep feeling that all life was sacred persisted through the whole of his life. He couldn't bear to kill *any-thing*, undoubtedly agreeing with the lady who observed, on seeing an office colleague kill a honey bee, mistaking it for a wasp, 'You can take life away, but you can't give it back again.' Stories are told of his seeing a moth fluttering around a lampshade, whereupon Eric would take one of his exquisite silk handkerchiefs, gather up the hapless creature gently into its folds, and take it to the very bottom of the garden, as far from the house as possible, and there gently release it into the wild.

His one-time neighbour, Violet Williams, tells an alto-gether charming story of having an ants' nest at the roots of one of her trees, and having to have it 'dealt with' by the local

Violet Williams, whose disposal of an ants' nest in her garden caused Eric great distress.

authority. She gave warning to Eric that there would be a muffled explosion sometime the next afternoon, whereupon Eric spent the whole of that afternoon in his music room, with his headphones on, listening to Beethoven.

All this makes it easy to understand that Eric Ball was a pacifist too. There is a 'Comment' column in *The British Bandsman* in which he displays his displeasure (the date of the issue is 26 December) at the wholesale slaughter of poor, harmless birds to provide the feast for the previous day, and of children being given toys which glorify conflict – and all to celebrate the birthday of the Prince of Peace. Not for nothing did he write his tone poem for Salvation Army bands, 'The triumph of peace'; it is one of his most powerful statements of faith.

The item is in strict sonata form, with the 'evil motive' as the first subject and the 'good motive' (his hymn tune 'Peace' written to carry words written by John Oxenham, commencing 'Peace in our time, O Lord . . .'). The 'development' section shows the two ideas in conflict, with, as befits the title and the sentiments of the piece, the 'good motive' having an unforgettable, ringing high B flat before it descends to its more manageable octave, on its final re-entry.

Joy Webb, a Salvation Army officer known for her work in the sphere of modern gospel-type music, has her own memories of Eric Ball.

She comes from a very musical Salvation Army family, with parents and others who were contemporaries of his, and it was not an uncommon occurrance for Eric Ball to be a visitor in their house. 'We often talked about common interests, music and things of the Spirit,' she told me. 'And with him there was never any feeling of "age" – do you know what I mean? We always talked as equals.

Joy Webb. 'I want you to know I'm praying for you,' Eric told her.

'He came into my office on one occasion. Unknown to anyone else – even my parents – I was going through a "dark night of the soul" experience. I was feeling persecuted and alone. Eric put his arm round me and said, "My dear, I have an idea you are going through a difficult time at the moment. But remember, I'm praying for you." '

The years went by. At the beginning of 1991 there were many anxious hearts, and Joy's was one of them. The Gulf Crisis was gathering momentum. The world held its breath as war threatened. Joy was leading meetings at Enfield Citadel. The atmosphere was tense in the meeting. Bandmaster James Williams came to her, greatly troubled, wondering what his band should play in the meeting. It was decided that the item should be 'The triumph of peace'.

The bandsmen played it as men possessed. As it came to

an end some of them, and their hearers, were weeping openly.

And Joy herself? What of her 'dark night of the soul'? 'I had by then learned to forgive the one who was persecuting me' she says, simply. She had learned, the hard way, of 'the triumph of peace'.

Not for nothing did Eric write his song, 'A prayer for courage', and afterwards his tone poem based upon it, 'Song of courage'.

He had listened, anxiously, Olive at his side, to a BBC broadcast given early in the year of 1940 by a well-known minister of religion, who said that he could not pray for happiness for his listeners, for no one knew what lay in store; neither could he pray for worldly gain for them, for of what use was that in such anxious times as they were living through then; but he could pray for courage – that they may face the challenges and the evils which surrounded them. The words sank deeply into Eric's soul, and he wrote a set of three verses, more or less paraphrasing those words. Afterwards he wrote music for them, music of great power, particularly on the words 'Courage to fight 'gainst the evils that now surround me, and temptations that would confound me.'

It was in the 1960s that Eric was asked to write 'something special' for a visit to the United Kingdom of the New York Staff Band. He thought and thought, and finally came up with the idea of a rhapsody on his tune, 'A prayer for courage'. He always thought it something of a joke that the opening *motif* for this piece – that is, after the introduction has been played – bore a very recognisable resemblance to the song, 'Oh, what a beautiful morning' – though he didn't realise it until the piece was well under construction, and he was working under some pressure to have it ready in time for the visit.

It can be said with truth that Eric was an encourager of life itself, as well as of an enjoyment of it; a lifter of hearts and minds to the Infinite by his music, his writings, his conversations, and by the very quality of his own life.

TWELVE

Eric OBE

For Eric Walter John Ball the journey back home through the wilderness was a long one.

When he resigned from Salvation Army officership a replacement had to be found for him on his department. Several names were suggested, but Bramwell Coles, the Head, insisted that Charles Skinner, a young officer of proven ability, and who was already producing work of note, be appointed. A quiet, studious man, though possessed of a dry sense of humour, Charles Skinner went on to become Head of the department, as well as deputy bandmaster and then executive officer of the International Staff Band. He is perhaps better known for his songs than for his band music, though this was always polished and well-constructed.

Relations between Eric and the Army began to improve, friends working to bring him back to the place where his roots lay. Kenneth Cook, for instance, arranged a programme at Regent Hall, at which 'Mr Eric Ball' (to quote *The Musician*) took the chair. The band and songster brigade performed his music, and, so the correspondent, Will Holmes, tells us in his report, 'Mrs Ball sang delightfully'. This was on 4 March 1951.

And Don Osgood, who, it will be remembered, had invited Eric to preside over one of his programmes, was untiring in his efforts on Eric's behalf.

Eric himself often told the story of how the British Commissioner of the day, Wilfred Kitching, himself a musician of considerable gifts, and thus in sympathy with Eric's aims and abilities, suggested that there was surely no reason why his name should not be put back on the roll of Hanwell Corps. Eric replied that he had never wanted it to be removed – but it had been removed by 'the authorities' in 1944, on the grounds that he was attending another place of worship, even though that was not strictly true.

Thus, in June 1953, Eric Walter John Ball became 'No 186' on the roll at Hanwell – without fuss or ceremony of any kind.

Olive Straughan remembers it well. She and her husband were the corps officers at Hanwell at the time, and she recalls the instruction her husband received that this should be, and his announcing it in the meeting. A contrast, this, to the occasion already related, when her husband received a reprimand from his divisional commander for asking Eric to take the chair at Acton, soon after the estrangement began!

For Eric Ball the way forward was now clear. Although he never again wore uniform, he often appeared as guest conductor at Salvation Army gatherings large and small. The fact that he did not wear uniform was a cause of embarrassment for at least one editor-in-chief, who, each time a picture of Eric appeared in a Salvation Army periodical wearing 'civvies' rather than uniform, as regulations require salvationists to do before conducting a musical section in public, received a critical letter from a certain reader.

Charles Skinner, who succeeded Eric in the International Music Editorial Department, of which he was later to become Head.

But as the years went by Eric only increased in stature so far as salvationists and others were concerned.

In 1956 Eric arranged a programme of Easter music at Chalk Farm, a chorus of 150 voices contributing such items as 'God so loved the world', 'Christ in his garden' and 'Jesus said,"I am the Resurrection"' (the last of these having words by his old colleague Charles Coller). Maureen Cooper, Sam Hooper and the Peterborough Male Voice Quartet, all well-known names in the fifties, also provided items, and representative members of each of the five brigades making up the chorus brought a Scripture reading to illustrate a point in the story. Michael Kenyon provided organ accompaniments.

Such planning was typical of Eric. This was the first of an unbroken series of such programmes arranged by him at that *venue* which continued up to and including 1962.

The congregation of women at the Royal Parish Church of Saint Martin-in-the-Fields on a March day in that year may or may not have been surprised to see the choir-stalls fill up with about 30 young women, whose neatly bonnetted and navy-dressed appearance denoted them as salvationists. They were the National Songsters of The Salvation Army, under the direction of Muriel Packham, who, in a service led by Violet Williams, chairman at that time of the Women's World Day of Prayer national committee, sang a special setting of 'The King of love' ('St Columba') by Eric Ball. Queen Elizabeth the Queen Mother was guest of honour. The gentle ebb and flow of the music will be remembered still by many present and by those who possess the recording made by the same

Three International Staff bandmasters: George Fuller (above), who was succeeded by Eric: William Stewart (above right), who himself succeeded Eric: Bernard Adams (far right), who came after William Stewart, and was to be its bandmaster for 28 years.

group at a programme given in Sheffield a couple of years later.

The delicate little 'ripple' in the music, in which Eric exploits a triplet which occurs *once only* in the original tune, occurs more than 20 times in his arrangement, always in the pianoforte accompaniment. This is enormously effective in creating the tranquil mood of still waters and green pastures of which the words speak. The music moves into the expected minor key for the verse about 'death's dark veil' and although the last line of the song has a triumphant mood as the soul moves into 'thy house for ever', the arrangement itself has a quiet close which is as unexpected as it is effective. Apart from (or, maybe, including) the pianoforte accompaniment, the arrangement is not difficult, and bears out Eric Wilson's assessment of Eric Ball's music when he said that 'even a simple hymn arrangement was done to perfection.'

For the same all-women group Eric was to write a setting of Mary's song, '*Magnificat*' for the centenary celebrations of The Salvation Army in 1965. How skilfully he catches the varying moods of this canticle in a setting as effective as any by a classical composer! How vividly he matches the wild joy of the vocal lines in the pianoforte accompaniment! The setting was given a new lease of life some years later (after having been featured as a female-voice item at numerous summer

Illuminated scroll presented in recognition of Eric's services to Salvation Army music in 1977.

schools of music) in an arrangement for mixed voices, still with pianoforte accompaniment, though it remains a matter of opinion whether that rearrangement enhances or lessens the impact of the original.

Honours and requests for special appearances and arrangements of music poured in. 'Milestone' birthdays such as his 75th and his 80th called for special tribute-articles and interviews in the Salvation Army press, and for 'evenings' with him and his music. In a dissertation, non-salvationist student Ida Meccariello called him 'The Beethoven of Brass'.

He was present, for example, at a composers' festival at Crystal Palace, held in 1968 as part of The Salvation Army's celebrations of 90 years of bands. General Frederick Coutts, one of the Army's masters of the right word in the right place, announced Eric on that occasion to conduct 'Songs of the morning' (which he did, to 'thunderous applause', so *The Musician* of the day said), and told the congregation that one of his earliest compositions, published in 1922, had had the 'prophetic' title of, 'Through storm to safety'.

In 1977, he was thanked publicly in a Royal Albert Hall gathering for 50 years of service to Salvation Army music, presented with an illuminated scroll, and invited to conduct the International Staff Band in one of his compositions. In 1978, at a composers' festival held as part of the congress of

Opposite: Front cover of *The Bandsman and Songster,* 11 February 1928, commemorating the composers' festival at which the then Duke and Duchess of York were present.

that year (when he was close on 75), he conducted the massed bands in his epic tone poem, 'The Kingdom triumphant'. 'The applause after this lifted the roof at least six inches!' Gwen Barnett, who was present, says with a chuckle.

At a composers' festival held in the Clapton Congress Hall 50 years previously, at which the then Duke and Duchess of York (later to become King George VI and Queen Elizabeth) were present, Eric had conducted his music. This fact was recognised by the Duchess (now Queen Elizabeth The Queen Mother) in a message sent to General Arnold Brown and read by him to the congregation:

> I learned with interest that in connection with your International Congress a concert was to be held to honour salvationist composers who would be meeting in London for the celebrations. . . .
>
> This event has been arranged to commemorate not only the centenary of Salvation Army bands but also to mark the 50th anniversary of your first international composers' festival in 1928. On that occasion, in your Clapton Congress Hall, my husband and I were privileged to be guests of honour. General Bramwell Booth graciously received us and shared our box to enjoy the lovely music. . . . I understand that one of the composers who conducted in that concert is to conduct again tonight – the lone survivor. I send a special greeting to Mr Eric Ball.
>
> Much has happened to the world in these 50 years but two things have not changed. The message of The Salvation Army remains vital and relevant. The music of The Salvation Army is still a vehicle of hope, happiness and spiritual enrichment. Both must survive to make the world a better place.
>
> My affectionate greetings to you all.
>
> ELIZABETH R
> Queen Mother.

Quite naturally, Eric was deeply touched by being remembered in this way. He replied to The Queen Mother, saying,

> Your Majesty,
> I have today received from The Salvation Army International Headquarters a copy of the message you so kindly sent to General Arnold Brown on the occasion of the concert honouring salvationist composers and in which you made reference to '. . . the lone survivor of a similar event held 50 years ago'. May I thank you for this special greeting, by which I was greatly honoured and deeply moved. Your message was received with great acclaim by the great number of musicians and listeners on that occasion. For me it was a very special day.
> God bless you.
> Yours sincerely
> Eric Ball.

No. 870—Vol. XXI   Registered at the General   **LONDON, FEBRUARY 11, 1928**   Post Office as a Newspaper   **Price One Penny**

Army Composers who will take part in the Clapton Festival, on Wednesday, February 15th, at which the Duke and Duchess of York are announced to be present, and over which the General will preside.

Message from HM Queen Elizabeth The Queen Mother to the International Composers' Festival at Wembley in 1978, with its special reference to Eric, and Eric's reply.

CLARENCE HOUSE
S. W. 1

General Arnold Brown,
   The Salvation Army,
      The Empire Pool, Wembley.

        I learned with interest that in connection with
your International Congress a Concert was to be held
to honour Salvationist composers who would be meeting
in London for the celebrations.

        The gifted few you are honouring tonight are
representative of all the composers of your glorious
musical past and of those today, in five continents,
who have been unable to make the journey.   The
descendants of Herbert Booth and Richard Slater provide
a veritable army within an Army.

        This event has been arranged to commemorate not
only the Centenary of Salvation Army bands but also to
mark the 50th Anniversary of your first International
Composers' Festival in 1928.   On that occasion, in your
Clapton Congress Hall, my husband and I were privileged
to be Guests of Honour.   General Bramwell Booth
graciously received us and shared our Box to enjoy the
lovely music.   We met the humble men who had written
that music, among them Bandmaster George Marshall, the
Durham miner in his wheelchair.   I understand that one
of the composers who conducted in that Concert is to
conduct again tonight - the lone survivor.   I send a
special greeting to Mr. Eric Ball.

        Much has happened to the world in these fifty years
but two things have not changed.   The message of the
Salvation Army remains vital and relevant.   The music
of the Salvation Army is still a vehicle of hope,
happiness and spiritual enrichment.   Both must survive
to make the world a better place.

        My affectionate greetings to you all.

                              ELIZABETH R
                              Queen Mother

8th July 1978

9 Milton Road
Parkstone, Poole. Dorset
BH14 9QL

Her Majesty Elizabeth R   3 August 1978
Queen Mother
Clarence House London S.W.1

Your Majesty,
I have today received from The Salvation Army
International Headquarters a copy of the
message you so kindly sent to General
Arnold Brown on the occasion of the
Concert honouring Salvationist Composers,
and in which you made reference to
"... the lone surviving of a similar event
held fifty years ago
May I thank you for this special greeting,
by which I was greatly honoured and deeply
moved.
Your message was received with great acclaim
by the great number of musicians and listeners
on that occasion   For me it was a very
special day. God bless you.
      Your obedient servant,
            Eric Ball

For his 75th birthday, 'a gala evening' was held in the
Poole Arts Centre, in which Rita Green and Maisie
(Ringham) Wiggins were, respectively, the soprano (vocal)
and trombone soloists. Boscombe and Poole Bands sup-
ported, together with Boscombe, Poole and Winton Songster
Brigades. Eric's own selection of gospel songs, 'Good news',
was included, as was Erik Leidzén's 'Concertino for trombone and band'. As part of the finale, Eric conducted the
united bands in 'The eternal presence'.

For his 80th birthday, Enfield Band and Boscombe Song-

Eric (left) with Bandmaster Herbert Mountain of Blackpool Citadel. Herbert Mountain composed a fair amount of music for The Salvation Army; popular in its day, it has not, however, due to changing fashions, stood the test of time, Eric was seldom happy being photographed; his lack of ease in this regard is, perhaps, visible in this snapshot.

sters presented a programme, at which the only exception in an 'all-Ball' programme was, at Eric's own request, Dean Goffin's 'Symphony of thanksgiving'.

In 1981 the International Staff Band presented a programme of his music at the Regent Hall, in which Phil Catelinet played one of Eric's all-too-rare published pianoforte solos, 'Sunshine', with its somewhat 'jazzy' interlude, and an arrangement for piano by Eric of an old march, 'Fighting soldiers'. Solos for cornet and euphonium were also included, as was a song by the male voice chorus (an innovation commenced by Eric when he was bandmaster of the ISB 20 years earlier). Replying to a spoken tribute to 'a man we love and admire' from Lieut-Colonel Ray Bowes, Bandmaster of the ISB, Eric said,

> I am really highly honoured tonight. The Salvation Army has given me a wonderful opportunity to work with its bands and songster brigades, and I give thanks to God for the wonderful life he has given my wife and me. Our lives have been over-ruled by his hand. What more could a composer want than for his music to be recognised as being of value? Sometimes I forget how I wrote the music but then I realise that it has been God working through me.

Following what *Musician* reporter Paul Mortlock called 'a resounding round of applause', Eric took up the baton to lead the band in its final items. 'Sanctuary', which was received in reverent silence, was followed by Geoffrey Havercroft's Scripture reading and exhortation, and this in turn by 'Song of courage'.

Not only did The Salvation Army lionise him in this way. His Christchurch cantata, for instance, was performed in an 80th-birthday concert at St John's, Smith Square, and London Collegiate Brass, under its conductor, James Stobart, paid tribute to him, with his rarely heard, 'Kensington concerto'. Neither of these was a Salvation Army occasion. The following January, Hendon Band played, 'The triumph of peace' in a broadcast – possibly the first time a non-Salvation Army band had broadcast a work published by The Salvation Army. Newham Band played 'The eternal presence', another Salvation Army publication in their BBC programme 'Bandstand' on 28 November 1985.

And on 8 December 1984, B. Mellors, of Sheffield, wrote, in *BB*, that 'The extent to which Eric Ball leads in the writing of music for brass bands was, I suggest, amply demonstrated on Thursday 11 October last when Grimethorpe gave the performance of a lifetime of "Festival music". When this gifted man finally lays down his pen, where, I wonder, will we find a successor?'

In 1985, the magazine *This England* awarded to Eric Ball and Harry Mortimer its own Silver Cross of St George. The nomination was made by 'an English exile in Canada', Mr Gordon McGowan, of Nova Scotia. Gordon McGowan was a member of the North American Brass Band Association, a body which has drawn so much from the example of the two men, and in his nomination he wrote of their 'truly gigantic role in creating the image of quality that appears now to be spreading the brass band to hitherto unimaginable areas.'

Also in the nineteen-eighties, in a very different connection, he 'adopted' the young son of an African salvationist, Samuel Nalonga, who named the boy 'Eric' after the composer. A brief, but engaging, correspondence ensued, Eric using opportunities afforded him when writing to Brother Nalonga to pass on greetings to local salvationist musicians.

In 1987 he was awarded an honorary graduate diploma in band musicianship by the Salford College of Technology. He wrote to the head of department with typical courtesy, saying that he was 'grateful and proud to have received this honour, and will keep the scroll [of his award] with my certificate for the ARCM diploma received many years ago. This is the sum of my collegiate achievements!'

In that year he received a letter from a correspondent, Eric Dobson, saying that he had changed the name of his boat from 'Pipe dream' to 'Star Lake', and that. . .

> As you know, Ellen and I do a considerable amount of cruising on the Thames and the name of our boat causes much attraction which gives me the opportunity to explain its origin. You may find it hard to credit it but a few weeks ago we were on the river between Henley and Reading when we saw a 70-ft narrow boat called 'Song of the morning'. . . . I am now looking out, although with not much optimism, for a boat named '*Resurgam*' or 'The eternal presence', but who knows. . . .

But before all these, in 1969, Eric Walter John Ball was mentioned in the Queen's Birthday Honours List as receiving the Order of the British Empire for services to brass band music. His good friends of many years' standing (he had conducted their wedding while he was still a Salvation Army officer), Tommy and May Silvester, drove Eric and Olive to Buckingham Palace for the investiture.

He was still paying visits overseas, touring Canada in 1972, New Zealand (for the New Zealand championships) and the USA (for Salvation Army meetings) from 12 May to 4 June 1973, Olive accompanying him; in 1975 it was announced that he would conduct Solna Brass in Sweden, and then travel to Massachusetts, USA, 'for a few days'. In February

1979 he was in New York for the 'Friday night at the Temple' series of meetings. He was by this time just turned 75 years of age.

The Canadian tour of 1972 was so special that it deserves particular mention.

The brass band movement is not strong in Canada, any more than it is in the United States, though there are places where great interest is shown, largely through Salvation Army bands. The wind band predominates in both parts of the continent. But it was to satisfy the demands of the interest which does exist that four of the best English bands were flown to Canada in July 1972 to give massed concerts in Niagara, and to tour extensively in the region as individual groups. These bands were Black Dyke Mills, CWS (Manchester), GUS, and Fairey Aviation. Each band took its resident conductor, and three guest conductors, Geoffrey Brand, Harry Mortimer and Eric Ball, accompanied them. Besides these a plane load of their supporters travelled to Niagara, some of them elderly enthusiasts who had never been out of the United Kingdom before; there were even visitors from mainland Europe, Australia and New Zealand. The tour was a tremendous success, musically and socially. It was not a financial success unfortunately, so that, although a return visit was planned for two years later, the idea was abandoned.

For Harry and Margaret Mortimer it was a special trip, in that their friendship with Eric and Olive Ball became even deeper than it had previously been. 'Come and join us for our daily devotions,' Eric and Olive said (Eric would read from the Scriptures, Olive from a devotional aid, and then they would pray together). For the Mortimers this became a very rich ritual indeed, and one they never forgot.

As late as 1978 he was taking Poole Salvation Army Band in rehearsal in the absence of Bandmaster Alwyn Green, who was on tour with the Bournemouth Symphony Orchestra.

And all these years he was writing. In 1971, for instance, his 'Celebration' was used as a test piece in the second section of the National Contest. Its four movements were intended to be played without a break, and consisted of a 'Festival prelude', originally composed for orchestral brass. According to one account, however, it was used before that as a fanfare in a cadets' pageant in the 1930s. Eric was at times as economical with his musical themes as the legendary George Frederick Handel! Now, two more lyrical episodes were included; a slow dance; a theme and variations, with solos for cornet and euphonium among others; and a march, based on the theme of the preceding movement. The *BB* reviewer said it was '. . . well scored, and typically Eric Ball'.

Opposite: With HRH The Duchess of Kent at the Royal Albert Hall, 1969.

Letter to Eric from Sir Arthur Bliss
thanking him for his arrangement
of his own 'Dances from
"Checkmate" ' for brass.

8, THE LANE,

MARLBOROUGH PLACE,

LONDON, NW8 OPN.

01-624 8441.

February 6th 1973.

Dear Eric.

I am so pleased to learn that it
is you who has arranged 'Dances from
"Checkmate"' for the Brass Bands.

My wife and I are coming to the
Albert Hall on April 14th to hear the
Concert.

with much gratitude
Sincerely
Arthur Bliss.

In 1972 he provided a cantata for the opening of the town hall of Christchurch, New Zealand. This received its first performance on 30 September of that year.

It was a setting of parts of three psalms and a full setting of Psalm 148, and had in addition one movement for band alone. According to one critic, 'that part of the work showed stark strength, expressed through cleverly coloured combinations of instruments. It had brightly rhythmical treatment. The Prayer, the second movement of the cantata, was sung with feeling. The unaccompanied "Affirmation" was sung lyrically and with meditative expression, and the last movement gradually piled on power and had a strong ending . . . The cantata is not a work which harmonically is likely to set ablaze rivers adjacent to the great academies, but it is interesting in showing how useful a brass band can be as an accompaniment to voices.'

The year 1978 saw the completion of an arrangement of four dances from the ballet *Checkmate* by Sir Arthur Bliss and

8, THE LANE,

MARLBOROUGH PLACE,

LONDON, NW8 OPN.

01-624 8441.

4th April 1979

Eric Ball, Esq.,
9 Milton Road,
Parkstone,
Poole, Dorset.

Dear Mr. Ball,

Denis Carr has sent me the Two-Ten recording
of CHECKMATE and I do want to tell you again what
pleasure I have from your arrangement of CHECKMATE.
The more often I hear it, the better I appreciate
how skilful you have been. Arthur would have been
delighted and very grateful to you.

With warmest greetings to you both,

Trudy Bliss

Letter from Trudy Bliss, widow of Sir Arthur, acknowledging receipt of a recording of 'Dances from "Checkmate" '.

there is in existence a copy of a letter from the composer's widow thanking Eric for his work and expressing her satisfaction in it.

But among the music belonging to this glorious 'Indian summer' of Eric's life belong his transcriptions of Elgar's 'Froissart' overture and 'Enigma variations'. Eric had always had a strong predilection for the music of Elgar, counting him next to Beethoven and Brahms in his personal favourite composers. Elgar himself had, it will be recalled, written to him, congratulating him on his *air varié* 'The old wells'. Perhaps it is the highest compliment one composer can pay another to arrange that composer's music for another medium, even though history is full of transcriptions being made from far less worthy motives. Eric had already arranged the prelude to 'The Dream of Gerontius' a number of years previously.

Bram Gay conducted Solna Brass in the arrangement in April, 1984, and Eric himself gave 'a truly radiant account' of it with the National Youth Brass Band in Ripon Cathedral on 11 August of that year. When Desford played it at St Mary's Church, Warwick, in June 1984, Peter Wilson said that it was an 'almost unbelievably faithful and sincere arrangement – integrity oozing out of every bar'.

By now Eric and Olive were living quietly in Dorset. They moved from Hanwell, west London, on 24 October 1969, taking up residence at 9 Milton Road, Parkstone – their last permanent address. They transferred as Salvation Army soldiers to Branksome. They were, for as long as they possibly could be, fiercely independent, refusing lifts to and from the meetings, though they lived quite a distance from the hall. Eric's letters to his old friend Victor Kingston often refer to Olive's walking to and from the home league, where she was an enthusiastic member. Olive Straughan remembers arranging a 'boats' afternoon for her home league (she was home league secretary at Parkstone in her retirement from officer-service) and Eric took part, 'reviving' his piano/organ fantasia, 'Stilling the storm', for the occasion.

Eric himself took long, thoughtful walks in the lovely district in which they lived. 'I find it easier to say my prayers when I'm out walking than I do at home, even in the silence of my own private room,' he often said. In a similar way he enjoyed mowing his lawn, for, although he never professed to be a gardener, he found that the rhythm of pushing the mower along, turning round and mowing another length, and repeating the process again and again, caused musical themes to form themselves in his mind, especially when he was in the throes of composition.

Latterly they became soldiers at Poole Corps. There Eric led several Easter Sunday meetings which were quite unforgettable in character. Towards the end of their lives they were cared for by friends in the corps, and others in the district. No praise can be high enough for Bandmaster Stan and Mrs Mary Randell of Winton, for instance, who cared for Eric devotedly during his months of widowerhood. Beryl Smith, a soldier at Boscombe, would take Eric and Olive for afternoon runs into the lovely Dorset countryside in her car, (sometimes they would return convulsed with laughter at Eric's quick wit) and Gwen Barnett, of Parkstone, would provide a taxi service to and from the station when Eric went on a train journey, or arrange his flight details when he went on longer journeys, as he did until he was turned 80.

Typical of the affection in which they were both held are the parties that were arranged for them at corps level for Eric's 80th birthday, and their diamond wedding. For the first of these there was a huge birthday cake (supplied by

Eric and Olive's last home at
Parkstone, Dorset.

Eric and Olive in the garden of
their home in Dorset.
(picture - Robin Bryant)

Eric's study at Parkstone.

Novellos, the music publisher, for whom Eric had supplied work from time to time) and of which everyone gathered received a piece. Apparently one elderly member of the congregation was heard to say to a companion afterwards, 'Just fancy – *Ivor Novello* sent the cake!' And for the second, which occurred when the nation was preparing for the wedding of the then Prince Andrew and Miss Sarah Ferguson, Poole Home League had a special 'royal wedding' occasion, and Eric and Olive's 'special day' was recalled and suitable presentations made.

From Sweden came a report of an 80th-birthday salute in two identical programmes given by Södertalje Band on successive evenings in Södertalje and Jönköping. An information sheet, running to six foolscap pages, was available, giving an account of his musical career, and listing the musical arrangements, vocal and instrumental, that had to that date been published by The Salvation Army. Two brass items, 'Pledged for service' and 'Meditation on a theme by Spohr' were included, as well as two songs, 'In the secret of thy presence' and 'Begin the day with God'.

In a written greeting, Eric referred to the enriching fellowship he had shared within the banding fellowship of the worldwide Army. Having visited both Södertalje and Jönköping, he could, he said, 'picture the scene and will join you all in spirit'.

The second event was at the Swedish Brass Band Contest in Växjö, where Retired Bandmaster Sture Petersson, of the Army's music department for Sweden, gave the audience an account of Eric's long musical career, his outstanding service and considerable influence.

Eric was always loyal to his friends, paying tribute in *BB* in January to Vaughan Morris (his item being 'felicitous as well as timely' according to one correspondent), and to Don Osgood, who, with others, had done so much to bring him back into recognition by the Salvation Army establishment. And of Dr Harold Hinde, for long a contributor to *BB*, he wrote in that periodical, 'I have long been grateful that Harold Hinde publicly commended some of my early works on more than one occasion; and during my years as editor (his contributions have been of great value), our contacts were entirely cordial and of mutual respect'.

Of particular interest with regard to Don Osgood are the visits Eric paid to him when he was gravely ill in 1981. Among other 'ministries' offered by Eric at this time was the following 'meditation' from the works of John Henry Newman, which is also interesting in itself, showing as it does the breadth of Eric's mind and soul:

Eric and Olive, with sister-in-law
Gertie and brother Don, in
Parkstone, on Eric and Olive's
diamond wedding anniversary,
1986.

God has created me to do him some definite service: he has
committed some work to me which he has not committed to
another. I have my mission – I may never know it in this world,
but I shall be told it in the next.

I am a link in a chain, a bond of connection between persons.
He has not created me for naught. I shall do good, I shall do his
work. I shall be an angel of peace, a preacher of truth in my own
place *while not intending it* – if I do but keep his commandments.

Therefore I will trust him. Whatever, wherever I am, I can
never be thrown away. If I am in sickness, my sickness may serve
him; if I am in sorrow, my sorrow may serve him. He does nothing
in vain. He knows what he is about.

He may take away my friends, he may throw me among strangers, he may make me feel desolate, make my spirits sink, hide
my future from me – still he knows what he is about.

During these years Eric built up a relationship with The
Salvation Army Social Services Centre in Southampton,

Olive and he visiting the centre to give talks on the spiritual influence of music. This ministry was greatly appreciated. Another ministry he undertook was the playing of the piano for the carol singing at the Christmas Day parties given to lonely people by members of Poole Corps.

Eric always had a great concern for the poor and 'unlovely'. Connie Clark tells of an occasion when she, with Eric and Olive, was leaving a Salvation Army festival given at Saint Martin-in-the-Fields Church, Trafalgar Square:

> There were several men lying on the ground just outside the side door of the church, in any space that gave them shelter. One man, with a blanket round him, was holding out his hand and bidding folk 'goodnight' as they left. Most passers-by were embarrassed and looked the other way. But Eric stopped and stooped to shake hands with the man and chat with him, asking if that was to be his bed for the night. When the man said that it was, Eric replied, 'Well at least you won't have far to fall if you roll out!' The old man laughed at Eric's remark and wished him 'goodnight'.

From Sidney Williams, a retired Salvation Army officer, who, with his wife, Violet, lived next door to Eric and Olive during their 'Parkstone period', come some quite enchanting stories of Eric and his influence in the district. He writes:

> As a next-door neighbour one could say that Eric touched nothing that he did not adorn. For example, he signalled to his wife that each new day had begun by accompanying coffee with the playing of a march. He enhanced my mornings by pushing through my letter-box his copy of the previous day's *Times*, a gesture I deeply appreciated, although initially he had hesitated to offer the arrangement in case it might offend. He felt it was a small way in which he could recompense me for the occasional lifts I gave him to the station.

Sidney Williams, Eric's neighbour. 'Eric touched nothing that he did not adorn' he says.

> It could be said of Eric in the road where we lived that his gentleness made him great. He was esteemed by the neighbours, who were the recipients of his concern in times of sickness and sorrow. A retired military officer who suffered a long illness was visited often by Eric, who enlightened him concerning The Salvation Army's beliefs and procedures. Being a military man he was interested in the salvationist's one-finger salute. As Eric bade him 'goodbye' on what proved to be a last visit, he managed a flicker of a smile and gave the Army salute.

> If Shakespeare's Duke could see sermons in stones, one gained the impression that Eric was finding symphonies in Parkstone's irregular paving stones as he took his regular evening walks. Nature had generously blessed him with a head of full and shapely hair to match his artistic gifts. To see it in its silver richness floating in the breeze marked him naturally as a person of distinction.

Sadly, his usual barber retired and all the skill the new man had to offer was a 'short-back-and-sides'. When Eric emerged from his first visit to the shop he looked like a sheep shorn of its coat, or Samson robbed of his locks. I took it upon myself to advise him of the 'tragedy' and offered on behalf of the brass band world to find another barber. The greatness of the musician was shown when he declined my offer stating that the young man was new, and needed the encouragement of his custom. Fortunately I managed to persuade him to change his mind.

Eric showed deep concern for all God's children, especially those who were weakest. A score of years before I became his neighbour, I was present at a band festival over which he presided in Melbourne Town Hall in connection with his visit to Australasia. Skilfully he interwove the musical items with touches of wit and wisdom. He told mothers to be sure to cover their babies' ears against the first impact of a band playing. 'It is apt to be a shock to baby ears and to incur a bout of crying' he said. The truth of it was well demonstrated during the evening! . . .

The Eric Ball home in Parkstone was a place of calm and a refuge to the many who availed themselves of Eric's healing ministry. Coffee cups were ready for all who came.

Eric became very exercised concerning the failing health of his much-loved Olive. In the issue of *BB* dated 2 December 1978, for instance, there is an announcement in which he thanks readers for their kind enquiries with regard to her stay in hospital. She later sustained a serious fall while out shopping and suffered a fractured hip. She never really recovered. It was on 10 July 1988 she 'entered the Summerland', to use Eric's own phrase.

But just prior to that there was a tender exchange of correspondence with Stanley Ditmer, an officer in The Salvation Army, well known for his musical compositions, and in particular for his deeply moving song, 'I'm in his [God's] hands', born out of suffering, and used by salvationists as a vehicle for their prayers of trust. Stanley Ditmer wrote:

Stanley Ditmer, whose song, 'I'm in his hands', was of such comfort to Olive latterly.

Every once in a while we do have chance to write and say 'Hello'. Recently Violet Williams . . . advised us that dear Olive is quite ill. . . . These burdens come with the ongoing years of life. The body fades away and ultimately dies, but the spirit soars with him who is eternal.

You can't imagine how gratifying it is to know that the great composer Eric Ball, with his wife Olive, finds some sense of meaning and comfort in a simple song like 'I'm in his hands', and yet the eternal truths are the most simple in statement, are they not? Faith is only necessary when it is severely tried through pain, sickness, and ultimate death. It is of the greatest comfort to know that with David there is no need to fear any evil and that his rod and his staff do comfort.

Many times I have shared the story and remember with joy our eating together the cold meat pies in the arena at Wembley Stadium. Such choice memories are more valuable than the many trinkets that we possess.

Our prayers are with you both.

Many of the letters Eric filed away have copies of the replies, almost always written by hand, and carbon-copied on the back of the letter being replied to. So it is here:

Dear Stanley

Very many thanks for your welcome letter. It is most encouraging, underlining as it does the fact of our Lord's continual Presence with us.

Until recently Olive was able to sing various verses or choruses quite clearly, and 'I'm in his hands' is a great favourite. Now she has some difficulty in communicating (a variable disability), but can still react to mention of your words. We have spoken often of our experience of his Presence, and now we experience deeply the value of acceptance and trust.

It is true, as you write, that the eternal truths are the most simple in statement. One comes to realise the value of simplicity and indeed economy in the use of words spoken or written. 'The common people heard him gladly', and he would have spoken in terms they could easily understand. We know too that there is a Divine Adjustment of all our affairs.

It applied also to that 'feast' of meat pies in the arena at Wembley. Even a simple crust is a feast when eaten with friends.

Thank you for your prayers. Your name will be on my prayer list, together with your dear ones, and for your work and witness.

General Eva Burrows. 'Thank you for the inspiration of your music', she wrote to Eric.

Letters from this time from admiring friends and acquaintances all round the world are deeply touching to read in retrospect. From General Eva Burrows comes the following, after a visit to the Southern Africa Territory at the beginning of 1988:

For me, one of the highlights was the festival on the Saturday evening when members of the chorus came from all races. Had the pitch of the instruments been compatible, the bands would have been able to unite also. It was a great musical occasion and I wish you could have heard the congress chorus and Johannesburg Citadel Band as they concluded the programme with 'The Kingdom triumphant'. It was thrilling and very much appreciated by the 1,000-strong congregation. I told them I would let you know what great blessing your and their combined effort had brought to the meeting. . . . Thank you for the inspiration of your music. You will see how world-wide is its influence, and salvationists everywhere are grateful to God for the ministry of your dedicated gifts.

Eric's reply is typical:

Dear General Eva,

Thank you very much for your very kind letter telling me of the presentation of 'The Kingdom triumphant' . . . and your report of all this practically drove me to kneel and thank God for all his goodness to me. I try to follow your movements through *Salvationist*, and I pray that God will continue to give you his grace and strength and the power of the Spirit as you carry out your great task and responsibilities. Although Olive is at present in a nearby nursing home she will join me in sending greetings and good wishes, and thanks for your kindness in writing.

From Haakon Dahlstrom, a retired Salvation Army leader living in Oslo, comes an account of a programme he is about to present on local radio of Salvation Army music, with the background to the items, including Eric's 'The old wells' and 'The King of kings'. He ends his letter 'God bless you, grand Maestro!' Eric replies, '. . . I am very grateful to our Lord that my work has brought pleasure and – more important – blessing to you and to other dear people. It is his Spirit who does the work! Your plan for broadcasting "The old wells" and "The King of kings" in such detail pleases me very much indeed. Especially I hope that "The King of kings" will make a spiritual impact upon the listeners. . . . It is good that a local radio station gives this opportunity for Army music and songs to be heard. God will bless you in this ministry. To him be the Glory. His presence is with us always.'

From Muriel Yendell, the well-known Salvation Army choral trainer, comes a letter dated 11 June 1989 (less than four months before Eric's passing):

> I was really thrilled to see you at Sunbury last Wednesday. What an inspiration you are and have been to me ever since I knew you. Your commendation of my choral work has meant more to me than anything said by anyone else. That I have been privileged to interpret your music, some of which you wrote specially for me, seems unbelievable. Thank you for everything you have done for me. I hope to have at least a few more opportunities to conduct your work.

Eric did not keep a copy of his reply to this note, but it was acknowledged only a week or so after it was received, on 21 June.

From Durban comes a letter from Esme Browning, asking for prayers for 'Cynthia' who has to visit a specialist in a few days' time. To this letter is clipped a list of her family, in Eric's writing, doubtless so that he could remember them all in his prayers.

Down through the years Eric kept up a lively correspondence with a number of old friends, such as Victor Kingston, long-since settled in Toronto, Canada, and whom he visited

Muriel Yendell. 'Your commendation of my choral work has meant more to me than anything said by anyone else,' she told Eric.

on several occasions, and with Bob Getz, in Detroit, Michigan. Bob writes of the final period in Eric's life:

> Eric had been 'awaiting the call' (his words) ever since his wife of over 60 years, Olive, had died on Sunday, 10 July 1988. The quality of the man and the marriage was seen in a letter he wrote to me soon after Olive had to go into a nursing home. He wrote of 'coping with chores for the first time . . . nothing overwhelming'. He then spoke of going each day to 'see my dear Olive . . . her mind is still variable, but she knows me, and expresses concern for my welfare. Our time together is spent reaching out and within – for a closer link with divine love, and it is an enriching experience.' I carried that letter in my pocket until it was about to disintegrate. Visiting a beloved wife of 60 years, suffering in this way, and finding it an enriching experience.'

Yet another powerful and moving expression came soon after Olive passed away. After apologising for taking so long to answer Bob's previous letter, he wrote, 'I have to tell you that following Olive's sojourn in hospital and nursing home since Christmas eve, she at last went to Heaven. . . . I was with her as she passed, and it was a wonderful, holy experience. The near presence of our Lord was very real. So now I have much to give thanks for.'

Eric's own tribute and copy of the order of service at her funeral have survived. He wanted it to be 'A joyful occasion', quoting the verse

> Angels now are hovering round us
> Unperceived amid the throng,
> Wondering at the love that found us,
> Glad to join our holy song:
> Hallelujah!
> Love and praise to Christ belong.

Then came his much-loved quotation from the Book of Wisdom which begins, 'The souls of the righteous are in the hand of God', which he had used so often at funerals when he was a Salvation Army officer, and which so profoundly influenced the writing of '*Resurgam*'. After this he thanked the corps officer and all present for their messages and remembrances of Olive in their prayers, before he said,

> Many present have experienced what the world calls the 'loss' of a dear one. But we are encompassed about by a great cloud of witnesses and there is no loss. They are with God and *we* are with God. I am thankful for all with whom I am linked in thought, word and deed, those here on earth and in Heaven.
> I am thankful to Olive for her natural goodness and consistent life, her gentle sense of humour, her understanding. She was alongside me – not behind me – and now gone on before.

I am thankful to God. Only looking back there is clearly an ordered progress in our lives, sometimes in spite of myself. So now, with angels and archangels and all the company of the Heavenly host, we entrust ourselves to the Divine Love manifest in our Master, Jesus Christ. All will be well. All *is* well.

Stanley Ditmer's song, 'I'm in his hands' was sung as a solo during the simple service.

A tribute, typical, I suppose of many which have been lost, and others which might have survived, is the following, from Don Morrison, musical director at that time of The John Laing (Hendon) Band:

> All of us who knew her had such great respect for her. She was very proud of you and your work, and her faithful support was something that we all greatly admired. I have precious memories of Olive singing her solos with your accompaniment at the piano; you were as one and that is how I shall always remember you both; you were as one in your love for each other, and in your service for others.

And between Eric and Houston Ellis, a retired American Salvation Army officer, there was an interchange of correspondence. The Ellises had lost a daughter in her early-twenties, a radiantly happy girl, deeply spiritual and highly artistic. Afterwards Houston Ellis collected together some of the tributes he and his wife had received to their daughter, and following the promotion to Glory of Olive, they sent a copy to Eric. It contained a letter from Elizabeth Brengle Read, a daughter of Samuel Logan Brengle, a Salvation Army 'saint' of earlier years, saying, among other things that her father used to say that '. . . he always felt that the veil between our world and theirs is very, very thin, but here we see through a glass darkly, and our earthly eyes are not meant to see future glories' – a sentiment with which Eric profoundly sympathised. 'They are with God and we are with God,' he replied.

To the end of his life, his faith remained secure. Indeed, it deepened. When his old friend, John Hunt, died in 1982, he paid tribute to him in *BB*, ending his item, 'Here's to our ongoing friendship!'

And to the end of his life belong the tenderest memories of the influence of Eric Ball. Connie Clark remembers visiting Eric and Olive often at their home in Parkstone, spending long periods of time with them during the last four or five years of their lives. Afterwards she wrote:

> It was a great joy to be in their home, which had such a peace-ful atmosphere – perfect harmony. It had a quiet 'busy-ness' yet there was plenty of fun and laughter, and much excitement at

times as they would have many vistors, especially during the summer months.

During the last few years of her life, Olive needed more help and attention. She had more than one fall in the home, and became very frail. Eric lovingly looked after her, helping with the domestic chores, coping with the washing machine, and wielding a duster with as much aplomb as he could a conductor's baton if necessary. However, they did have much help in their later years.

Eric was very fond of the radio, especially Radio 3. He listened to much orchestral and chamber music, and regularly to 'Choral Evensong'. Each morning there would be coffee (made by Eric) and biscuits, and he and Olive and I would sit back and join in spirit with other listeners to 'The daily service'. They also listened to 'Sunday half-hour' and 'Your hundred best tunes'. It goes without saying that brass band programmes were a must. He was very selective with regard to television, greatly enjoying orchestral concerts and opera productions. One of my last memories of sharing a radio programme was on the Good Friday afternoon just a few months before he died. A choral work of the Good Friday story was being performed, and we listened to the complete work, following the full score and the words. Eric remarked afterwards, 'What better way could one spend Good Friday than listening to such an uplifting and inspiring work!' It was certainly a spiritual experience for us both.

Another memory I have is of about a week before Eric entered hospital. He was very tired and weak in body. I answered the telephone and the caller wished to speak to Eric, who insisted on going to the phone. After the receiver had been replaced I became concerned as Eric did not return to the lounge. I found him sitting by the telephone, praying for the caller, who was ill

Winton Salvation Army Band plays to Eric, at 'The Chines' Nursing Home a few days before his passing.

and in much pain. Eric was himself a very sick man, with very little physical strength left, yet he gave of himself in order to bring comfort and healing to another. He thus cared for other people right to the end.

And Bob Getz has similar things to say:

I was privileged to visit Eric at The Chines Nursing Home in Poole, Dorset, in the last two weeks of his life. The three days I was able to call on him were among the best days he was to be given after the operation. I brought him greetings from so very many who were far away, and from a different time. He was only concerned with *their* welfare, not his own. 'Bless them. Tell them I shall pray for them.'

As I was honoured to hold his hand, and to join in prayer with him and our dear friend Mary [Randell], I was drawn to his words and music in 'A prayer for courage' – 'I pray not for happiness . . . I pray, Lord, for courage: courage to fight 'gainst the evils that now surround me, and temptations that would confound me . . . naught shall turn my glad heart from the way of the cross.' I was also challenged by the beautiful thought expressed in his music 'Constant trust'. I prayed fervently that we would each be able to trust constantly in our Lord, the Christ, Jesus.

As we finished our prayers, Mary and I both sensed that Eric was totally still. His waxy-pale and emaciated little body showed no signs of life at all. We stared at him and at each other, tears flowing. Had he passed on right before us? A sigh of breath fluttered, and he began to pray, with considerable difficulty, and with vast pauses between phrases. 'Dear Lord . . . Thank you for these dear ones . . . hold us together . . . until the end, which is the beginning . . . of a closer walk with our Lord . . . (a very long silence) Bobby . . . Jeannie . . . Barbara – bless them, Amen.' Lying near death, in pain and weak, he prayed for *us*, and for my family, by name.

It was very shortly after this, on Sunday 1 October 1989, that there dawned for Eric Walter John Ball the 'some glad sweet day' of which the song in his selection 'Songs in exile' spoke. His exile from his heavenly home was over.

Epilogue

He was born on a Saturday. 'Saturday's child works hard for his living' the old rhyme tells us. More than 120 works for brass band, three of them with choir (published in Great Britain); over 100 other brass works published by The Salvation Army; more than 120 songs published by that organisation; more than 50 pieces for continental bands; too many special arrangements in manuscript to recall; thousands of proof pages read; millions of words written and spoken; countless millions of notes played on the pianoforte and organ – all of these add up to an impressive output of work.

Harry Read, a commissioner in The Salvation Army, and responsible for its evangelical work in England and Wales, conducted Eric's funeral which took place in the hall of his adopted corps at Poole. His own tune, 'Peace', was used for one of the songs, 'Peace in our time, O Lord'. Norman Bearcroft, whom he had known as a boy in Southall Citadel days, and by this time National Secretary for Bands and Songster Brigades in The Salvation Army, paid tribute. A song by another of his old friends, John Hunt, opened the committal service at the local crematorium. Here the local Salvation Army band played, and his good friend, Mary Randell, who with her husband had done so much for him in latter days, read from the Scriptures.

Tributes were to flow in from all round the world. Writing in *Salvationist*, Malcolm Bale said that 'his music had a distinctive quality which appealed to performer and listener alike, satisfying the former with his musical craftsmanship yet never failing to reach even the musically uneducated in its spiritual and emotional dimensions', and that 'his faith was the inspiration of his music and his music was the servant of his faith'. The reporter of a tribute festival held at the Regent Hall, in which the International Staff Band and Songsters of The Salvation Army played and sang his compositions, had

Opposite: Two favourite pictures taken at The Salvation Army's Central Music Institute, USA, around 1962. That of Eric and Olive together accompanied Eric during his final days in the nursing home.

his report headlined 'Thanksgiving for man who gave ordinary folk "a sense of belonging" '. During this meeting, Harry Mortimer's tribute was read by Norman Bearcroft (Harry himself being in hospital). He referred to the profound impression made upon bandsmen by '*Resurgam*', and paid further eloquent tribute to the man 'whose musical criticism was always accompanied by words of encouragement'.

The British Bandsman paid warm tribute to its former editor. Peter Wilson said, among other things, that he was 'dignified, economic in word and deed, modest, yet not unaware of his charisma and influence . . .'; that he 'never refused an invitation to compose a work, be it for some great international occasion or for the local village band or choir, and he always made time for those who sought his counsel and teaching. To the privileged ones who were counted among his friends, he was a wise and loyal companion – warm, yet reserved; positive but open to the views of others.'

Peter's son, Eric, wrote just as perceptively in *The Independent* newspaper, that he 'will be remembered as perhaps the most significant contributor to the repertoire of the brass band. In quantity as in quality his output may never find an equal. . . . As a musical architect, Ball excelled. His sense of proportion and balance ensured that his music flowed no matter how the level of his inspiration varied.'

In March 1990 the Cornwall Brass Band Association met to compete on test pieces selected from Eric's compositions, 'Festival music', 'Tournament for brass', 'St Michael's Mount', 'Devon fantasy' '*Petite suite de ballet*' being the titles chosen, and an 'own choice' being allowed. The National Youth Brass Band included his 'Sunset rhapsody' in its concert in Salisbury City Hall on 20 April, Eric having conducted the band in public on 10 occasions between 1953 and 1984. In Australia, Willoughby Senior and Junior Bands joined Sydney Congress Hall Salvation Army Band and Songsters for a programme which included parts of his 'Enigma variations' arrangement, 'Songs in exile', 'Psalm 150', '*Magnificat*', and '*Resurgam*'.

More lasting memorials than those expressed in written or spoken word were planned. The British Territory of The Salvation Army instituted an Eric Ball Scholarship for students of its National School of Music; in the United States of America, the Central Music Institute decided to construct and dedicate a fountain in his memory; *The British Bandsman* and Rosehill Publishing jointly presented an 'Eric Ball Music Award' to encourage young composers.

Perhaps the last word on Eric Walter John Ball should remain with Connie Clark, in a tribute prepared for a pro-

gramme of Eric's music arranged by Noel Frost at Stapleford
Citadel a year after Eric's death:

> . . . I called to mind Brindley Boon's telling in his book *ISB*,
> of the installation of Eric as bandmaster of the ISB in 1942. . . .
> 'Eric confided to the congregation – "The International Staff
> Bandmastership is not my highest ambition. I have another
> ideal. It is to attain to Christ. Toward that I press forward." '
> I believe Eric kept faith with that vow right to the end of
> his earthly life, by his conversation, his dignity, his grace, his
> humility, and his self-disciplined workmanship. Much has been
> said and written about the influence Eric Ball's music has had
> both in Salvation Army and non-Salvation Army circles. He did
> influence for good and for the Kingdom of God, many people
> by his music, but I think a greater influence was Eric Ball – the
> man.

Appendices

APPENDIX A
Music for Brass Band

1 – Original Works

Akhnaton
American Sketches
Angel voices (fantasia)
A psalm for all nations
Call of the sea
Celebration
Contest day
Cornish festival overture
Devon fantasy
Divertimento
English country scenes
Everybody's child
Faroe Islands rhapsody
Festival music
Four preludes
Fowey River
Free fantasia
High Peak
Holiday overture
Holiday suite
Homeward
Impromptu
Indian summer
In Switzerland
Israel rhapsody
Journey into freedom
Kensington concerto
Main street
Meditation on St Columba
Morning rhapsody
Oasis

Peniel
Petite suite de ballet
Prelude, song-variations and finale
Princess and the poet
Resurgam
Rhapsody on American gospel
    songs
Rhapsody on negro spirituals
Rhapsody on negro spirituals
    (No 2)
Rhapsody on negro spirituals
    (No 3)
Salute to freedom
Scottish festival overture
Sinfonietta – 'The wayfarer'
Sinfonietta No 2 (Waratah)
St Michael's Mount
Sunset rhapsody
Swiss festival overture
Thanksgiving
The ancient temple
The conquerors
The English maiden
The pilgrims (meditation)
The undaunted
The young in heart
Three songs without words
Tournament for brass
Youth salutes a Master
Welsh festival overture

2 – Marches

Excelsior
October festival
Rosslyn
Royal salute

Sure and steadfast
Torch of freedom
Wollongong city

3 – Ensembles

A new song (euphonium, piano,
    organ and voices)

Bortom Gyllere (cornet trio and
    band)

Friendly giants (quartet for tubas)
Herald angels – fanfare
Pastorale and rondo – humoreske

Second quartet for tubas
Quid pro quo (double trio and
  band)

4 – Band and choir

A Christchurch cantata
For all mankind

Hail to the Lord's anointed

5 – Solos

Concita (cornet)
Legend (trombone and piano)
Mountain melody (horn)

September fantasy (horn)
Woodland song (flugelhorn/cornet
  and piano)

6 – Arrangements

A French suite (Boely)
Alleluia (Mozart)
All in the April evening
  (Roberton)
Amen chorus (from 'Messiah')
  (Handel)
Andaluza (Granados)
Angel's farewell (from 'The dream
  of Gerontius') (Elgar)
A rural suite (Woodhouse)
Ave Verum (Mozart)
Chorus of the Hebrew slaves
  (Verdi)
Cossack patrol (Knipper)
Dances from 'Checkmate' (Bliss)
Easter hymn (Mascagni)
Egmont overture (Beethoven)
Eine Kleine Nachtmusik (Mozart)
Enigma variations (Elgar)
Entracte from 'Rosamunde'
  (Schubert)
Fascination (Marchetti)
Favourite hymn tunes (13)
Fugue in E flat ('St Ann')
  (J.S.Bach)
Galantia (Scull)
Golliwog's cake walk (Debussy)
Goodnight beloved (Pinsuti)
Hansel and Gretel (Humperdinck)
Harry Lauder songs
Imperial March (Elgar)

In this hour of softened splendour
  (Pinsuti)
Jesu, comfort of my heart (J.S.
  Bach)
Let the lower lights be burning
Melody in F (Rubenstein)
Orb and Sceptre (Walton)
Prelude to 'The dream of
  Gerontius' (Elgar)
Rhondda Rhapsody (Jones)
Softly sounds the little bell
Suite Gothique (Boellmann)
The homeland (Sullivan)
The long day closes (Sullivan)
Themes from Symphony No 1
  (Beethoven)
Themes from Symphony No 9
  (choral section) (Beethoven)
Themes from Symphony No 5
  (Tchaikowsky)
The wizard of Oz (Arden)
Three hymn-tunes from the 20th
  century folk mass (Beaumont)
Two preludes (Chopin)
Two chorales and final chorus
  from Saint Matthew Passion (J.S.
  Bach)
Waltz memories of Schubert
We wish you a merry Christmas
  (Scull)
Worthy is the Lamb (from
  'Messiah') (Handel)

7 – Solos

Andantino (Stradella)
Berceuse de Jocelyn (Godard)

The one-note bugler (Scull)
To a wild rose (McDowell)

APPENDIX B

Publications for continental brass bands

Allein Gott in der Hoh'
Amazing grace
Am Kreuze meines Heilands
Anbetung
Befiehl du deine Wege
Bibllesebund-Marsch
Christustag
Das Kreuz von Golgatha
Der Fels
Du grosser Gott
Du meine Seele singe
Die Heilige Stadt (Jerusalem)
Die Ehre Gottes
Ein einig Volk
Ein' feste Burg
Eins in dem Namen Jesu
Engelstimmen
Er lebt
Es gibt eine Heimat
Festmusik Berner BB-Musik
Festival-Marsch
Frieden mit Gott
Frohe Botschaft
Gewissheit
Gideons Sieg (Festmarsch)
Gnade
Gott preisen

Halleluja dem Erretter
Heilig, heilig, heilig
Heimwarts (Marsch)
Herr, deine Gute
Herr wir bitten
Israel
Ist jemand – JT 77
Jesu Name nie verklinget
Jesus kennen
Jesu meine Freude
Jugend fur Christus (Marsch)
Lob und Anbetung, Menschen, die zu
    Jesus fanden
Namen uber alle Manen
Nun danket alle Gott und Grosser Gott
    wir loben dich
O Gott, dir sei Ehre
Prelude
Sicher in Jesu Armen
Seine Gute und Gnade
Vertau auf Gott
Vorwarts Christi Streiter (zu
    Jehovahs Ehren)
Wag es mit Jesus
Weihnachtsmusik
Welch ein Freund
Wir singen von Jesus

APPENDIX C

Brass music published by The Salvation Army (SP&S Ltd)

Adoration
All in the April evening
Alleluia!
An Appeal
The Awakeners
Beethoven (transcription)
Break forth into joy
A carol fantasy
Centennial review
The challenge
Challenge and response
Christmas music
Clear skies
Consecration
Constant trust

Departure
Devoted service
Ellan Vannin
The eternal presence
Exodus
Fantasia on Lobe den Herren
Fight on
Forward to the fight
Glory songs No 1
Glory to his Name
The golden stair
Good news
The good old way
The gospel feast
The day of victory

Hanover
Hoist the flag
Hold thou my hand
In the Army (1)
In the Army (2)
In the light
In the power of the Spirit
In the ranks
Invitation and warning
The joy of the redeemed
The King of kings
The Kingdom triumphant
Lessons from nature
Meditation on 'Spohr'
More than conquerors
My longing heart
Never give up
Night of wonder
O God, our help in ages past
O'er mountain and valley
Oh, remember Calvary
The old wells
On service overseas
Our Saviour's praise
Peace with God
Perfect trust
The pilgrim way
Pledge for service
Praise and exaltation
The prospect before us
Psalm 150
Rays of sunshine
Remember me
Resurgam
Safe in the arms of Jesus
Sanctuary

Saviour and friend
The Saviour's invitation
Serenity
A sinner's plea
A soldier's experience
Song of courage
Songs for pilgrims
Songs in exile
Songs of the fight No 1
Songs of the morning
Songs of the valiant
A soul's awakening
A soul's triumph
Sound out the proclamation
Star Lake
Star Lake No 2
Swiss melodies
Through storm to safety
Torchbearers
The greatness of God
The solid rock
The triumph of peace
The whole armour of God
To the rescue (arr from Leidzén)
True life
Trust in God
The victory of love
A warning message
War songs No 2
The warrior's sanctuary
A warrior's testimony
The warrior's reward
We will fight!
With verdure clad (transcription)
World-wide witness

APPENDIX D

Songs and other vocal music published by The Salvation Army

A life victorious
A prayer ('God be in my head . . .')
A prayer for courage
A song of harvest time
A 'Unison' song
Ah, then I knew!
All ye that labour
Alleluia! ('All creatures of our God and King . . .')

And now, beloved Lord
And will the Judge descend?
As the palmtree
Balm in Gilead
Bethlehem bells
Break forth into joy
Child of Mary
Christ my companion

Christ was the Shepherd (arranged
    from Slater)
Come back
Come!
Come, Holy Ghost
Consecration
Contrition
Deep within
Eternity
Faith is a banner
Faith, hope and love
Fight the good fight
Fishers of men
For all who serve
For quiet places
Forward to the fight
From the heart of Jesus flowing
Guide me, mighty one
Hail to the King!
He gave me pardon
He will not leave you
Healer of yesterday, Healer today
Hear us, O Lord
Help us follow thee
Help win the world for Jesus
Heroes of yore
Holy flamelight
If anyone thirst
In the secret of thy presence
In the secret of thy presence
    (rearranged)
Into thy likeness
Jesus looked on me
Joyful hallelujahs
Just one more day
Look upward
Love stands the test
    (rearrangement)
Love stands the test
Love's demand ('My life must be
    Christ's broken bread')
Make a joyful noise today
Morning song
My deliverer
My Father's at the helm
Nothing I withhold
O fire of the Spirit
O tell it once again
Old Tom's yarns
Our Saviour-King
Our vocation – winning souls
Out of the depths
Peace ('Peace in our time, O Lord
    . . .')
Pleasure complete
Plunge in the fountain

Praise him with psalms
Psalm 150
Ready to pardon
Rejoice, again I say, rejoice
Service and sacrifice
Sessional song – Crusaders
Sessional song – Dauntless evan-
    gelists
Sessional song – Enthusiasts
Sessional song – Guardians of the
    covenant
Sessional song – Heroes of the
    faith
Sessional song – Hold fast!
Sessional song – The awakeners
Sessional song – The liberators
Sessional song – The witnesses
Sessional song – Torchbearers
Sessional song – Valiant
Shout salvation!
Sing while marching on
Song of truth
Supplication
The best is yet to be
The Christmas bells
The day of victory
The door sergeant
The fight
The great physician
The greatness of God
The hands of Jesus
The heart's desire
The lifeboatman
The lifegiver
The Lord of harvest praise
The Master's charge
The pilgrim song ('He who would
    valiant be . . .')
The prayer of St Francis
The river pure
The song of the angels
The song of the tambourine
The three-fold blessing
The way of holiness
The whole armour of God
The world so deceiving
True life
Trust, rejoice and sing
We will fight!
We'll keep on singing
Welcome! happy morning
Were you there?
What hinders you
When wounded sore
Why wilt thou die?
Will you not accept salvation?

APPENDIX E

Analysis of selection 'Adoration'

(*Festival Series 26*)

The piece opens in the key of E flat, with a chord which, commencing *pianissimo*, rises in force to *fortissimo*. A slow *cadenza* for euphonium adds to the atmosphere of majesty already created. This is repeated in the relative minor, C minor. His actual introduction is 16 bars in length, but there is no recognisable theme until letter B, so that the music is swirling around in various keys, related and unrelated, until this extended introduction closes on a gentle *piano* – and with a *diminuendo* marking.

Then comes a cornet solo, 'O thou, whose word created worlds'. This is only a degree louder (*mezzo-piano*) to begin with, and with careful gradations of sound throughout the verse, until a *fortissimo* is reached. The chorus of the song is developed in an episode at letter E, where there are a few fireworks, especially for soprano, solo cornet, first baritone and euphonium. In his own score notes, the composer asks that 'the music sound brilliant without becoming flippant':

The following movement introduces one of the most beautiful Salvation Army songs of the 1920s, 'The fairest of ten thousand', as a baritone solo, with muted *second* cornet and trombones to accompany:

A hushed, ethereal atmosphere is created here by very simple means. The chorus builds up towards a climax, adding more instruments to the scoring as it goes along, keeping the trombones until the final repetition of 'Giving up my all to follow, just to do my Master's will.' The composer suggests that the *obbligato* for euphonium 'be brought well forward, and take care not to develop a waltz rhythm'. This would be somewhat difficult to do, and if there is any criticism of this selection it would be with regard to this *obbligato* which sounds somewhat dated.

This leads to a movement of great charm: the song which gives the selection its title – 'Adoration'. Also known familiarly as 'The Swiss psalm', it was a great favourite in times past. The composer suggests that interpreters of the selection look up the words of the first verse:

> When the morn in glory breaks,
> When the bird to song awakes,
> All to voice thy majesty,
> Lord, our God!
> When the sun's soft, soothing pow'r
> Lifts the dewdrop from the flower,
> We will lowly bend the knee,
> Hearts attune to worship thee.

Horns, baritones and basses sing the first four lines, and are joined in the harmony by trombones at line three. First cornets *divisi* and second cornets join them in lines five and six, leaving them to 'lowly bend the knee' by themselves, joining them again for 'Hearts attune', only to leave them on the repetition.

The final section is an arrangement of a male voice item. It is a straight-forward-enough movement which needs no comment, and leads into a coda in which reference is made to the euphonium *obbligato* used in the introduction, nicely rounding off the piece.

APPENDIX F

Analysis of *air varié* 'The Old Wells'

(Festival Series 58)

The composer suggests that 'as a simple *air varié* this piece is hardly true to type, as it relies more upon *thematic* (as opposed to *melodic*) development than is usual, hence it approximates more nearly to the form known as 'symphonic variations.' These are formed from the chorus only of the song; the verse appears merely as the introduction to the piece. This is marked *Andante*; perhaps *semplice* might, with effect, have been added. The scoring is, initially, simple enough, with the melody in the solo cornet for the first half, transferring to trombones (firsts divided) on the line 'Other waters may fail you' with an entrancing, tiny *obbligato* for the flugelhorn, leading to the tune being taken over again by the solo cornet. The theme proper now appears, scored for full band, in letter A:

Key F

Letter B brings us the first variation, with cornets and basses 'having important work to do' in the composer's own words, little florid passages alternating between them, giving almost a *scherzando* effect. The composer asks for the music to be played 'as delicately as possible – even by the basses! The general effect of this section should be that of happiness and laughter.'

The second variation, in letter C, is most unusual in Salvation Army music, introducing a ground bass, though this is a recognised classical form. The initial figure of the theme is repeated three times in all, and is followed by a pedal G (dominant) – the music being in C. The theme is then turned upside down, first in solo cornet, and then in euphonium and bass trombone, before the movement comes to a very quiet close on a *pianissimo* sustained tonic chord. The movement is very thinly scored, thereby adding greatly to its effectiveness:

Key C

Letter E brings the third variation, with the air, such as it is, for the music is becoming more and more broken, in the euphonium. It is a rollicking, boisterous movement, typical of its period with the *bravura* euphonium line and other instruments taking up his lead. This section, with letter F, owes much, it would seem, to the third movement of Beethoven's second symphony:

Scherzo

The fourth variation, introduced at letter G, requires a complete change of mood, great, fat chords (noticeably *without* solo or soprano cornets) imploring the pilgrim to 'Go back to the old wells' with the air of command rather than supplication. After three bars there is a most delicately scored interlude with the air (again a mere fragment) in the solo horn, with tiny, florid *embellimenti* in the solo and soprano cornets, which were silent before, but now seem to tempt the rest of the band away from their intention. This alternation of styles continues until three bars before the end of the movement, where a euphonium *obbligato* (so much more subtle and meaningful now than in 'Adoration') seems to suggest that the pilgrim has missed his way: that the mirage of the solo and soprano cornets has been successful in deflecting him from his purpose.

Confidence seems to be restored by the last variation (letters H, I and J). Are we perhaps a little over-confident, in the harsh braying of 1st trombones? The falling-away figure in the solo cornet in the first half of letter I might seem to suggest so. A solo for E flat bass at letter J should be played with 'some amount of abandon' the composer tells us in the notes to the score, and he suggests the B flat basses should play their *staccato* notes *quasi pizzicato* 'in the style of the plucked string on the cello or double bass'.

Any lack of confidence we might have felt earlier disappears on the lead into letter K where the initial theme is recapitulated in full, almost in a *con trionfale* style, taking us into a boisterous *coda*, in which the composer tells us to 'note the indication *non rall* [ie do not slow down], and let the finish be played in a spirit of exuberant happiness.'

This brings us into letter K where the initial theme is recapitulated in full, almost in a *con trionfale* style, taking us into a boisterous *coda*, in which the composer tells us to 'note the indication *non rall* [ie do not slow down], and let the finish be played in a spirit of exuberant happiness.'

APPENDIX G

Analysis of anthem 'Break Forth into Joy'

(published in 1930)

The initial words are set in the style of a fanfare, this being followed by a contrapuntal treatment in smoother style in 'For the Lord hath comforted his people', returning to the earlier fanfare figure for the repetition of 'Break forth'. The key is a stirring B flat.

For the next verse of the psalm, a new key is introduced, the closely-related E flat, and a contrasting, smoother style for 'The Lord hath made bare his holy arm'. A gently-scalic passage, overlapping in the middle, matches perfectly the sentiments of 'And all the ends of the earth shall see', while the little suspension on 'see' adds interest for the altos.

Finally, a return to the first 'movement' and the key of B flat, before a tiny *codetta*, based on the opening fanfare idea, and three full, fat chords, on 'in - to - joy' complete the piece.

APPENDIX H

Analysis of sessional song 'Hold Fast'

(published in 1940)

The opening is in a militaristic C minor, with the voices in *unison*, though accompanied in full harmony, a full harmony in which the voices join after the first two lines:

Led by Satanic Majesty,
The armies of the enemy,
With martial mien, in wanton war,
Encompass thee behind, before!
Hold fast and conquer gloriously.
Lift up thine eager eyes to see
Where streams an Ensign stained with Blood,
The Emblem of the Son of God!

Then follow three verses in a strongly contrasted musical style. The same broad, sweeping melody is used, the first verse by the women's voices, the second by the men, both in *unison*, the whole choir in harmony for the third. The key is C major:

> The day is breaking! War shall cease!
> The Kingdom of the Prince of Peace
> At last shall dawn.
> Kings to his feet their crowns shall bring,
> And men and angels own him King;
> Oh, glorious morn!

Now we return to the militaristic mood of the first subject:

> Rages the conflict fierce and fast,
> And timid spirits stand aghast.

until a four-bar linking passage brings us to the last verse, with another of Eric's 'broad', 'open-airish' tunes:

> Called by our God and equipped with his might,
> Boldly we enter the glorious fight!
> We will fight on till we lay down the sword.
> God's own 'Well done!' is the victor's reward!

Finally, instruments and voices are used together in a *stringendo* coda to reach a splendid climax:

> We will hold fast
> Hold fast!

APPENDIX I

Musical analysis of selection 'Songs in Exile'

(Ordinary Series 1460)

In the note to the full score, Ray Steadman-Allen writes, 'The inspirational idea of this music may be found in the last verse of a gospel song,

> "Though exiled from home, yet still I may sing:
> All glory to God, I'm the child of a King."

It is imperative that continuity be maintained; the music must flow, gathering up the themes in its progress, until the final bars with their reminiscent, "I'm the child of a King".'

The item is one in which the mystical side of Eric Ball's nature is revealed. There are figures in the music which build up this feeling. For instance, there is nothing so prosaic as the first four notes of the central melody, 'Toil on just one more day', when played in straight crotchets as the tune requires. But play them *as quavers* as is needful in the first four bars of letter F and the effect is completely different, and is quite hypnotic:

Key B flat   *p*

And before this, when the first line of the melody introduces the piece, on baritones and horns, echoed a fourth lower on basses, still in crotchets, the effect is extraordinary:

Later, at K, when the horn sings his 'song in exile' *par excellence*, 'Oh, how I'd like to see his face, my Lord beholding', the accompaniment is spare in the extreme. Solo cornets mainly in octaves have a delectable *obbligato* over a held tonic third from first and second cornets:

After a bar or two, trombones intone delicate, tiny horn calls, like Bunyan's 'trumpets sounding for him, on the other side', only faintly and far off:

Troms.

Even further into this section, when the melody achieves a confident *forte*, for 'I'll hear the music of his voice' there are tiny falling figures, like those Eric employed many years before in his *air varie* 'The old wells' which seemingly seek to destroy this sense of confidence. Gratefully, however, all is well by the time the final chords are reached.

APPENDIX J

Musical analysis of selection 'The Eternal Presence'

(*Festival Series* 314)

'The composer seeks to capture the moods evoked by reading verses from Psalm 139. Although only once used in its entirety the hymn "Still, still with thee" appears in derivative forms as a "head-motive" as at the very commencement. There are three opposing movements subtitled "The Imprisoned Spirit", "The Heart's Grief" and "Tribulation". As if a continual reminder of the Eternal Presence, an important ethereal theme is interpolated and linked to the "head-motive" [fragments of the main theme] (muted cornets and trombones or horns); the addition of a soprano voice as indicated on the score may well heighten its effectiveness.' (Score note by Brian Bowen)

These vocalised *embellimenti* have great power in creating the atmosphere of mystery and 'eternal presence' of which the title of the piece speaks. It is in similar vein to the last movement, 'Uranus', of Holst's 'Planets' suite:

At letter E a fragment of the hymn tune is reintroduced, just as in 'Songs in exile' the figure 'just one more day' in notes of half the value, and this helps to give a sense of mystery and heart-longing to the music:

The innovative writing for *obbligato* glockenspiel is extremely effective here. A *poco accel* marking halfway through this section introduces a feeling of tumult until the 'head theme' is heard once more. This gives way to a new section, and a new mood, 'The heart's grief', with an original setting by the composer of the hymn, 'When our heads are bowed with woe'. Significantly, the 'head theme' is heard once more, before the final mood, 'Tribulation', comes to the soul.

Significantly, too, the composer adds a scriptural reference at the top of the score: John 16:33 ['These things I have spoken unto you, that in me ye might have peace. In the world ye shall have tribulation: but be of good cheer; I have overcome the world' (*AV*)].

The excellent score note continues, 'In its conception this movement is more violently opposed to its neighbours; technically it will be found more demanding. A rhythmic and at times vehement impact is made representing the testing helter-skelter and whirl of life, or, as the composer says, "the wheel of life". To obtain a convincing welter of sound, and at times suppressed clamour, very firm control is necessary. There is a sinister element in such ordered hubbub which the interpreter may well exploit. From the ninth bar of M very forceful, muted rhythms are set up which, if they are to become sufficiently venomous, will require uninhibited playing. The 'head-motive' is worked into the scheme at O; through the turmoil the spirit acknowledges its awareness of the Eternal Presence – the Calming Influence. The tribulation rapidly dispels and the spirit is fleeting toward a haven suggested by the verse 'When sinks the soul, subdued by toil and slumber'.

But always it is the 'headmotive' which conveys the eerie, yet comforting effect, of the tireless follower, who pursues the soul and is never at peace with himself until the soul is at peace with him.

APPENDIX K

Musical analysis, including part of programme note (by Eric Ball) of tone poem 'Resurgam'

(Festival Series 302)

Any composition which is intended to be at all 'serious' is bound to illustrate in some measure the sense of conflict inherent in all aspects of life. Light and darkness, joy and sorrow, life and death are reflected in some degree in all works of art. Even the simplest of compositions – a hymn tune for example – relies for its effect upon the contrast, the antagonism between discords and concords: for without such a principle at work there could be nothing but sterility in any manifestation of life.

The title of this tone poem – 'Resurgam' – can be translated 'I shall rise again' and throws the idea of contrast and conflict into high relief. The following quotation from the ancient Book of Wisdom, on which the music is based, accentuates this idea still more:

> The souls of the righteous are in the hand of God,
> And no torment shall touch them.
> In the eyes of the foolish they seemed to have died;
> Their departure was accounted to be their hurt,
> And their journeying away from us to be their ruin:
> But they are in peace.

But it should not be thought that the music is intended to illustrate these words specifically. It is not a 'descriptive fantasia'. The idea behind it can be interpreted in many different ways, and upon various planes of thought or consciousness; as a personal affirmation having regard to present life or that to come.

The opening tune (which fits part of the quotation above) [and which is also a quotation from his sessional song 'The awakeners' – 'Awake thou that sleepest, and arise from the dead, and Christ shall give thee light'] may be called the 'faith' *motif*:

It recurs again and again and at the end is heard triumphantly when all the intervening tumult is over and in contrast there occurs music charged with high emotion, sometimes harsh and discordant, in moods despairing, sorrowful, fearful. The tone poem will evoke differing moods and images in the mind of each individual performer and listener, some personal, some universal.

The stories which have evolved around this particular piece are legion. More significantly for us, here, is the composer's own comment, again included in the full score, that 'At figure 2 the music reflects a frustrated, despairing 'what's the use?' mood. The *Adagio e lamentoso* (cornet solo) speaks of deep sorrow (one has often asked soloists to think of the words, "Death took my love away"):'

He goes on to advise the bandmaster in preparation of the music that 'From 12 there is an atmosphere of fear and even hysteria, interspersed with sudden silences and a sinister, fateful "knocking at the door". Sometimes this section has been subtitled "Fear of Judgment", for here also is heard part of the ancient hymn *Dies Irae*:

and a quotation from an earlier tone poem "Exodus" – the "death" theme:

All this sounds grim and forbidding. Some of the music is in fact discordant and even ugly; but this falls into its rightful place, and the general effect of the whole work should be one of serenity achieved in the face of sorrow and fear.'

Note: the analyses which form appendices J and K are not intended to be comprehensive, but merely to illustrate the mystical element in some of Eric Ball's music. They could have been extended, but might then have been tedious to the general reader.

APPENDIX L

Analysis of test piece 'Akhnaton'

(publisher: R. Smith & Co)

The opening statement, a descending, scalic figure marked *Grave*, with a crotchet = 63 speed, sets the scene. The scoring is rich and dark: melody in first and second horns, first baritone, first trombone and 'first' euphonium (euphoniums being divided and sharing their second line with second baritone and second trombone. E flat basses are also divided for the first two bars. Eric suggests that 'the idea of passionate yearning after light and truth may help . . . with perhaps an impersonal, priestly chant suggested by the trombones in Section A:'

Key E flat

The 'priestly chant' soon transfers itself to flugelhorn and E flat horns, repiano and soprano cornets quickly joining them, while solo cornet has its own work to do:

Key C minor

Then the temple doors open, and we come out into the light, with music of great delicacy, soprano and repiano cornets playing in duet, and with the marking *quasi flauto* – 'like a flute':

Solo (quasi flauto)

Key E flat

But dark forces are at work. Under a charming little theme marked *dolce con espressivo*, for cornet, which we are to imagine represents Akhnaton's family life, the euphonium is stirring up trouble in a theme we shall hear later:

Solo   *dolce e espress.*

Key F

Key D min

Then the basses take up the 'trouble' theme, and a new figure is introduced at D, beginning with horns and baritones, to be taken up by the cornets a bar or two later:

Key D min

f

The conflict extends through D, until a quieter atmosphere is invoked,
at E, by a cornet solo, a kind of *cadenza*, to be followed by a resumption of
the 'family life' theme heard previously at C. This is, in turn, followed by a
resumption of the flute-like duet between soprano and repiano cornets
which we first heard at B, until the mood is broken by one of ferocity,
where the music is intended 'not to sound very nice' (in the composer's
own words). Several things are happening at letter G: the 'priestly-chant
theme' against a 'martial tread', in open fifths, from the basses, and the
repiano cornet doing its own aggressive 'thing' against everything else. Eric
suggests 'a vein of cruelty' may be discerned here, with the effect sounding
taut and not ragged. The cruelty is thus calculated and not accidental.

The 'impersonal priestly theme' is now heard again in the trombones at
I, but with other aggressive rumblings, until the introductory descending-
scale figure is heard once more, to bring this part of the composition to a
conclusion.

If Eric Ball himself suggests that his music is a companion-piece to
'Exodus', then the closing pages perhaps remind one of the 'Song of triumph' section at the end of Handel's oratorio 'Israel in Egypt'. It consists
of four variations on a six-bar theme heard initially in the horns:

ff
Key C

The composer suggests the first statement of the theme is to be played in
choral style (the theme reminding one of those great melodies he had composed in the thirties for his sessional songs – 'Hold fast' in particular). The
first variation is scored for cornets only; horns have it in the second, while
euphonium and basses have a rolling, triplet counter-theme; and the third
variation gives the theme to the whole band, with a striding bass line and
an *embellimento* line in the solo cornet. The soprano cornet is, noticeably,
silent here.

A second episode begins at letter L, where the texture of the music is
darkened by references to themes we heard earlier in the work. The final
presentation of the theme is marked *Nobilmente*, and brings the highest
emotional climax of the work in its train. The music, Eric tells us, must
sound 'free and unfettered' and the mood must be one of 'overwhelming
praise and adoration'.

APPENDIX M

Words by Songster Will J. Brand **Praise Him with Psalms** Scottish air – *Turn ye to me*
Arr. ERIC BALL

APPENDIX N

The World so Deceiving

Words by Brigadier H.J. French

Irish air
Arr. ERIC BALL

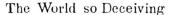

1 Has sin, with its charms so al-lur - ing, At-tracted thy way-ward feet, With
2 The treasures that win and al-lure thee Are tin-sel and quick-ly face? No
3 There's glo-ry that van-ish-es nev - er, And joy nought can e'er ef - face, There's

pro-mise so fair and as-sur - ing Of joys all so gay and sweet? No cloud shall e'er dim with its
shel-ter the world can as-sure thee From judgment so long de-layed. Thy hun-ger of heart is far
hope that is giv-en for-ev - er To those who are saved by grace. Oh, yield now thy heart to the

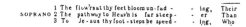

1 The flow'rs at thy feet bloom un-fad - - ing, Their
SOPRANO 2 The pathway to Heav'n is far steep - - er, Than
3 To Je-sus thy foot-steps be speed - - ing, Who

shad - ing Thy noon-day of pleasure su bright,
deep - er Than stay'd with the trifles of time.
plead-ing Of mer-cy so tender and free;

1 The flow'rs at thy feet bloom un-
TENOR 2 The pathway to Heav-en thou
3 To Je-sus be speed-ing, Who

beau-ty un - dimmed with blight.
thy falt'ring feet can climb.
lov-ing-ly waits for thee.

-dimmed with blight.
cannt not climb. Oh, rouse thee from dreams so de-ceiv - ing, From fan-cies that can but en-
waits for thee.

-slave (en-slave). There's life, endless life in be - liev - ing On Je-sus Who died to save.

Index